Off Script

MASTERING THE ART OF
BUSINESS IMPROV

10/25/21

*Be Bold and
Go Off Script!*

PRAISE FOR *OFF SCRIPT*

"This book will help you survive and grow in uncertain times. It offers practical tools and instructive examples of how to thrive in business (and life) in a COVID World. In the pages of *Off Script*, Peter Margaritis builds upon his past books to serve up fresh, powerful, relevant insights — exploring unique lessons about the day-to-day use of improv and arguing (convincingly!) that thinking and behaving like an improviser can help you grapple with uncertainty and change. Don't wait for your future to be determined by someone else or by the events around you; read this book. It will help you take control."

Steve Makredes
Vice President of Construction
Target Corporation

"*Off Script* is a book infused with the personality and fun of improv, and it jumps at you and takes hold of your attention with the same energy Peter delivers during his live events. Practical, funny, and always had me thinking: 'I could do this! Why am I not doing this?' Peter's improv experiences offer us ways to enhance our day-to-day interactions ... from the Zoom meeting to the boardroom."

Don Craig
Chief Financial Officer, Haley & Aldrich, Inc.

"*Off Script* provides the perfect path for every presenter to engage with participants, not just talk at spectators. With a wink and a smile, Pete Margaritis once again demonstrates why he's the funniest accountant since Bob Newhart. This book is a must-read — you'll revel in the storytelling and ultimately be better prepared to elevate your own personal impact."

Jamie T. Richardson
Vice President, White Castle Management Co.

"In his must-read book, *Off Script*, Peter Margaritis takes the concepts underlying successful improvisation and relates them to the roles and differing styles of successful leaders, and to the world of organizational leadership at large. Through the lessons in this book, Pete prepares leaders to successfully apply the principles of improvisation to the situations they face every day. I highly recommend this book for every leader and those who aspire to be leaders."

J. Clarke Price, FASAE, CAE
Retired CEO, Ohio Society of CPAs

"As Peter's brother, I can confirm that his improv isn't funny and neither are his jokes. He did, however, accomplish the authoring of three non-fiction books (including this one) that didn't put me to sleep. That should suffice as a ringing endorsement. Yes, and ... have you called your mother?"

Stephen C. Margaritis
Pete's Only (and Formerly Favorite) Brother

"I found the stories and examples in this book to be incredibly compelling, especially the correlation between the author's improv classes and the reality of scenarios we all face in the real world. It reminded me to stop and reflect before running with assumptions, and instead take better stock of the entire situation. The moments required for that reflection allow you to see many potential outcomes and make better decisions about next steps."

Michael Sherlock
Author of *Tell Me More: How to Ask the Right Questions and Get the Most Out of Your Employees* and *Sales Mixology: Why the Most Potent Sales and Customer Experiences Follow a Recipe for Success*

"Tired of fitting in like everyone else? Ready to face the new challenges of leading with new tools instead of the same old ideas that you have used for years? In this book, Peter provides a new and different approach to the new situations we face in organizations today. He does more than just provide theory — he provides ideas that he has tested. He has practiced and honed the approaches and skills presented in *Off Script* and found success — the same kind of success you can find as you apply the lessons of this book."

Dr. Merle Heckman, CSP
Manager of Organizational Development, Regal Power Transmission Solutions

"Peter Margaritis is not only one of the most genuine and authentic humans I've ever known, he is also a virtuoso — a maestro — in the world of leadership, business, and the power of improvisation to drive both. In writing *Off Script*, he has created the perfect orchestration of all three. From the first page of this book, I was drawn in and became immersed in (and fascinated by) the realization of how powerful and necessary improv is in every aspect of our lives. We are all doing it every day and we just don't realize it. When we do, and we do it on purpose, new possibilities and new worlds open up. This book is not just a game-changer — it is a life changer. Practical, fun, deeply profound, and powerful, it takes us *Off Script* and guides us in learning, opening our minds and hearts, and mastering the power and art of improv in business and in life."

Roxanne Kaufman
President & CEO, ProLaureate Ltd; Certified Leadership Master, Speaker, and Author

"Who would *ever* think an HR Leader would say 'Improv is absolutely the way to go?!' Yet here I am! Peter does a fantastic job of helping us understand why we *do* need to improvise as leaders and he helps us see that to be a bold leader we need to say 'yes, and ...' Employees don't want to follow a leader who constantly gives the 'textbook' answer. Does that mean we don't prepare for those difficult conversations? Absolutely not! We prepare in advance *and* we work on listening and finding the way to YES for our organizations, ourselves, our employees, and our families. Be open — try the tools in this book. Be ready to become a better, stronger, more respected leader. Thank you, Peter, for helping us all realize we can improvise with strategy and purpose!"

Karen A. Young, SPHR, SHRM-SCP
Author, *Stop Knocking on My Door: Drama-Free HR to Grow Your Business*

"Peter Margaritis is a true gem in the world of authentic leadership. By keeping an open mind, open ears, and an open heart, Peter serves as the confident guide for any leader ready to go '*Off Script*' to leverage improv as a powerful business growth strategy."

Theresa Rose
Speaker, Emcee, Corporate Comedian, Brand Expert, Content Crystallizer, and Award-Winning Author

"In his powerful 2021 book, *Off Script: Mastering the Art of Business Improv*, Peter Margaritis bridges the gap between preparation and improvisation. Peter argues that, while often seen as disparate concepts, effective improvisation is only possible following solid and purposeful preparation. The powerful combination of the two — preparation and improvisation — leverage both conscious and unconscious forces to yield the potential for peak performance even given uncertain and ambiguous circumstances. Stir in a set of well-integrated leadership concepts and you have an unusually powerful and relevant read. This book might just change all your ideas about how to strengthen your own performance."

Jay Young, PhD
President, College Bound Advantage

"My good friend, Peter Margaritis, has written another thought-provoking book, *Off Script*, which helps leaders to have real conversations. Known for his fun, upbeat manner, Peter encourages leaders to improvise in their communications by paying attention to and getting participation from their audience ... which allows them to be more creative, innovative, and collaborative. Doing this will help to build a stronger corporate culture. What a great resource for leaders in any field and at any level!"

Jeanie Price, PAFM
Partner and Director of Administration, DeLeon & Stang, CPAs

"Peter Margaritis is a man after my own heart! Writing about the benefits of preparation, presence, collaboration, engagement, and taking risks, he makes the concept of improvisation accessible and approachable for any business leader seeking to create — in Peter's words — a 'dynamic and vibrant culture for your business.'"

Lisa Braithwaite
Public Speaking Coach, Trainer, and Author of *Presenting for Humans: Insights for Speakers on Ditching Perfection and Creating Connection*

"I really enjoyed wandering *Off Script* into these powerful lessons of 'Yes, and ...,' embracing failure, and building a more resilient mindset. Peter Margaritis has created a fun, practical and effective resource for business leaders."

Stephen Morris
Business Performance Navigator, Catylator.com

"A must-read book for leaders and aspiring leaders in any industry! Improv skills improve communication and leadership skills in such a dramatic fashion. Peter will show you how."

Brannon Poe, CPA
Founder of Poe Group Advisors & Creator of Accounting Practice Academy™

"When Peter Margaritis talks, people listen because he always has something important and meaningful to say. His sense of humor is a bonus. Leaders — pay attention. Read this book."

Alan Patterson
President, Mentoré

"*Off Script* got me thinking .... how often do I legit think along the lines of, 'Yes, and ...' Well, I'm embarrassed to admit that even as a two-time best-selling author and successful entrepreneur, I don't prescribe to that theory *nearly enough*! Peter's recommendations especially hit home for me because I have an accounting degree, like he does. I mean, this is speaking to me — I'm a self-professed Numbers Nerd, yet I wasn't utilizing this powerful tactic?! Yes, and ... I'm going to use it from now on!"

Ken "Mr. Biz" Wentworth
Speaker, Author, *Fractional CFO*

"As a corporate training director and leader, I am constantly in situations where being able to pivot is crucial. Improv leadership is a necessity in my field and Peter brilliantly teaches readers how to improvise strategically and with a purpose! In rapidly changing times, this book is a must read for anyone in leadership!"

Michelle Wyatt
Corporate Training Director, First Southern Bancorp

"Peter does a masterful job of weaving the tenets of great improv into the elements of high-level leadership. *Off Script* is engaging and a must-read for leaders in all walks of life."

Bob Dusin
Keynote Speaker, Author, and Coach

"Peter Margaritis shares with readers the secret to successful improv-based leadership and communication. Business leaders will surely be saying, 'Yes! And ...' to Peter's valuable techniques and insights."

Stacey Horan
Author and Host of *The Bookshop at the End of the Internet*

"I found Peter Margaritis's third book, *Off Script: Mastering the Art of Business Improv*, to be riveting! As a leadership consultant, I like Peter's application of the art of improvisation to business and leadership. Many leaders may initially dismiss improvisation as a skill for comedians but Peter does an excellent job of providing historical and practical reasons why leaders everywhere — especially here in the 21st century and post-COVID — need to embrace the chance to master uncertainty and to skillfully use the art of improv to lead in business and life."

Eddie Turner
#6 Ranked Motivational Speaker in the World and Preeminent Authority on Emerging Leaders

"Peter Margaritis has done it again with his third book, *Off Script*! What a great book for leaders on ways to 'go with the flow' — whether speaking, communicating with teams, or developing business strategies. I love Peter's use of stories to bring the learning alive. Highly recommended!"

Cathy Fyock
Author, *The Speaker Author: Sell More Books and Book More Speeches*

"Two simple words — *'Yes, and ...'* — can change a culture and spur ideas and conversation throughout an organization. One word stops everything ... *NO!* I love what Peter teaches us, using two simple words and how he invites us to work on exercises that help us better understand the impact of leading like an improviser. If you want to be an effective leader, start with *YES AND*!"

Adam Kratzert, CMA, CPA
Vice President of Finance, Parker Hannifin Corp.

"Preparation is key and the more prepared you are, the more poised for success you are. That's what this book is all about — being ready to answer the call when opportunity knocks. Peter's extensive career as a speaker gives him the experience, expertise, and acumen to provide real-life (and personal) examples of how improvisation can help us in the business world."

Jeffrey Hayzlett
Primetime TV & Podcast Host, Speaker, Author, and Part-Time Cowboy

Off Scr!pt

MASTERING THE ART OF
BUSINESS IMPROV

PETER A. MARGARITIS, CSP, CPA

FOREWORD BY JEFFREY HAYZLETT
Chairman, The C-Suite Network

PREFACE BY JAY SUKOW
Founder, Today Improv

SILVER TREE
PUBLISHING

DEDICATION

This book is for all the improvisers in the world — the amateurs, the aspiring experts, and the truly established "improv leaders."*

Are you an improviser by virtue of just doing what you are doing ... and having picked up this book? Yes! And I'm inviting each of you to go **Off Script** to achieve better results and to build and maintain stronger relationships. When you embrace the principles of improv leadership and gain the courage to go "off script," you will become more of who you are — more successful in life and career, positioned to thrive in ways you have never imagined.

Here's to you, dear readers and fellow improvisers, and here's to mastering the art of business improv!

* *This means you too, Stephen Michael Margaritis.*

TABLE OF CONTENTS

The Case for "Improv" in Improving Organizational Cultures

Rewriting the Script: Leadership, Improv, and a World of Opportunities

Off and Running: Vulnerability and Generosity as the Fuel for Selfless Leaders

Flipping the Script: Making It All About Them and Not About You

Way Off Base: The Death of the Ego in Modern Leadership

FOREWORD

by Jeffrey Hayzlett

Primetime TV & Podcast Host, Speaker, Author, and Part-Time Cowboy

To be successful in business, and life, you must continuously plan —
preparing for every occasion and often practicing your actions and your
words. Planning is key. However, you've got to leave room to be nimble
enough to pivot at a moment's notice and be malleable enough to adapt
to any situation. You must be willing to let the plan go. It seems like
a contradiction of terms, but the fact is that if you do one (plan carefully) and
not the other (seize the opportunity to go "off script"), you're going to fail.

When we think of the word "improv," we think of comedians, *Saturday Night
Live*, or The Second City in Chicago. The truth is that business leaders like
me and you use improv all the time — we just don't call it that. We've all
been in situations that don't go as planned and what do we do? We change
course, or tactics, that align with the new direction. We adjust and react
and go off script. It's not about making stuff up — although we do that from
time to time.

The key is being prepared for any eventuality. That's what great leaders do — they're always thinking three steps or five steps ahead and they have contingency plans in their back pocket. It's not required to use those plans every time, but it's always great to have.

> ## The truth is that business leaders like me and you use improv all the time — we just don't call it that. We change course, or tactics, that align with the new direction. We adjust and react and go off script.

As a Hall of Fame speaker, I'm ready to wing it every time I step on stage — not because I think things will go wrong, but because that's what every speaker worth their salt would do. It's not just about anticipating, it's about being ready to change your delivery, your presentation, your tone, and even your planned jokes or stories. Read the room. What's your audience's reaction to your first attempt at humor? Didn't go well? Pivot. Does your audience look bored or confused? Pivot.

Preparation is key and the more prepared you are, the more poised for success you are. That's what this book is all about — being ready to answer the call when opportunity knocks. Peter's extensive career as a speaker gives him the experience, expertise, and acumen to provide real-life (and personal) examples of how improvisation can help us in the business world. Business is always changing, and so are our approaches and the technologies we use to get ahead.

So, the next time you think improv isn't for "real" business leaders, think again! You might be missing out on a great opportunity to be even better and to reach a wider, more engaged audience.

There's so much more outside the business realm (like improv!) that we can use to make ourselves better. The sports world can teach us about mental toughness, perspective, and endurance while the arts can teach us that often the best moments we experience are not scripted.

Lose your fear of the unexpected, dive in, and stretch your boundaries. That's how you win!

PREFACE

by Jay Sukow

Founder, Today Improv

Hi friends!

First off, I'm guessing that — like most folks — Peter is never going to read this part of the book. So, let me be honest with you about who he is and give you a little back story. Truth be told, I have learned as much from him (if not more) than he has learned from me.

If you are reading this, don't tell him!!! It'll be our little secret.

Who is Peter Margaritis? Father, bourbon lover, part-time cyclist, multi-published author, semi-pro sunset watcher, Accidental Accountant, underrated speller, and improv evangelist. Peter is someone who lives and breathes improv. And he wants to spread the word to the masses! When it comes to "the art of improv," he gets it.

Our mutual friend Annie Conderacci introduced me to Peter, who wanted to interview me for the *Change Your Mindset* Podcast. Peter and I immediately hit it off and our conversation seemed to flow like water. I thought, "What a great guy. Too bad he lives in Cleveland. Oh well, I guess we will never talk again."

But imagine my surprise when Peter signed up for one of my improv workshops in Chicago! People sign up for a variety of reasons and most of those reasons are related to a desire for self-improvement. We had people in that class from all over the world with reasons ranging from "My daughter signed me up" to "I want to be a better performer" to "I have no interest in performing — I just want to have fun." Peter was there to get better at improv and, whether he knew it at the time or not, to get better at this thing called "life."

Cue the music and the song stylings of Prince:

> *Electric word life*
> *It means forever and that's a mighty long time.*
> *But I'm here to tell you*
> *There's something else …*

Sorry, I digress. Those are lyrics from "Let's Go Crazy" — from the incredible Prince. Catchy, right? Of course it is … IT'S PRINCE!

But let's get back to my story about Peter. Hmmm … this transition might be clunky. How to get back to our story?? I GOT IT!

He soaked up (see what I did there??!!) all the learnings he got from me and he also learned from watching and playing with his fellow students. What I noticed is that people felt safe on stage with him. He took care of them by supporting their ideas. He displayed empathy, listened well, put their ideas ahead of his own. A true improviser.

People felt safe on stage with him. He took care of them by supporting their ideas. He displayed empathy, listened well, put their ideas ahead of his own. A true improviser.

After the weekend workshop, I just assumed we would go our separate ways and maybe be lucky enough to run into each other again at some point. "What a great guy," I thought. "Too bad he lives in Cleveland. Oh well, we will never talk again."

Well, imagine my surprise when I got a call from Peter. And imagine my surprise when he said he was from Columbus, not Cleveland. Then, imagine my surprise when he said he wanted to continue studying with me! He wanted to have monthly one-on-one sessions. My first thought was, "Columbus? Huh. My bad." My second thought was, "With me? Why?" So I asked him. He wanted to learn as much as he could about improv and how he could apply the learnings to the business world. So I said, enthusiastically, "Yes! And ... we can start now!"

> **Perhaps it was destined that Peter would one day write a book in which he lays out simple, yet effective, tools for developing that same improvisational mindset in the workplace that Peter has seen transform people on stages and in relationships.**

Peter and I started a monthly coaching session that continues to this day and we have never looked back. The main focus on our work together still remains how to use improv philosophies to become a better person. What's been really powerful is Peter's willingness to expand the goals of our collaboration — his eagerness to dive deep into these improv philosophies and apply them to the business environment.

And so perhaps it was destined that Peter would one day write a book about the art of business improv — a book in which he lays out simple, yet effective, tools for developing that same improvisational mindset in the workplace that Peter has seen transform people on stages and in relationships. Throughout this book, aptly titled *Off Script*, Peter shares proven exercises designed to help you work certain mental muscles and get you to where you need to go — to a kind of leadership acumen that you know you're capable of and that you know your team deserves.

Still with me? Great! If you got this far, keep going! This is just the beginning.

And remember: Don't tell Peter what I said about him. It'll be our little secret.

INTRODUCTION

I love a good challenge. Convincing business leaders that improv (i.e., improvisation) isn't just something that comedic actors do but that it's a powerful business tool — and an overall leadership method or mindset — has been one of the more difficult challenges of my career. I remain undeterred. The first part of the challenge starts with convincing executives, directors, and managers that I'm not suggesting they develop their team into the next ensemble cast of the American TV show *Whose Line Is It Anyway*? The second part of the challenge involves busting the pervasive myth that people who improvise are just "winging it" and "making stuff up" as they go along.[1] And this is where I want to start our conversation about business improvisation — addressing the "winging it and making stuff up" myth in the improv process of preparation, practice, and letting go.

---

1   Fun fact: One of my trusted advisors suggested I title this book *Winging It!* I loved the playfulness of the title, which helped inspire me to choose *Off Script*. But, as you're about to learn, what the magic of "going off script" results when the speaker or leader is over-prepared and confident, not under-prepared and pulling off the bluff. Keep reading. This is about to get fun!

Preparation is a key to success and, if you've read my second book (*Taking the Numb Out of Numbers*), you know that I'm the king of preparation. Unfortunately, however, when most people think of improv, they think of off-the-cuff comments and unplanned behaviors; they don't associate improvisation with preparation. If you're approaching this book and are thinking the same thing — that "But Peter, improv is all about winging it!" — I promise to do my level best in changing your mindset. In fact, great leaders are masters of improvisation.

Great leaders are masters of improvisation.

By way of example, let me give you an insider's view of how I prepare for speaking engagements (a topic about which I know a thing or two, as I make my living as a professional speaker). When I prepare for any speaking engagement, I research the topic, take tons of notes, prepare my slide deck, rehearse the words and content, and practice the delivery of the presentation. Along the way, I think of questions that might be asked (and objections that might be raised!), obtain and study the demographics of the audience, develop a backup plan for travel delays, and discuss with the meeting planner the tech/AV requirements and room set-up details. When I'm preparing to deliver a virtual program, I do the same preparation but put extra focus on the development of a backup plan just in case I lose power in my home or off-site office, if the internet goes down, or if the computer crashes. Co-working spaces and hotels are the best alternatives. While much of this pre-event work is practical, part of this preparation sits in my subconscious mind — remembering prior experiences that went awry and the solution I applied to correct the issue. Mindset is part of preparation too. For me, this preparation gets very granular, and no stone is left unturned. Go ahead and say it — I know what you're thinking. I'm perhaps obsessed with preparation. But if I could be so bold as to advise you on this matter, I'd suggest you double-down on preparation too.

Practice Makes Perfect (or Close Enough)

In addition to preparation, an equally critical part of success when you're about to communicate (about an important topic, with important stakeholders, or during important moments) is practice. It doesn't matter whether you're getting on stage for a keynote address, stepping into the board room to make a high-stakes presentation, or broaching an important conversation with a colleague or customer, practice matters. I was asked recently to give a five-minute presentation. "What's the big deal," right? Five minutes sounds easy! Not so much. After I figured out how many words are spoken in five minutes (about 750 words), I wrote out my presentation to only have 400 words. I wanted enough time to allow for pauses and to keep my pace at a regular rate. So, I started to practice. I spent about five hours practicing for a five-minute presentation. I wasn't trying to memorize the presentation; I was working on the cadence, tone, pauses, body language. And all the while, I was placing tiny memory seeds in my brain. The worst thing you can do when giving a presentation is to go into it with no memory of having done it before. Pacing around your office or a hotel room or your living room, practicing what you're going to say is, indeed, giving your mind and your body (and even your tongue) the benefit of "having done this before."

> **It doesn't matter whether you're getting on stage for a keynote address, stepping into the board room to make a high-stakes presentation, or broaching an important conversation with a colleague or customer, practice matters.**

When it came time for me to speak on the fateful day of the five-minute presentation, I took a deep breath, trusted my preparation (not my instincts but my preparation!), and put all my notes and written text into a trash can. Then I leaned into the unknown and started speaking. The result was amazing — and the five-minute presentation was a huge success. I felt great — energized and confident and accomplished — and my audience got what they bargained for and what they deserved. Because I let go of perfection and had fun — because I had prepared and practiced — I was able to guarantee a most exhilarating experience.

> *"Greatness is in the preparation, not the performance. Greatness is in the preparation."*

– DR. JACK HYLES

But what does preparation have to do with improv? Everything! You see, preparation and practice give you the foundation to be able to improvise. To be able to successfully go "off script," you must first master the script (then throw it away).

When it came to that five-minute presentation with the five-hour practice session, I was able to bring passion into the conversation that I was having with the audience because I was well prepared. If I had been anxiously trying to read a script or remember what bullet points were in my notes or on my slides, I wouldn't have been able to bring my best, most authentic, and most relatable self to that moment. I shared a couple of PowerPoint (PPT) slides with a few words and two pictures so the key points would be visible for the audience through the short presentation. At one point, I was actually able to slip in an inside joke (a mention of a "onesie") just as it popped into my head at the right time. When I said it, I heard a huge laugh from the colleague for whom that the joke was reserved. *That* is improvisation!

Even when I tell this story to business leaders, they give me a polite "I get it" and start moving on. Then I ask them if they have ever delivered a scripted presentation to the board of directors, or a sales pitch to an important prospect, and if they've ever panicked when they sensed that their message was not being received accurately or with the intended emotional response. "Have you ever seen the crossed arms or the distracted glances toward the clock or the door or the raised eyebrow?" When given the time to reflect on the presentations they have given that didn't quite hit the mark, the business leaders I'm talking to change that polite but disinterested look of "yeah, I kind of get what you mean" to "Oh, yeah ... I remember that time when ..."

Then I tell them about Martin Luther King.

Off-Script Moments in History

Did you know that the Reverend Dr. Martin Luther King, Jr., improvised his iconic "I Have a Dream" speech? Most people (when asked this question — which I am prone to ask often) stop dead in their tracks and reply, "Seriously?" or with a confident, "No, he didn't." But it's true. The historic "I have a dream" portion of King's brilliant oration was not in his prepared speech that day. Dr. King had used the powerful "I have a dream" language in several speeches months before the March on Washington, but it was not planned for inclusion in his speech on that particular and historic day. It had been cut out ... because he had used it before.

Many people have told the "King improvised the speech" story, and all the credible accounts sound pretty much the same. Let me introduce you to (or help you revisit) a few facts about King, his speech-writing skills, his first forays with improvision, and the "I Have a Dream" speech — facts and observations that are relevant to our conversation here about the value of "going off script" as a modern leadership strength. Let's step back in time, long before the March on Washington, to see how a leader who loved his scripts learned to throw them away when the moment called for a different kind of leadership.

The Reverend Dr. Martin Luther King, Jr., began honing his speechmaking craft when he was 14. He won a speaking contest as a teen and an oratory award in college, and he was destined to deliver the kinds of remarks that would change lives and even a nation. He was meticulously prepared when it came to every word he spoke from a stage or a pulpit. Indeed, he was anything but an improviser. When Dr. King began his career as a preacher, he was known to spend 15 hours crafting each sermon and then committing it — word for word — to memory. He delivered those sermons to his congregation exactly as he had planned and scripted them. He did *not* go "off script."

Then came an unexpected moment when there was no time to write and memorize a detailed speech. Rosa Parks, in December of 1955, was arrested for refusing to give up her seat on a bus to a white man in Montgomery, Alabama. Four days later, with just 20 minutes to prepare what he later called "the most decisive speech of my life,"[2] Dr. King spoke to an audi-

---

2   "Chapter 7: Montgomery Movement Begins," Stanford, The Martin Luther
     King, Jr. Research and Education Institute, https://kinginstitute.stanford.edu/

ence of 50,000 people at the Holt Street Baptist Church. He was responding to the news and to current events as they unfolded; the moment was now and there was no time for scriptwriting and a dozen hours of preparation, practice, or memorization. With just a few ideas planned in advance and with the pressure of a large crowd and several television cameras, he improvised brilliant moments like: "You know, my friends, there comes a time when people get tired of being trampled over by the iron feet of oppression." King was learning to improvise in real time.

"As he spoke, King listened to the crowd, feeling out their response, speaking in the moment," explains bestselling author and renowned broadcaster Tim Harford. "His early sentences were experiments, grasping for a theme, exploring how each sounded and how the crowd responded. Each phrase shaped the phrase that followed. His speech was not a solo. It was a duet with his audience." [3]

Eight years later, the Civils Rights Movement in the United States was in full force and Dr. King had since enjoyed the benefit of more experience when it came to trusting himself to go "off script" in front of big audiences. The night before the March on Washington, Dr. King and his inner circle were working on the final version of his speech for the next day. Dr. King felt that this needed to be a finely tuned speech — precisely crafted and with nothing left to chance. Dr. King wanted the speech to have a similar impact on the nation as the Gettysburg Address, so he had included the "I have a dream" paragraph because it had elicited positive results with previous audiences. But a member of Dr. King's inner circle, Wyatt Walker, convinced King to cut the practiced segment because Walker felt that it had been used too many times in the past. [4]

On August 28, 1963, Dr. King was delivering his prepared remarks (a speech originally titled "Normalcy: Never Again") to a quarter million people who

---

king-papers/publications/autobiography-martin-luther-king-jr-contents/chapter-7-montgomery-movement.

3   Tim Harford, "Martin Luther King, Jr., the Jewelry Genius, and the Art of Public Speaking," February 26, 2021, Podcast Episode, *Cautionary Tales with Tim Harford*, https://timharford.com/2021/02/cautionary-tales-martin-luther-king-jr-the-jewelry-genius-and-the-art-of-public-speaking/.

4   Rachel Chang, "Martin Luther King Jr.'s Famous Speech Almost Didn't Have the Phrase 'I Have a Dream,'" *Biography*, January 15, 2020 (updated January 19, 2021), https://www.biography.com/news/martin-luther-king-jr-i-have-a-dream-speech.

had marched to and through Washington, DC, when about two-thirds of the way into the speech, he decided to go "off script." Perhaps he remembered that a great speech is a duet, and not a solo. He started improvising when he reached a sentence that felt clunky. Instead of calling on the crowd to "go back to our communities as members of the international association for the advancement of creative dissatisfaction" (quite a mouthful, indeed!), he went with:

"Go back to Mississippi; go back to Alabama; go back to South Carolina; go back to Georgia; go back to Louisiana; go back to the slums and ghettos of our Northern cities, knowing that somehow this situation can and will be changed."[5]

He paused for a moment, looking at his script, when Gospel singer Mahalia Jackson, who was standing near Dr. King, shouted out, "Tell them about the dream, Martin! Tell them about the dream!" Few people, it has been recounted, heard Mahalia's words except for Clarence Jones (Dr. King's advisor and speechwriter) and, of course, King. It's up for debate whether Jackson's words triggered King's "off script" moment or whether he was headed for that improvisation on his own. But what we know for sure is that he didn't deliver several paragraphs of the originally scripted speech. And the confidence and instinct to improvise allowed King to inspire a nation.

Just after the moment when Jackson shouted to him, which you might notice if you watch film footage of the speech, Dr. King leaves his prepared notes behind to improvise the entire next section of his speech — the historic section that began:

"And so even though we face the difficulties of today and tomorrow, I still have a dream. It is a dream deeply rooted in the American dream. I have a dream that one day this nation will rise up and live out the true meaning of its creed: 'We hold these truths to be self-evident: that all men are created equal.'"[6]

---

5   Emily Crockett, "The Woman Who Inspired Martin Luther King's 'I Have a Dream' Speech," Vox, January 16, 2017, www.vox.com/2016/1/18/10785882/martin-luther-king-dream-mahalia-jackson.

6   Carmine Gallo, "How Martin Luther King Improvised 'I Have a Dream,'" Forbes, August 27, 2013, https://www.forbes.com/sites/carminegallo/2013/08/27/public-speaking-how-mlk-improvised-second-half-of-dream-speech/.

Six minutes of Dr. King's 17-minute speech, now famously known as the "I Have a Dream" speech, were improvised.

Long after the March on Washington, Dr. King was asked about that moment of improv, and he said, "I started out reading the speech, and I read it down to a point ... The audience response was wonderful that day ... and all of a sudden this thing came to me that ... I'd used many times before ... 'I have a dream.' And I just felt that I wanted to use it here ... I used it, and at that point I just turned aside from the manuscript altogether. I didn't come back to it."[7]

Not all moments of improvisation make history. But learning to go "off script" can certainly lead to new opportunities and vital evolutions (and revolutions) in your life.

Not all moments of improvisation make history. But learning to go "off script" can certainly lead to new opportunities and vital evolutions (and revolutions) in your organization, your career, your relationships, and your life. Dr. King went "off script," and so can you. This book will teach you how.

Creating Participants, Not Spectators

I once had the opportunity to speak with retired Ohio Judge Patricia Blackmon, who has delivered the "I Have a Dream" speech with the Cleveland Orchestra, and I asked her about Dr. King's speech. Blackmon, who was Ohio's first African-American female appellate judge, told me that the Mahalia Jackson story is truth and not folklore. Then she asked me if I had ever been to a black church. I replied, "No." And that's where our conversation began to sparkle with insight. Blackmon told me that the ministers at predominantly black churches are nearly always wanting the congregation (the audience) to participate in their sermon. She has seen several ministers go "off script" when they are not getting the anticipated feedback from their congregation. Judge Blackmon believes that Dr. King

---

7   Gary Younge, "Martin Luther King: The Story Behind His 'I Have a Dream' Speech," The Guardian, August 9, 2013, https://www.theguardian.com/world/2013/aug/09/martin-luther-king-dream-speech-history.

did the exact same thing when he went "off script" and inserted the "I Have a Dream" monologue into his March on Washington speech. Participants, not spectators. To me, this suddenly made so much sense.

I have often explained to clients and to other stakeholders, especially if I'm teaching them how to deliver impactful presentations, that the goal is to create and engage *participants*, not spectators. I have joked that presentations are like football games — with 22 people on the field who desperately need some rest and 40,000 or more people in the stands who desperately need some exercise. Dr. King got the masses of people in Washington to participate. Ministers seek to get their congregations to participate (with an "amen!" or much more). Good professors and good presenters and good motivational speakers and, yes, even good *business leaders* can and do seek to get participation from their audiences. Being willing to improvise is foundational to creating that kind of interaction and dialogue.

You see, improv is not about making stuff up or just winging it; improvisation is about deviating from your prepared remarks, thoughts, and ideas and adapting to what your audience is wanting or missing ... to inspire them into action. That's what happened for Dr. King in August 1963. Winging it? Not a chance! He was drawing from previous speeches, previous experiences, and from the significant preparation and practice that preceded that historic day.

> **You see, improv is not about making stuff up or just winging it; improvisation is about deviating from your prepared remarks, thoughts, and ideas and adapting to what your audience is wanting or missing ... to inspire them into action.**

Executive leaders, senior leaders, and aspiring leaders, there is a lot to learn from Dr. King's speech and the power of improv. While reading this book, keep an open mind to the world of improv and its timely application in a modern world — in *your* world. Whether you love or hate the acronym, you likely know all about operating in a "VUCA world" — a business climate that is volatile, uncertain, complex, and ambiguous (VUCA). Dr. Ronald

Dufresne, management professor at Saint Joseph's University, suggests that, "The critical skills needed for leaders in the face of volatility, uncertainty, complexity, and ambiguity are self-awareness, listening, communication, adaptability, critical thinking, and collaboration."[8] Mastering the art of business improvisation can teach us these very skills, and so much more.

Improv is Not About Being Funny: How It All Began

Back in 1998, I performed stand-up comedy in the big cities of Ohio — Cleveland, Cincinnati, Dayton, and Columbus. One day after an open-mike performance, I was approached by a comedian friend and asked if I would be interested in an improv comedy workshop. I replied, "Sure, why not?" Little did I know that my life was about to change forever.

I showed up for the improv class not knowing anything about improv comedy, other than what I had gleaned from watching the TV show *Whose Line Is It Anyway*. The class — truth be told — was bizarre. We played these crazy exercises, immersing ourselves in skits and doing what felt, to me, like acting. Coming into this experience as I newbie, I had mistakenly thought we would spend the afternoon *writing* comedy. The instructor kept harping on two words — "Yes! And ..." I wasn't quite sure why those two words were so important. Oh, was I in for a lifechanging lesson!

Before that first class was even over, I was looking to cut and run. I wasn't sure if I was coming back the following week. *Was this really for me?* I was intrigued about the concept of improvisation and yet still very confused. Then the instructor gave us an assignment for the next week: study the 1970s. "Absorb everything that you can — movies, TV shows, news events, everything," he said. Hearing that the class came with homework assignments somehow made me feel better, like I knew now why I felt like a fish out of water. That must be what I missed — the homework assignment from the week before. Now, I was catching up. *I could do this!*

---

8   Ronald L. Dufresne, PhD, "Using Improvisation to Develop
     Leadership for a Volatile World," *Journal of Leadership Education*,
     2020, Vol. 19, Issue 4, https://journalofleadershiped.org/jole_articles/
     using-improvisation-to-develop-leadership-for-a-volatile-world/.

I wasn't about to give up. The following week, I showed up to the improv comedy class, once again, this time having done my homework. We were hilarious during the exercises — for those who did our homework. And those who didn't? Well, they sucked. This was my first "art of improvisation" ah-ha moment. The lightbulb of insight burned brightly. To be funny in improv, you have to have a solid baseline of knowledge and information; to adapt to these exercises, you need material from which to draw.

Without realizing it, I was learning to collaborate with "colleagues" (in this case, the other men and women on the improv theater stage) and to provide meaningful experiences for a broader audience as well. It would be a long time before I understood how to apply improvisation techniques in the workplace and in real life (and longer still before I'd be writing books about it for leaders like you), but I was on my way.

Improvisation, as it turned out, wasn't "winging it" – it was mastering it.

Rule #1 for becoming an effective improviser is that you must live and die by the open-minded and collaborative concept of "Yes! And ..." To take conversations forward (and during comedy sketches, to take the comedy storyline and impact further), I needed to draw upon the education, knowledge, and life experiences of my teammates and myself. I had to validate their vantage point with "yes!" and then build upon it with "And ..." I had previously been performing stand-up comedy, where my success on stage followed a comedy-writing formula: premise + punchline + tag.[9] But improv was so very different. It was hard, and it required a lot of homework (*who knew?*) and it required a sort of "script" that had to be researched and practiced and then, in the final moment, modified or thrown away altogether. Improvisation, as it turned out, wasn't "winging it" — it was mastering it.

Within just a few of those improv-comedy classes, I knew I was falling in love with a new craft and a new way of thinking about (and communicating in) the world around me. So I threw myself into the experience. First, I decided to learn more about the history of improv. I started reading about the

---

9   In comedy, a tag is a short add-on punchline to keep the laughs going.

godmother of improvisation, Viola Spolin, who was an actress and educator, an author, director, and creator of theater games. In the very same year that the Reverend Dr. Martin Luther King, Jr., spoke famously at the March on Washington, Violin Spolin published the first edition of her book entitled *Improvisation for the Theater*. She and her son, Paul Sills (who ultimately popularized her methods and her work), were affiliated with iconic organizations, like the Young Actors Company in Hollywood and founded The Second City (from which many notable entertainers got their start, like Bill Murray, Gilda Radner, John Candy, John Belushi, Dan Aykroyd, Del Close, Eugene Levy, Catherine O'Hara, Nia Vardalos, Colin Mochrie, Ryan Stiles, Mike Myers, Steve Carell, Tina Fey, Amy Poehler, Chris Farley, Stephen Colbert, Aidy Bryant, Jay Sukow, and many others.

During her time as a drama supervisor in Chicago (1939-1941), Viola Spolin worked with children and recent immigrants in low-income neighborhoods. And the magic of the work she did intrigued me:

"She felt the need to establish a form of theater training that incorporated what she'd learned about the benefits of play from Neva Boyd, one that could reach across divisions of culture and language. Lectures about traditional theater techniques were useless with children or adults with limited English skills. Still, when those lessons became the focus of a game, the students were able to incorporate them organically, full of the spontaneous physical expression needed for true theatrical communication."[10]

For me, reading about Spolin's work with children delivered another "ah-ha moment." Spolin was a communicator, not a comedian! The theatrical teachings to children and immigrants were designed to help improve their communication skills; they weren't meant to be funny or to "entertain for entertainment's sake." Today, I fully understand and embrace that improvisation is a method of communication that has as many merits today in the business world as it did back in the late 1930s and early 1940s in low-income, urban neighborhoods.[11]

---

10   www.ViolaSpolin.org

11   I would be remiss if I didn't mention that Viola Spolin's son, Paul Sills, and Compass Players were active from 1955 to 1958 in Chicago and St. Louis. Like The Second City, the Compass Players was the launchpad for some incredibly talented professionals. Two of the members of the Compass Players were Michael Nichols and Elaine May. You may or may not recognize their names, but they were best known as the comedy duo of "Nichols

So is this book, *Off Script*, about theater or acting or comedy? Not really, and not much. It's about proven methods that organizational leaders like you — whether you work in a Fortune 1,000 company, a small business, a nonprofit, a government organization, or anything in between — can apply to your work every day. It's about learning to let go of the control we all so desperately cling to as leaders and instead embrace the opportunity to go "off script" in our conversations and negotiations. It's about being present instead of rushing to the future, and about collaborating in authentic, empathetic ways.

Most books written about improv have been from the theatrical perspective. However, the more you dig into understanding the theatrical principles, it becomes clear that improv is a leadership technique based on collaboration, play, taking risks, acceptance, and positive outcomes.

Improv, in short, is good business. I happen to think you can't achieve your leadership potential without it.

Since the publishing of my first book, *Improv is No Joke: Using Improvisation to Create Positive Results in Leadership and Life*, I have been curating business articles, videos, and books, all which support the viewpoint that improv is a viable leadership strategy to increase productivity and profitability, improve morale, and decrease turnover. Improv, in short, is good business. I happen to think you can't achieve your leadership potential without it.

---

and May." Here is a partial list of achievements they earned based on what they learned in the early years of improv comedy.

Michael Nichols (director): Neil Simon's *Barefoot in the Park, The Odd Couple, Arthur Miller's Death of a Salesman, The Graduate, Silkwood, The Birdcage, Primary Colors,* and Charlie Wilson's War. He won six Tony Awards and five Academy Awards.

Elaine May (screenwriter): *Mickey and Nicky, Heaven Can Wait, The Birdcage,* and *Primary Colors.* As an actress in *The Waverly Gallery,* she won the Tony Award for Best Actress in a Play.

Understanding the Improviser's Brain to Generate Better Business Results

Dr. Charles Limb is a neuroscientist, a surgeon, a jazz saxophonist, and one of only a few people who have studied the improvising brain. Dr. Limb conducted research on people as they improvised inside brain scanners called fMRI machines. And what he found, as he watched oxygen-rich blood flow to different areas of the brain — and oxygen-depleted blood flow away) while musicians played experimental jazz or performed freestyle rap, was that you can actually see differences in brain function between improvisers and memorizers. The freestyler/improviser's brain (the person we would think of as having gone "off script") lights up the "visual" areas of the brain while the memorizer (the person who sticks to a script or to the music or lyrics as they are written) has a brain that lights up the "language" areas. Indeed, something different and special happens in the brain when we "go off script." In a TEDx Talk, Dr. Limb explains:

> "These are multifunctional areas of the brain; these are not the jazz areas of the brain. They do a whole host of things that have to do with self-reflection, introspection, working memory, etcetera. Really, consciousness is seated in the frontal lobe. But we have this combination of an area that's thought to be involved in self-monitoring, turning *off*, and this area that's thought to be auto-biographical, or self-expressive, turning on.
>
> "We think that at least a reasonable hypothesis is that, to be creative, you should have this weird dissociation in your frontal lobe. One area turns on, and a big area shuts off, so that you're not inhibited, you're willing to make mistakes, so that you're not constantly shutting down all these new generative impulses."[12]

An improviser's brain is developed over time as one continues to train their instincts in new ways.

An improviser does three things differently from how other people might. They:

---

12   Charles J. Limb, MD, "Your Brain on Improv," TEDxMidAtlantic, November 2010, https://www.ted.com/talks/charles_limb_your_brain_on_improv/transcript.

1. Silence their inner critic and allow creative thoughts and ideas to flow out.

2. Are very curious about everything and love to learn about things that might be foreign to them.

3. Create lists of associations (things similar or related to a specific topic).

The improviser's brain is curious and calm, educated and connected, open-minded and deeply focused all at once. What happens in the mind of an improviser is strikingly similar to what a stand-up comedian does. But improvisers don't summon this kind of energy or gather these associations to be used in a joke; improvisers don't make jokes but instead they use these associations to help build more creative thoughts.

> **The improviser's brain is curious and calm, educated and connected, open-minded and deeply focused all at once.**

The Case for Mastering the Art of Business Improv: A Wealth of Leadership Impact

So, how do we tap into the wealth of leadership impact that improvisation offers and bring it into our business world? Start with curiosity, and with four big questions.

Curiosity is my strong suit. Over the past two years, I have been doing much research on the topic of improvisational leadership. I have curated 70 articles, 28 books, and 26 YouTube videos based on improv or improv leadership characteristics. Before I wrote this book, I had some homework to do (just like for that improv class! So much homework!). In his book, *Getting to "Yes And,"* Bob Kulhan argues that influential leaders can fully and effectively answer four questions about themselves:

1. Why this?

2. Why now?

3. What do I have to do?

4. What's in it for me?

I like Bob's simple, powerful questions very much. So let me answer them for you here, in the contexts of why you should consider bringing improv into your organization.

QUESTION #1: WHY THIS?

Why business improv for your organizational culture and your leadership style? Because it's where the proverbial rubber meets the road. Improv is where strategy and planning meet implementation. Improvisation is a communications technique that requires leaders to be present and, in the moment, to listen as if the business depends on it. Business improv requires that we respond honestly, put the thoughts and needs of others ahead of our own, and adapt to the unexpected challenges and opportunities.

Focus on the things you can control and ignore the things you can't. Doing so will bring you clarity during chaotic times.

Improvisational communication lets you as a leader focus on the things you can control and allows you to ignore the things you can't control. Doing this will bring you clarity during chaotic times. With practice, your brain will slow down to focus on the details, the context, and subtext of the conversation to guarantee nothing is missed. The foundations of improvisation will guide and strengthen you and your teams.

The 7 Foundations of Improvisation

1. Respect
2. Trust
3. Support
4. Listen
5. Focus
6. Adapt
7. Maintain the "Yes, and ..." mindset

Improvisation is all about reacting and adapting to a changing landscape by accurately assessing a given situation's needs, which allows the conversation to move forward in a positive new direction. Improvisation is about building more substantial teams, being creative and innovative, collaborating with others, negotiating from a place of win-win, becoming highly focused during times of stress, setting your ego aside for the good of the organization and others, demonstrating empathy, and being very comfortable with the uncomfortable. Improvisation strengthens your emotional intelligence and interpersonal skills.

Business improv is about letting go of your own agenda to listen intently — to be empathetic and open-minded in the present moment — so you can truly connect with colleagues and other stakeholders to generate optimal results.

> **Business improv is about letting go of your own agenda to listen intently – to be empathetic and open-minded in the present moment – so you can truly connect with colleagues and other stakeholders to generate optimal results.**

Improv will help you:

- ➤ Push conversations forward and explore new possibilities

- ➤ Tackle delicate situations and improve internal and external negotiations

- ➤ Manage personal and organizational change

- ➤ Deliver impactful presentations

- ➤ Create space for innovation, process improvement, and profitable, sustainable growth

- ➤ Reduce stress, increase joy, improve productivity, and transform cultures

When it comes to "Why this?" and business improvisation, I could regale you with justifications and stories all day. But, as you can see, improv at work changes the culture and the communication in a way that generates positive, measurable results.

QUESTION #2: WHY NOW?

I began writing this book during the height of the COVID-19 global pandemic. If ever there was a time to adopt the improviser's mindset, it was in that moment of chaos and unpredictability. The rules were changing every day. Stakeholders were scared and confused; some were very sick; others were grieving. Employees were struggling to adjust to new safety protocols and even new places of work, and people's personal lives (including the loss of daycare or a school routine for their children) were bleeding over into their work lives. I have a friend who is a communications coach and the pandemic made her services all the more critical to her clients. She shared with me that her phone was ringing off the hook with questions from leaders (people like university deans and small business owners and corporate C-suite leaders) with questions like: "How do I stand up in front of everyone and give a speech with no script? They want to know when we're coming back to work and 'what happens if' — and I don't have any answers." The world has always been chaotic, but the pandemic forced the entire world "off script" and only the lucky few (i.e., the prepared and practiced) were ready.

We are all busy and there never seems to be enough time to read an entire business book, to complete the exercises it suggests, to make the personal change it inspires us to pursue, and to put our new learning into action at work. But the longer you put off to tomorrow the commitment to mastering the art of business improvisation, the more your workplace relationships will flounder, the more negotiations will come up short, the more innovation will be lost to the status quo. Opportunity, growth, success, profit, and even happiness are on the other side of change. And, like it or not, change is happening all the time — imposed changed and designed change. As leaders, we need to be adaptable, collaborative, creative, innovative, and willing to embrace risk. And the time is now.

The world has always been chaotic, but the pandemic forced the entire world "off script" and only the lucky few (i.e., the prepared and practiced) were ready.

Change is a constant. You can either lead change, follow change, or ignore change. Leading change gives you a voice in the conversation. Following change allows you to be a witness in the conversation. Ignoring change will lead to pain, dissatisfaction, and even unemployment. Which do you prefer?

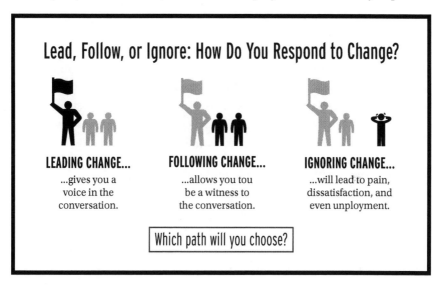

Lead, Follow, or Ignore: How Do You Respond to Change?

LEADING CHANGE...
...gives you a voice in the conversation.

FOLLOWING CHANGE...
...allows you tou be a witness to the conversation.

IGNORING CHANGE...
...will lead to pain, dissatisfaction, and even unployment.

Which path will you choose?

QUESTION #3: WHAT DO I HAVE TO DO?

Leaders need to learn to live in the moment and become *engaging* and engaged *with* their teams. An improvisation mindset helps you do precisely that. An "off script" attitude helps in building and maintaining relationships while strengthening the focus of those relationships. Can you park your ego and suspend judgment? If not, give it a try. I'll show you how. First, cross your arms over your chest in whatever way feels natural to you. Now cross your arms the opposite way. Uncomfortable, right? Of course, it is, *and* if you began crossing your arms differently every day for a long period of time, at some point, it would be *comfortable*. You would adapt. That is precisely what change feels like. Uncomfortable at first, *and* you will eventually get comfortable with the uncomfortable.

So that's the first step when it comes to "what you have to do" to begin embracing business improv. While you are attempting to live in the moment and lean into uncomfortable situations, you must be respectful, be trustworthy, and provide support to others. Influential leaders are better communicators because they "listen to understand" not just "listen to respond." Empathize with your team and be more vulnerable. Embrace the foundations of improvisation into your leadership style and the way you live your life. This sounds simple, and it takes work. Whenever I'm taking on large tasks, I think to myself: "How do you eat an elephant? One bite at a time!" And then I take one bite or one step, or I check off one thing on my "to-do" list. Before I know it, I've made big progress. The same can be true of your decision to become a leader with an improviser's mindset. Don't be overwhelmed with all there is to master. Simply practice improvisational leadership every day and watch your team respond positively and become more productive. And guess what? It doesn't cost a thing to change your mindset, your behavior, your attitude, or your communications. You can just get busy doing it ... and then start reaping the rewards.

To be sure, improvising is the exact opposite of the traditional methods of learning and development. And that's a good thing! Sitting in a classroom or a board room, being lectured to for hours upon hours does not increase retention. It increases boredom. It is just a mind-numbing data dump of facts, figures, and content that is uninspiring.   We have lost the motivation to engage the audience in action so we need to fight our way back. When you take the improviser's mindset, we turn the content into stories, analogies, and metaphors so the audience will pay attention, which increases retention of information (and, in turn, reduces rework and improves productivity).

It doesn't cost a thing to change your mindset, your behavior, your attitude, or your communications. You can just get busy doing it ... and then start reaping the rewards.

In Question #2 above, I argued that the answer to "why now?" hinges on the urgency of addressing risks as they arise and not hiding from them. So what exactly do you need to do now? You need to embrace risk. That means being open to lots of new ideas, even the ones that make you initially respond with negative emotion. Embracing risk is all about not being punitive to those who come up with new ideas (even the ones that initially strike you as silly or stupid or impossible or inappropriate); a leader who embraces risk is one who celebrates those ideas even when they "fail." I like to think of the word "fail" as an acronym — FAIL — that stands for "First Attempt In Learning." If you don't allow your team (or yourself) to FAIL and if you punish your colleagues (or yourself) for taking a risk, all you will achieve is a delay in your ultimate success. Because it will take you longer to solve the problem once everyone is living in the fear of being punished. Give your team the freedom to fail and watch them grow.

Without fear, there is safety. And safety creates opportunity. Improvisational leadership provides psychological safety to the team, allowing everyone to speak their minds and to feel safe taking risks in front of each other. Don't take my word for it — just ask Google, the powerhouse company that believes that psychological safety is "far and away" the most crucial dynamic of a successful team.[13]

Give your team the freedom to fail and watch them grow.

What else do you need to do? Be vulnerable. Showing vulnerability as a leader makes you relatable and human. Your leadership inspires your team, in turn, to become vulnerable and allows the team to set aside their individual and collective egos for the good of the organization. Indeed, the improvisational philosophy is what modern leadership requires of us today. It's not the command-and-control "I will tell you what to do" leadership style of the 1950s and 1960s (and even the 1970s and 1980s and beyond!). Improvisational leadership is a collaborative and inclusive leadership style that focuses on the team and not the leaders themselves.

QUESTION #4: WHAT'S IN IT FOR ME?

It's a fair question and not a selfish one, so go ahead and ask it. What's in it for you? When it comes to improvisational leadership, there is a lot in it for you, as the leader — in short, you are rewarded with more tremendous respect from your team and from others in the organization. You will be the

---

13   Julie Rozovsky, "The Five Keys to a Successful Google Team," re:WORK, November 17, 2015, https://rework.withgoogle.com/blog/five-keys-to-a-successful-google-team/.

improviser/leader who others admire and want to work with. I have never felt that people work for a boss — leadership is earned and it has nothing to do with a job title. Being a skilled and authentic improviser allows you to earn the respect and relationships you (and your organization) need for success.

Today's leadership demands more collaboration and less of an "it's all about *me*" approach. You may have the authority and the power to hire and fire or to bark out orders, and that is not leadership. (By the way, if you were thinking "*but* that is not leadership," you're correct. *And* I'm doing my best to practice what I preach when it comes to "yes, and ..." instead of "yes, but ...") I've always loved Simon Sinek's definition of leadership; he says that being a leader has nothing to do with rank or authority, but that a leader is "someone who embraces the awesome responsibility to see those around them rise."[14] When you adopt that mindset, you teach everyone in your organization that they are all leaders, no matter their title or seniority. So if you're wondering "What's in it for you?" — which is exactly what I've asked you to ponder — the answer is "a whole lot!" Let me offer just a few examples of what's in it for you.

When you commit yourself to a new way of being at work — an attitude and set of behaviors that is driven by an improviser's mindset — the rewards are significant and many.

→   You will create a culture that inspires others to action

→   Your influence will be contagious to all

→   You will be the spark of innovation as your willingness to ask for bad ideas will ultimately lead to good ideas.

Let's talk about why I think asking for "bad ideas" is such a good idea, shall we? In the world of improv, "bad ideas are bridges to good ideas — and having no ideas lead to nothing." Imagine watching an episode of *Whose Line Is It Anyway* in which Drew Carey as the host sets up an exercise with detailed instructions and then the cast members stand there quietly, scratching their chins, devoid of ideas ... good or bad. "No ideas" is

---

14   Simon Sinek, Facebook Photo Caption, October 4, 2020, www.Facebook. com/SimonSinek.

a disaster in entertainment improv just as it is in workplace improv. So how do you get people to share their ideas at work? Think like an improviser!

When you ask your colleagues for ideas, it's important that they feel prepared, empowered, and safe to speak up. If you have an initial idea to share, go ahead and share it, but show that your idea is the setup, not the end solution. Go ahead and say, "This might be a crazy idea but let's be open to crazy ideas." Or "Help me think this through." Or "Can you offer some ideas that build upon this initial idea or blow it up entirely to replace it with something better?"

Involve your employees in decision-making, problem-solving, and strategy. Listen to their ideas, their issues, and their feelings with empathy. Increase your emotional intelligence, along with your team's capacity for respectful, compassionate collaboration. Don't be afraid and, if you are, push forward anyway. The only way to become comfortable with the uncomfortable is to face it, head on. By doing so, your turnover will reduce, engagement will increase, problem-solving will require less time, and your bottom line will grow in ways you could never have previously imagined.

> **Involve your employees in decision-making, problem-solving, and strategy. Listen to their ideas, their issues, and their feelings with empathy. Increase your emotional intelligence, along with your team's capacity for respectful, compassionate collaboration.**

There's nothing worse than feeling uncomfortable at work (or on a stage); and yet that discomfort is something that the greatest leaders learn to lean into rather than flee from. Improv teaches us how to be comfortable with the uncomfortable, how to be present, to take risks, and to draw upon our knowledge base. When you think about it, we all are improvisers in our personal and professional lives. Now, it's time to improvise with intention.

ASK YOURSELF

➤ How can you and your organization begin to adopt these improv foundations — asking for bad ideas, listening with empathy, leaning into discomfort, and throwing away your scripts?

➤ What will it take to go beyond just testing out the foundations to actually incorporating them into your culture to ultimately create leaders who lead and adapt in a very challenging business climate?

➤ What can you do or decide *today* that gets you started?

The Journey Through *Off Script:* What to Expect in the Chapters Ahead

Okay, readers, you have been fully oriented and introduced to the concept of "going off script" in business and embracing an improviser's mindset. Now, it's time to dig in. So let me tell you briefly about the chapters that await you, and then let you turn the page, grab a notebook and pen, and get started mastering the art of business improv.

The overall intention of this book is to change your mindset as it relates to the words "improv" and "improvisation" so that you can apply them in meaningful ways in your careers, companies, and lives. The first goal is to bust the myth that improv is all about making things up, that it's only a comedic tool, and that' it's not meant for the business world.

The second goal is to create a vision in your head to see that improv creates a dynamic and vibrant culture for your business.

Here's what to expect in the chapters ahead ...

Chapter 1 — Rewriting the Script: Leadership, Improv, and a World of Opportunities — begins with a discussion about the philosophy and power of the phrase "Yes, and ..." as well as a discussion of how "No" is appropriate in limited use.

Chapter 2 — Off and Running: Vulnerability and Generosity as the Fuel for Selfless Leaders — takes you through an exploration of how to move the focus from the leader or boss and to the team, the collective, and the stakeholders.

Chapter 3 — Flipping the Script: Making It All About *Them* and Not About *You* — invites you to examine why empathy is essential to being a leader.

Chapter 4 — Way Off Base: The Death of the Ego in Modern Leadership — outlines why ego-based leadership is outdated and improv-based leadership is a more preferred way to lead an organization and a team.

Chapter 5 — Off Key: Learning to *Listen* to Avoid Tone-Deaf Leadership — is all about becoming a better listener by eliminating internal and external distractions, parking your ego, and truly listening to the other person so you can learn and not just respond.

Chapter 6 — Mastering Authentic Leadership: The Art of Monotasking and Being Present — explores the term "being present" and why leaders need to be more present, offering an alternative to multitasking and distraction.

Chapter 7 — Scripted for Safety: Letting Go of Negativity and Dismissal — introduces you to the concept of psychological safety and outlines its relationship to improvisation, helping you see what is possible when professionals stop condescending to or dismissing one another.

Chapter 8 — Turned Off: Walking Away from Your Inner Critic — describes how your inner critic can be detrimental to your leadership effectiveness and the impact it can have on the team at large.

The third goal of this book is to provide you with practical tips on how to use improv in your daily business life so you can be impactful in what you do. The day-to-day realities of improv at work are explored in the book's second part.

Chapter 9 — New Scripts: Communicating and Collaborating for Better Results — teaches you how to use improv in corporate conversations.

Chapter 10 —Unscripted Give-and-Take: Using Business Improv to Resolve Disputes and Negotiate Deals — unveils how improv is used effectively when negotiating or moving issues and conversations forward.

Chapter 11 — Off Course: Mastering Change Management with a New Mindset — is all about how to use improv when dealing with change.

Chapter 12 — Taking a Load Off: Stress Relievers for Overwrought Leaders — offers a juicy list of tips for reducing stress at work and in general.

Chapter 13 — The Art of Innovation: Deploying Improve Techniques to Arrive at Creative Solutions — and **Chapter 14 — Better Off Together: Inspiring a Creative, Idea-Generating Workplace —** are chapters that work together to make the case that we need to innovate differently, and that improv is the key.

Chapter 15 — The Ultimate Pay-Off: Leveraging Your Leadership to Build the Best Team — provides you with ways to use improv in resolving conflict, problem-solving, and building cohesive teams.

Chapter 16 — Facing Off: You, the Audience, and the Art of the Imperfect Presentation — is a primer on how to use improv to help you prepare and deliver more effective presentations.

Chapter 17 — Off Site: Making Sure Your Virtual Presentations and Meetings Don't Suck — is full of ideas for the Zoom generation.

Chapter 18 — Off Kilter: The Pandemic as the Ultimate Improv Exercise — celebrates you and reflects on all we endured and learned about improvisation during the COVID-19 crisis.

Chapter 19 — Off Color: An Improviser's Journey in the American South — is a final story told in hopes of helping all readers of this book understand that we come from different upbringings and vantage points and that opening our minds and mastering the art of improv can be challenging in a variety of ways (but oh so rewarding in the end!).

The last goal of this book is a bit of a bonus — but (and!) a big, practical one I think you'll enjoy. It's my final goal to help you stretch your new improv wisdom and take the "Yes, and ..." approach to exploring how your financial conversations (up, down, and across your organization) can be more powerful. Talking about sales and profits, operating expenses, and capital investments are often the heart of "doing business" and improv can help you do it more effectively.

So let's dig in! Turn the page to learn how mastering the art of business improvisation is the power — the driver — behind extraordinary leadership. It allows us to be our best, most genuine selves and it empowers us to go "off script" to make a difference ... to create impact and to manifest a legacy of excellence.

PART I

The Case for "Improv" in
Improving Organizational Cultures

> *"There are people who prefer to say 'Yes,' and there are people who prefer to say 'No.' Those who say 'Yes' are rewarded by the adventures they have, and those who say 'No' are rewarded by the safety they attain."*
>
> – KEITH JOHNSTONE

CHAPTER 1

REWRITING THE SCRIPT: LEADERSHIP, IMPROV, AND A WORLD OF OPPORTUNITIES

Picture it …. There are two people in an improv workshop performing a popular improv exercise called "two lines." One person is standing and pretending he's casting a line from a fishing pole then settling in to wait for a bite. He turns to the other person on the stage and says, "What a great day to be fishing!"

The other person replies, "We aren't fishing — we're riding horses in the Kentucky Derby."

Then the teacher, clearly annoyed, says: "STOP! Pete, you just negated his reality. Craig said something, and you went NO." He sighs and then continues, "You and Craig try the scene again."

And so we did.

Once again, Craig was standing there, pretending he was casting his line and was fishing. He turned to me and said, "What a great day for fishing." And I replied, "Craig, how can we be fishing when we're at the pool, catching some rays?" The teacher said, "STOP! You negated him again. Sit down, take a break, watch the others, and next week you can try again."

> ## Negating the experiences, ideas, or feelings of others rarely helps us build relationships, reinforce meaningful cultures, ignite innovation, or solve problems.

I sat down to think it over. I should have said, "Yes, it *is* a great day to be fishing, and I brought us some cold beers." I needed to adopt the "Yes! And …" philosophy. I needed to agree with Craig's statement and add on to it instead of hijacking the conversation away from him. In other words, my ego got in the way. Not a huge deal in an improv workshop, perhaps, but in the real world, negating the experiences, ideas, or feelings of others rarely helps us build relationships, reinforce meaningful cultures, ignite innovation, or solve problems.

"Yes! And …"

Let's start this discussion around the key foundation of improv, which is found in these two powerful words: "Yes! And …" or sometimes less emphatically "Yes, and …" For me, "Yes! And…" is more than a coupling of words, but is a way of working, and way of thinking, and a way of being. "Yes, and …" (with or without the exuberant exclamation point) has many applications. First, "Yes and …" is about the agreement but not always agreeing. It is about pushing forward a conversation and exploring the possibilities. "Yes, and …" is the opposite of "No, because …" or "Yes, but …" because those second two

alternatives are negative responses that invoke a negative emotion and —
let's be honest — they are used far too often in today's corporate environment.
"No, because ..." and "Yes, but ..." are dismissive and even punitive whereas
"Yes, and ..." is validating and open to possibilities.

"Yes and ..." is about the agreement but not always agreeing. It is about pushing forward a conversation and exploring the possibilities.

ASK YOURSELF

→ How many times in an average day or week do you say to your
colleagues, "No, because ..." or "Yes, but ..." in an unconscious
need to elevate your own ideas, expertise, or authority?

→ How many times, conversely, do you respond to a question or
suggestion with "Yes, and ..." — affirming your colleagues and
then building upon their ideas?

→ Keep a literal or mental tally of how often you use these phrases.
Opting for "Yes, and ..." even 20% more often than you do now
could fundamentally change the workplace experience for you,
your peers, your direct reports, and even your customers.

For "Yes, and ..." to be effective, you must suspend your judgment and park
your ego. That's right — and let me say that again — *suspend your judgment
and park your ego.* Period. Push the conversation forward through a series of
questions and positive comments to gain a better understanding of the issue
the other person is experiencing. This is called empathy. It's about understanding the issue from *their* point of view, not yours.

The process of listening and being empathetic involves a set of decisions and
behaviors that lets the other person know that you appreciate what they are

saying. This is powerful because appreciation (or the lack thereof) is often the foundation for workplace satisfaction and healthy workplace relationships. In fact, studies have shown that in the year 2019, 79% of people who quit their job said it was due to "lack of appreciation."[1] Don't be part of that statistic. How do you feel when you know someone is listening to you and trying to gain a better understanding of your perspectives versus shutting you down by saying "no" (in those words or ones that look like no, such as "Yes, but ...")?

To be clear, I am not saying that the word "No" should never be used in the workplace when someone presents an idea. Certainly, there are times where "no" or "not now" is appropriate. For example, if someone is trying to push you into an unethical situation, the response should be "no" (you can add an adjective in front of "no" to give it an extra bounce). When you are leaving a meeting and going into another meeting, and an associate stops you to ask you a question, your answer should be, "This isn't the best time. Let me find a break in my day when we can discuss it without any major distractions."

I believe that most conversations we have in the corporate environment should explore using the "Yes, and ..." principle as the driving force of the dialog. But how do we get there? By learning and practicing in a safe space. "Improv exercises" (yes, like the ones I've performed in improv comedy classes!) are a great way for you and others to come to understand the power of "Yes, and ..." So let's try out our first exercise, shall we?

Please note that all the improv exercises that are in this book, when taken together over time, should help instill the improviser's mindset into you and anyone with whom you choose to practice these exercises.

---

1   O.C. Tanner Learning Group, "Performance: Accelerated – A New Benchmark for Initiating Employee Engagement, Retention and Results," White Paper, p. 3, www. OCtanner.com.

EXERCISE #1: "No, because ..." / "Yes, but ..." / "Yes! And ..."

This exercise is used to demonstrate the difference between responding with "No, because ..." "Yes, but ..." and "Yes! And ..." This exercise is done in pairs.

ROUND 1

Improviser A: Pitch an idea to Improviser B. For example, "After this class, let's go out to dinner."

Improviser B: Respond to the pitch with "No, because ..." and give a reason. (You can use the word "thanks" after "no" if that feels more polite or comfortable for you.) For example, "No (thanks), because I want to avoid crowds so I can avoid COVID-19."

Improviser A: Respond back with "No, because ..." and give a reason.

Improviser B: Respond back with "No, because ..." and gives a reason.

This round is no longer than 60 seconds

ROUND 2

Improviser A: Pitch the same idea that you explored in Round 1 to Improviser B.

Improviser B: This time, respond to the pitch with "Yes, but ..." and give a reason. (You can use the word "Sure" or "Okay" if that feels more authentic to you.)

Improviser A: Respond back with "Yes (sure/okay), but ..." and give a reason.

Improviser B: Respond back with "Yes, but ..." and give a reason.

This round is no longer than 60 seconds

ROUND 3

Improviser A: Pitch the same idea from Rounds 1 and 2 to Improviser B.

Improviser B: Respond to the pitch with "Yes, and ..." (or an enthusiastic "Yes! And ...") and give a reason.

Improviser A: Respond back with "Yes, and ..." and give a reason.

Improviser B: Respond back with "Yes, and ..." and give a reason.

This round is no longer than 60 seconds

You can observe this exercise on my website at https://petermargaritis.com/ improv-video-exercises.

When the exercise is over, you may want to debrief with your partner or with the participants (if you were teaching two other people and not participating yourself) by first asking the improvisers how they felt during the "No, because ...." round. They may respond with words or phrases like: *negative, no progress, confrontational, defeating,* and *argumentative.* Then ask them how they felt during "Yes, but ..." They might respond with words or phrases like: *It feels a little better,* or *It feels like lip service because they initially agree, but then they add their ideas without fully understanding where I am coming from.* Then finally, ask them how they felt during "Yes, and ..." If you and your coworkers are anything like the thousands of people I have worked with over the years, you're apt to get responses of: *positive, found a solution, inspiring, motivating,* and *it felt so much better.*

Wouldn't you rather have a leader listen to you and try to help solve a problem using "Yes, and ..." versus shutting you down or making you feel bad? One of my favorite leadership quotes speaks to this feeling we get when we're led by those who listen, acknowledge, and appreciate.

> *"Leadership is not about being in charge. Leadership is about taking care of those in your charge."*
>
> **– SIMON SINEK**

"Yes! And ..." and Its Influence on the People Around You

Brainstorming solutions to problems is another application of the "Yes! And ..." method. Let me start by saying you can't create something and be critical in the same space. Criticism and creation can't co-exist. When I hear the word "innovation," I separate it in my mind into two separate pieces, activities, or steps: creativity and ideas into action. Creativity or the initial search for the solution (brainstorming) requires divergent thinking. Divergent thinking is the process of generating as many creative ideas as possible (what is often known in business-speak as "ideation"). Divergent thinking is about *quantity,* not quality. The more ideas, the better. Once we have gathered all our ideas during divergent thinking, now is the time for those ideas to be critiqued, analyzed, and scrutinized (convergent thinking). The effectively applied creativity quality assessment comes next and is accomplished through *convergent* (as opposed to divergent) thinking; we search for the right solution from the myriad ideas we've already generated.

You can't create something and be critical in the same space.

"Yes, and ..." in a brainstorming session is about agreeing with an idea and adding to it. In improv, we say, "bad ideas are bridges to good ideas; no ideas lead to nothing." Take a moment and think about that phrase. It makes perfect sense. *Yes!* And those bridges only work if you have created a culture that accepts *terrible* ideas. Once you have that type of culture in place, then you can take it up another level and ask for *crazy* ideas. The crazier idea allows us a lot more bandwidth to find the solution. Realistically speaking of course, we aren't likely to institute the *insane* idea but will walk it back to the middle to find a workable solution. Sometimes being able to see a full spectrum of ideas — from the fledging ideas that don't go far *enough* to the out-of-this-world ridiculous ideas that go way *too* far — allows us to see the perfect solution somewhere in the middle.

While I've got you thinking about bridges, let's keep talking about building materials, shall we? Another famous phrase in the improv world is "bring a brick, not the cathedral," which means bring an open mind with lots of ideas (i.e., individual ideas and building blocks) and not the fully devised solution (i.e., the cathedral). My improv coach, Jay Sukow, reminds me that, "Your idea is not the end idea; it is the setup." Those of us who have shown up with cathedrals instead of bricks have learned the hard way that it's imperative to dial back our egos and accept that someone else's idea is possibly (even likely) better than our own. I have been known to wear out the phrase: "The collective knowledge outside your office far exceeds the collective knowledge inside your office." Because it's true! We all have participated in a brainstorming session where the boss has already decided what the solution is but solicits everyone's ideas only to shoot them down. I call this kind of boss in this kind of situation an "ask-hole."

> ## "Bad ideas are bridges to good ideas; no ideas lead to nothing."

"Yes, and ..." Can Help You Deal With the Unknown (Like COVID-19)

You may be reading this book in late 2021 or perhaps you've picked up a copy in 2026. No matter what the calendar says today, you will remember acutely the uncertainty and constant change inherent in living through (and working during) a global pandemic. Since the moment the World Health Organization declared the pandemic in mid-March 2020, there was something new to learn and absorb and abide by every day (or at least it felt like it). Lockdowns and quarantines, border closings, mask mandates and hand-washing protocols, "flattening the curve" and moving workers and children and even college students to "remote work." Then there were temperature checks and nasal swab (PCR) tests, antibody testing and antigen testing, hundreds of protocols and theories about how to treat symptoms and save lives, and a mad dash to develop a vaccine. We learned about supplemental payments for unemployment benefits, about SBA loans and PPP loans and small-business grants. We stockpiled toilet paper and hand sanitizer while our neighbors scrounged up scraps of fabric to sew into masks. And, with few exceptions, we all learned to use Zoom and other video conferencing and streaming technologies for work meetings, stage presentations, family holiday parties, first dates, concerts, graduation ceremonies, and doctors' appointments. Eventually, there were vaccinations (Pfizer-Biontech, Moderna, and Johnson & Johnson, oh my!), vaccination cards, new rules for restaurants and airplanes, and a resurgence of cases (hello, Delta variant!) just as people in many countries were feeling hopeful and getting "back to normal."

> ### Without realizing it, every single one of us who lived through the SARS-CoV-2 pandemic was practicing improvisation, every day and in every way.

Without realizing it, every single one of us who lived through the SARS-CoV-2 pandemic was practicing improvisation, every day and in every way. We were learning to give up control, to listen better, to have empathy, to collaborate, to let go of our egos and sense of being the smartest person in the room. We were living in the moment, knowing the moment was going to change yet again when we least expected it. We were — by and large — accepting that we "didn't know what we didn't know," learning to silence our inner critics, and getting comfortable with the uncomfortable. The COVID-19 pandemic provided perhaps the most powerful real-life exercise in mastering the art of improv that we could never have imagined.

ASK YOURSELF

➜ What did you learn as an amateur or even an expert improviser during the COVID-19 crisis?

➜ What lessons will you put to use far into the future and perhaps forever? How can you ensure you "don't waste the crisis," as my friend Kate often asks leaders who want to pandemic-proof their businesses for the future?

In some ways, improvisers were made for the moment when COVID-19 hit our communities. Without notice, we lost control of so much. Yet improvisers were undeterred because they have been trained and have practiced how to focus on the things they have control over and to accept for now the things they don't have control over. Another way to think about it is that during a crisis or organizational disruption, it's best "to improvise the scene you are in, not the one you want to be in," and focus on today as much as possible.

In March of 2020, when the country was shutting down, we stepped into a state of unknown and uncertainty. At first, my mind went to a dark place as I imagined the future and I felt lost when my business was completely shutting down. (I speak and train for a living, and suddenly there were no clients inviting me into training rooms and no conferences inviting me onto their stages. My business world, as I had known and enjoyed it for many years, was suddenly knocked off its axis.) But then my improvisation skills kicked in and discarded those dark thoughts and just focused on the issues at hand. I took it literally one day at a time. Each day, I would shed the reality of yesterday and accept the new facts facing me today. The deeper we went into quarantine, the more I realized that the pre-COVID-19 world would no longer exist, and I needed to accept that fact and adapt.

> **During a crisis or organizational disruption, it's best "to improvise the scene you are in, not the one you want to be in," and focus on today as much as possible.**

With all due respect to the iconic *Friends* episode with the couch and the stairs, I'd love for us all to stop using the term "pivot" when it comes to what we've done at work because of the pandemic. The short definition of a pivot is "to turn upon." Pivoting is about shifting, with or without intention or comfort about where we're headed next. To adapt, on the other hand, is "to become adjusted to new conditions." We are adjusting to our new conditions every single day. At the time this book went to press, more than 700,000 people in the United States had died from COVID-19 and more than 43 million people in the U.S. were known to have contracted the virus. The crisis raged, and we adapted as best we could. As of October 3, 2021, more than 186 million people in the United States (57% of the population) were fully vaccinated against COVID-19 and schools and other public places were re-opening.

Whether the next crisis that shuts down the world is a viral pandemic, global flooding, a series of cyber-attacks, or something else, it's coming. And knowing how to adapt will be key.

Throughout 2020 and 2021, I worked feverishly to adapt my business model to the "new normal" because that was the only thing I could control. The facts were stark:

➔ 85 percent of my speaking business either canceled or was postponed by 6-18 months

➔   65% of my speaking revenue in a typical year occurred during the
months of August through December. During this timeframe for
2020, I had only nine scheduled engagements, a drop-off in business of 70% from the previous year.

My world had changed, just as yours — I am sure — had. So what were
we to do? We improvised! I used my time in lock-down, quarantine, and
work-from-home to re-create my business so that it would never again be as
dependent on "live," face-to-face speaking engagements to generate growth
and revenue. I got busy building a consulting practice, sketching out this
book, moving my face-to-face presentations to a virtual format, and creating
a virtual improv workshop (which launched in November 2020 — register at
PeterMargaritis.com/Virtual-Workshop).

Luckily for me, virtual presentations weren't new to me when the pandemic
struck; I had been doing them for more than five years, either pre-recorded
or live. I am familiar with Zoom, WebEx, and GoToMeeting. I am a certified
virtual presenter through eSpeakers, a business partner of the National
Speakers Association. I knew I was going to be okay, and I kept focusing on
what was in my control.

The mindset of an improviser is always adjusting to the new landscape and
letting go of past realities. Think for a minute about the fact that most people
initially thought the internet was just a fad and, years later, that online shopping would never replace "brick and mortar" shopping. Just ask Sears, Toys
"R" Us, Neiman Marcus, or Macy's if they might take online shopping more
seriously if they could go back in time. I think we all know that answer.

How about working remotely? I used to hear that people who worked
remotely couldn't possibly be as productive as those who worked in an
office setting. Those employees were sitting at home eating bon-bons
and watching *Ellen,* remember? However, during the pandemic, when
offices were closed, we learned that we could be *more* productive working
remotely. When forced to improvise, companies learned valuable lessons
about the power of a remote workforce — to the point that many companies
began trying to reduce their corporate real estate footprint and shed excess
overhead. If people wanted to work from home, could do so productively,
and it saved the company a ton of money, that was win-win-win.

Leading like an improviser and embracing the power of "Yes, and ..." will allow you to adapt to the changing landscape, to become more creative and collaborative, and to demonstrate your appreciation for the people you work with through empathy and active listening.

When you think about the work we're undertaking here together as author and readers, it's easy to see that this, too, is a critical moment in time ... a moment when, *yes*, you can sharpen your own skills as a leader *and* generate unforetold results at work. So, call it what you will — off-script leadership, improv leadership, or even "leadership in hyperdrive powered by improv™" (a term I coined several years ago) — and know this: leading like an improviser and embracing the power of "Yes, and ..." will allow you to adapt to the changing landscape, to become more creative and collaborative, and to demonstrate your appreciation for the people you work with through empathy and active listening. This kind of leadership will produce the most significant results in our volatile, uncertain, complex, and ambiguous (VUCA) landscape.

BONUS BITES!

Throughout this book, I'll be going "off script" myself to offer you fun, interesting, informative, and tasty "bonus bites" — resources that can stand alone, or augment your learning, and that might be fun to share with your colleagues and friends. Enjoy!

THE FOOD NETWORK'S *GUY'S GROCERY GAMES (GGG)*

Have you ever watched The Food Network's *Guy's Grocery Games*? If not, you may want to tune in for (or stream!) a few episodes because this is improv at its best (reality-TV style). The premise of the show is that four highly trained and skilled chefs will create a themed meal from items in a grocery store around some interesting challenges that the host, Guy Fieri, imposes upon the contestants. Prior to the episode/contest, the participating chefs don't know the theme of the theme they will be cooking or the constraints they'll have to contend with.

In season 23, episode 31, titled RAW (behind the scenes), the overall theme of the meal was "Big Baller Championship Meal" because it ran during that big football championship I can't mention by name and that is always played on a Sunday. The grocery game challenge was promoted on air and online as an "over-the-top" gourmet meal. The four chefs competing in that episode were Antonia Lofaso, Jet Tila, Aarti Sequeira, and Michael Voltaggio, and the constraints to the challenge were as follows:

➤ Each chef chose a mystery can item (with just a number on the label) and the chefs had to incorporate this item into their "big baller" meal. The selection of the can was a blind choice. The contents of the cans (one of each) were spaghetti and meatballs, three-bean salad, macaroni and cheese, and lasagna.

➤ Each chef was not allowed to use a shopping cart but only a very small, wired basket to collect additional grocery items to round out the ingredients for their meal.

- ➥ Each chef was limited to shopping for only nine items, and the 10th was the mystery can.

- ➥ Each contestant had just 30 minutes to shop, cook, create, and plate their meal.

The chaos that occurs once Guy says "GO!" is just crazy fun and stressful to watch. Viewing from an improviser's viewpoint, I find it quite fascinating. The chefs didn't have time to think in detail about what they wanted to cook so, instead, they had to go with their instincts. They had to step up to the kitchen with old scripts, ready to modify them and deviate from them and even throw them away altogether. They were drawing on their past experiences and knowledge in the creation of their meal. (Remember, they had no preparation time at all. Contestant Jet Tila said, "If you can't process things quickly or think on your feet, don't do this.")

Here is what each chef produced from the nine ingredients they assembled:

- ➥ Chef Antonia Lofaso — Bone-In Ribeye with Morels and a Baked Potato with Spaghetti & Meatball Puree

- ➥ Chef Jet Tila — Miso-Marinated-Black Cod with Canned Lasagna and Spot Prawn Risotto

- ➥ Chef Aarti Sequeira — NY Strip Steak with Green Peppercorn Sauce, Grilled Lobster and Fried Mac N' Cheese Balls (*WINNER*)

- ➥ Chef Michael Voltaggio —Filet, Three Bean and Truffle Vinaigrette, and Avocado Confit with Smoked Salmon Roe

Take what you just read and think about your organization (which, for most of you, isn't a restaurant or a catering business) and your leadership style. Are you willing to go "off script" and improvise to take your organization to the next level? (And when life gives you metaphorical canned goods, can you still deliver gourmet meals? A great improviser often can!)

> *"Status is what you do to someone, not what you are — it's the positive effect you have on others, not the job title you hold."*
>
> **- JAY SUKOW**

CHAPTER 2

OFF AND RUNNING: VULNERABILITY AND GENEROSITY AS THE FUEL FOR SELFLESS LEADERS

For many years now, I have been studying improv, I've participated in countless workshops, I've delivered many big-stage and boardroom presentations on the topic, and I've facilitated workshops with teams who are eager to embrace the art of improv. And through it all, what resonates most strongly is that the power of improv (even if I'm the one teaching it) is not about *me*, it's about *them*. Every suggestion, every exercise, every big "ah ha moment" is about the team, the group, and the organization. Unlike stand-up, which is a truly solo performance (and which, I am sorry to know, many of you have seen the business equivalent of bosses and other colleagues who stand in front of the room and tell it like it is without listening to the experts all around the conference table), improv is — at its finest — about being vulnerable and generous. Improv is all about the relationships. I can hear my fellow improv instructors say: "It's your job to make your teammates look good every time you step on the stage."

ASK YOURSELF

➜ When you step onto a stage, or into a boardroom, or take your seat at the conference room table, or stand in the front of the classroom, do you have a little "pre-game" mantra that goes through your head? Maybe you think, "Let's do this!" Or "It's a great day to learn something new." Or "Deep breaths, you've got this."

➜ Consider how your entire attitude (and, as a result, the conversations/scripts and outcomes) might change if your pre-game mantra was, "Okay, time to let my teammates shine!"

There's a powerful scene in the movie *Remember the Titans* in which Denzel Washington, in the role of a football coach at a high school that's facing the racial tensions of integration, leads his players on a 3:00 a.m. run through the woods that lead to the Gettysburg battlefield, studded with headstones. "This is where they fought the Battle of Gettysburg," he tells them. "50,000 men died right here on this field, fighting the same fight that we're still fighting amongst ourselves today. This green field right here was painted red, bubbling with the blood of young boys, smoke and hot lead pouring right through their bodies." At Gettysburg, brothers fought against brothers; fathers fought against sons.

The players — a group of young men both black and white — stand exhausted and riveted as their coach talks about soldiers who fought side-by-side to the death, brothers in arms ... brothers white and black. Gettysburg was a battle in which black slaves fought against their own interests in loyalty to their white masters, and it was a battle in a larger historical context — a Civil War in which brothers fought brothers, and fathers fought sons. It was a war largely about white America seeking to continue to enslave black America; a war about a fractured nation where ideological lines were drawn that either respected African Americans or dehumanized them altogether.

In the movie, Coach Herman Boone goes on, "You listen. You take a lesson from the dead. If we don't come together, right now, on this hallowed ground, then we, too, will be destroyed. Just like they were. I don't care if you like each other right now, but you *will* respect each other. And maybe — I don't know, maybe — we'll learn to play this game like men."[1]

As movie speeches about teamwork go, it's possibly my favorite. Because it addresses how we have a choice: To come together — despite our differences — to fight for or serve a common cause or, instead, to fall apart (and even die) because we refuse to see ourselves as one team. And respect is the key. A team can achieve its objectives only if each member can achieve respect for the others. Whether we *like* one another isn't as important as whether we give one another support — and that's as true in the workplace or in a family as it is on a sports team.

A team can achieve its objectives only if each member can achieve respect for the others.

This type of "respect for team" can be embraced anywhere in our lives. You might not like your neighbor, for example, and might dread the prospect of chatting with him over the fence, but if you have reached any level of maturity you aren't going to heckle and disrespect him and his family. You won't engage in petty arguments or disrespect him in word or deed. You won't meet his comments with "Yes, but ..." or "No, because ..." You'll improvise your way through the relationship as strong leaders can and do. Because you are that kind of leader (or are on your way to becoming that kind of leader — I believe in you!).

---

1   Yakin, Boaz. 2000. *Remember the Titans*. United States: Buena Vista Pictures.

Ultimately, *this* is what individuals need in a leader; they need a unifier and someone who believes in each individual contribution. Trust is the virtue required to achieve this kind of respect and unity, and — when it comes right down to it — it's up to the leader to create that environment of mutual trust and respect.

Turn the Spotlight to Others

In this chapter's "Ask Yourself" moment, we explored what it might look like to step up to your communications interactions at work with a spirit of "Okay, time to let my teammates shine!" Imagine yourself, if you will, as a proverbial Oprah Winfrey, inviting others onto the stage or the couch and turning the spotlight on *them*. Great leaders shine the light and draw the attention to others.

We can shine the light in obvious ways — through praise and through complimenting or giving attention to others in public forums. But "turning the spotlight on others" happens every day, not just at big speeches on "Employee Appreciation Day." One critical way of embedding a "shining the light" mindset into your organization is through helping your people excel and look good. And when your people achieve and excel and when they exceed expectations, the spotlight shines upon them in a natural, long-lasting way. Simon Sinek — whose TED Talks on the power of "starting with why" have been viewed by tens of millions of people — has continued to explore this notion of what I call "shining the light" … of reminding leaders of the value in seeing to the needs of others before themselves. In a recent book, *Leaders Eat Last* he touches on the military mindset of "officers eat last" — the idea that leaders are willing to forgo their immediate needs in the interest of first serving others.[2] No matter where you work (and, no, it doesn't have to involve a battlefield or a military uniform), success starts with the team. When your team sees your commitment to *them*, they are more likely to meet their commitments to *you* … which increases engagement and overall performance. And like the football players in *Remember the Titans*, you'll be off and running (but hopefully not at 3:00 a.m. through the woods!) on your journey to true teamwork and better organizational results.

---

2   Simon Sinek, *Leaders Eat Last: Why Some Teams Pull Together and Others Don't*, Portfolio, 2017.

This is where improv so perfectly prepares an individual to lead: It is built on the very ideas of team dynamics and teamwork, respectful give-and-take, adaptation, vision, and the willingness to accept risks associated with certain decisions. Imagine yourself participating in an improv sketch with a few other individuals. Your overall success requires the collective efforts and individual victories of everyone involved. And so it is with leaders in the business world too. Every trip to the conference room or the board room is an improv sketch with real-world, bottom-line consequences.

In the movie *Don't Think Twice* — a 2016 film about The Commune, an improv troupe in New York — the improv team is eventually disbanded because the theater is shutting down and two of the seven cast members get selected to be part of a TV show around the same time the theater closes. The two events (closing the theater and the group losing two cast members) creates fractures in the entire cast — jeopardizing their various relation-ships with one another.[3] When it comes to rock bands, we've all heard the term "going solo." It happens with musicians, improv troupes, and — yes — it happens with teams of all types and sizes within places of employment (i.e., corporations, medical practices, universities, nonprofits). "Going solo" isn't always the end of the world, but it usually *is* the end of the team. And that end can come too soon (or unofficially, when colleagues keep trying to function inside a broken team that doesn't have the luxury of disbanding) because one person isn't playing fair. To prevent one person from going rogue on a team of any type, the leader needs to create a group that is built upon trust, knowing that over time, that trust will allow the group to redefine itself and even develop new and different levels of trust when one or more members leave.

Everything Comes Back to Improv ...

I don't care where you work, what industry you serve, and what your area of functional expertise (e.g., accountant, marketer, technologist) — your success as a leader can always be mapped back to your adherence to or deviation from the improviser's mindset. And here's why ... Being a selfless leader who can earn the respect and cooperation from a dynamic team of individuals requires a certain emotional maturity and strength. I sometimes see a dismissive look

3   Birbiglia, M. (Director), *Don't Think Twice*, 2016.

in people's eyes when I mention the word "improv," as if to say, "What are you trying to sell me here?" They soon learn that improvisation involves a lot more than comedy. Leaders must respect, trust, support, listen, focus, and adapt. They need that "yes, and ..." attitude. Like the thousands of leaders I've worked with in my career, you can build and strengthen your teams by encouraging colleagues to regard one another with respect — helping them see each other as inextricably linked and vital to the achievement of the team's goals. You can deliver your own style of Coach Boone speeches and demonstrate, every day, that mutual respect is the foundation of your efforts.

Being a selfless leader who can earn the respect and cooperation from a dynamic team of individuals requires a certain emotional maturity and strength.

In today's business climate, successful leaders must be able to accomplish the following:

➔ Communicate your vision and your ideas, while adapting to the changing business landscape

➔ Be able to move forward even within an arena of uncertainty

➔ Process information quickly — all while being creative, innovative, and willing to see different perspectives

➔ Strive to make your teammates look good

➔ Think on your feet and adapt to changing situations

➔ Listen to *understand*, not just to *respond*

Each of these objectives can be accomplished by practicing improvisation. Once you understand that, the effect is transformative. Improv can be funny, but it works in situations that aren't very fun or humorous at all, regarding matters that could flare into confrontation if handled the wrong way and even regarding major institutional crisis or disruption. If you apply these principles, you promote healing and growth instead.

BONUS BITES!

A BITE OF TOAST, SORT OF ...

On the evening of May 14, 2021, I attended a dinner gathering at a restaurant (for the first time in 14 months because of the pandemic!) with 10 colleague who, like me, are active members of the National Speakers Association. The restaurant was packed and there was a lot of excitement in the building and at our table. When the waitress brought everyone their cocktail, one of our members, Jon Petz, CSP, stood up and said: "We all are going to make a group toast and here is how we are going to do it — three words per person." Jon started us off with three words and then the person to his left added three words, then the next person added three more — round and round until all 11 dinner guests had participated. We did accomplish the goal despite some people adding four words instead of three.

Most people when they make a toast don't include anyone else except to look to them for nods and smiles and to queue them to raise their glasses. By its very nature, the modern-day toast is a soliloquy ... with some revelers giving a little speech that's all about themselves, spoken with a whole lot of "I," "me," "my," and "mine." What Jon did for our group of friends was to make it inclusive to everyone at the table, making us all feel engaged and of equal importance to the evening ahead. What a great improvisational business dinner icebreaker! Might you try it at your next business event?

"*When you increase empathy toward others, their defensive energy goes down, and positive energy replaces it. That's when you can get more creative in solving problems.*"

– STEPHEN COVEY

CHAPTER 3

FLIPPING THE SCRIPT: MAKING IT ALL ABOUT *THEM* AND NOT ABOUT *YOU*

When it comes to the art of improv, The Second City in Chicago is the gold standard. Learning with and performing with The Second City is downright exhilarating. It's an improv experience that I have always taken very *seriously*, ironic as that might sound. Several years ago, I took a 32-week sketch-writing course from The Second City, in an online format comprising four 8-week sessions. It was exhilarating and tough. As I began to develop my sketches, the instructor would provide me with this feedback: "Quit trying to be funny" and "What is the relationship with the other characters?" It took a bit of time for me to learn how to develop the relationships and, even then, I was still coming up a bit short when it came to human connection. The feedback I received on a couple of my sketches,

"Pete, you need to build the relationship with your characters so your audience can empathize with them." The difficult part of developing empathy for my character was that I had to understand how they felt — what it might be like to actually walk in their shoes. So, I had to create a backstory for the character so I could better understand their world, empathizing with their feelings and experiences, and imagining how I would feel if I were in their place. That was a huge learning experience that I still use to this day. I still often ask myself, "What must it feel like to be them right now? How would I feel or act or speak if I were in their shoes?"

ASK YOURSELF

→ How many times at work, when faced with an interaction that has high stakes (in terms of project outcomes or interpersonal relationships), do you take at least 30 seconds of contemplation to imagine what the other person is going through?

→ How might your experience at work (and, in turn, the experiences of the people around you) be transformed through these moments of empathy ... 30 seconds at a time?

Don't take my word for it. Look around and you'll discover dozens of remarkable leaders and scholars singing the praises of empathy in the workplace. Geoff Colvin, *Fortune Magazine*'s Senior Editor at Large, is one of those leaders. In his 2015 book entitled *Humans Are Underrated: What High Achievers Know That Brilliant Machines Never Will,* Colvin argues that as workplaces evolve and leadership models change, the most important skill that leaders must have is empathy. And he goes on to say that women will have more leadership opportunities than men because they are much more empathetic than men. You know what? I happen to think he's right.[1]

Some might argue that women, in most regions of the world, have been socialized to hone their empathy skills. And the data and stories from the

---

1   Geoff Colvin, *Humans Are Underrated: What High Achievers Know That Brilliant Machines Never Will,* Portfolio (a division of Random House), 2015.

world of business demonstrate how empathic female leaders are setting the bar for us all. In an article published in the *Harvard Business Review* after a survey of 60,000 leaders, Jack Zenger and Joseph Folkman revealed that: "Based on our data, [direct reports] want leaders who are able to pivot and learn new skills; who emphasize employee development even when times are tough; who display honesty and integrity; and who are sensitive and understanding of the stress, anxiety, and frustration that people are feeling."[2]

When it comes to a crisis where human lives are at stake or where human suffering might be on the horizon, women leaders are often far more decisive than their male counterparts in doing what is necessary (even if it's not easy and not popular). Perhaps a talent for empathy translates, in these cases, to stronger, swifter decision-making. You might recall that at the beginning of the COVID-19 pandemic, world leaders were being scrutinized closely as it related to their efforts (for better or for worse) to flatten the curve (i.e., to ensure that the number of SARS-CoV-2 cases that required hospitalization didn't outpace the number of hospital beds available to patients). And time and again, we saw that countries with women leaders — like Sint Maarten, New Zealand, Norway, Iceland, Germany, and Taiwan — put their citizenries into lockdown more quickly and that COVID case rates in those countries were quickly managed, at least for the time being.

Empathy vs. Sympathy

We have all signed, with heartfelt concern, a "sympathy card" for someone who was mourning a loss. And, if you're like most people, you tend to use the terms "sympathy" and "empathy" in overlapping or interchangeable ways. But there is a distinct difference. And, not to confuse matters more, most "sympathy cards" are actually really empathy cards.

So, what is empathy? Empathy is the ability to put yourself in someone else's shoes and actually feel what they feel, not what you *think* they feel. Empathy involves feeling grief and pain when (and because) someone else feels it. The empathetic friend or coworker feels your frustration or anger or exhaustion when your car breaks down on the way to work or when you

2   Jack Zenger and Joseph Folkman, "Research: Women Are Better Leaders During a Crisis," *Harvard Business Review*, December 30, 2020, https://hbr.org/2020/12/research-women-are-better-leaders-during-a-crisis/

are passed over for a promotion because of internal politics that are unfair. Every single day, in our roles as leaders, we encounter situations where empathy would serve us (and others) well. It always matters to be thinking and saying, "I feel for you" or "I appreciate where you are coming from and that's awful (or amazing or exciting or scary)." But when it comes to most situations where empathy is important, is it always the case that we truly *do* empathize? No, it is not. Usually we miss the chance for empathy because we're too busy or too rushed, we're not present, our egos are in the way, or we're too focused on projects and deadlines and sales figures to be thinking about (and feeling for) the humans who make our organizations possible. Often, we simply don't take the 30 seconds the occasion calls for. And many times when we say we empathize with someone, we may just be *sympathizing* with them. What is the difference?

> **We miss the chance for empathy because we're too busy or too rushed, we're not present, our egos are in the way, or we're too focused on projects and deadlines and sales figures to be thinking about (and feeling for) the humans who make our organizations possible.**

Consider what Michael Miller presents in his article, "Empathy vs. Sympathy: What's the Difference?" on *Six Seconds: The Emotional Intelligence Network*. Miller delineates the two terms like this:

> *"Empathy means experiencing someone else's feelings. It requires an emotional component of really feeling what the other person is feeling. Sympathy, on the other hand, means understanding someone else's suffering. It's more cognitive in nature and keeps a certain distance."*[3]

---

3   Michael Miller, "Empathy vs. Sympathy: What's the Difference?," Six Seconds: *The Emotional Intelligence Network*, https://staging.6seconds.org/2021/01/20/empathy-vs-sympathy-what-the-difference/.

Sometimes, when we sympathize with others, we are trying to help them find the proverbial silver lining and make them feel better. Sympathizers go straight for the "Look on the bright side" instead of pausing in the emotion to feel it, even if it's hard.

To show empathy, you must be vulnerable, authentic, and put your ego aside.

To show empathy, you must be vulnerable, authentic, and put your ego aside. It's about making a human connection and not just pushing the conversation to conclusion so you can get on with your day and get back to work. Being vulnerable is putting yourself out there for others to see. It takes courage and it takes time. Far too often, leaders feel that being vulnerable is a sign of weakness ... and I disagree with that attitude. Being vulnerable is a sign of being human, authentic, genuine, and honest — and by being vulnerable, you create stronger human connections. Isn't that what great leaders do — make meaningful and authentic connections? In my life and career, the men and women I have considered to be the strongest leaders have been the ones who exercise vulnerability to the point of excelling at it.

Two Separate Personalities

It can be hard to teach leaders to "flip the script" when it comes to being more empathetic and even vulnerable if those leaders are wearing a thick protective armor over their humanity in the workplace. You've met leaders like this. Heck, maybe you have been this kind of leader. It's not uncommon for leaders — when they're climbing the corporate ladder and when they claim the corner office — to be guilty of presenting two separate personalities to the world: one personality inside the office and the other outside the office. Their inside-the-office personality is often very rigid and authoritative and hinges on a "nothing personal, just business" approach to getting things done. When they say "nothing personal, just business," they believe their ability to be aloof allows them to "rise above" — that their inhumanity and inaccessibility puts them in the upper echelon of the non-vulnerable. They revel in the "strength" it takes to never show any vulnerability in most circumstances.

Being vulnerable is a sign of being human, authentic, genuine, and honest – and by being vulnerable, you create stronger human connections. Isn't that what great leaders do – make meaningful and authentic connections?

They (we) use phrases like "never let them see you sweat" and they see friendliness as weakness (i.e., "I'm not here to make friends; I'm here to get the job done."). Two-faced, empathy-devoid leaders think that businesspeople need to be cold, order-barkers who should never fully connect with others in the business. They take pride in their distance. And, sadly, they often continue on this path until something happens that makes it all come crashing down. Their aloof and impersonal workplace behavior starts degrading relationships, and then projects start to fail. Terrifying numbers on the institutional balance sheet can sometimes be tied back to these failures to listen, connect, and care.

"Self-absorption in all its forms kills empathy, let alone compassion. When we focus on ourselves, our world contracts as our problems and preoccupations loom large. But when we focus on others, our world expands. Our own problems drift to the periphery of the mind and so seem smaller, and we increase our capacity for connection - or compassionate action."

–DANIEL GOLEMAN

ASK YOURSELF

➜ Have you ever walked into a conference room or jumped on a video conference preoccupied with a problem you were facing, and then had to make a critical decision when asked the simple question, "So how's your day going?" Can you think of a time when you answered the question honestly but with too much ego, making the meeting all about you and possibly derailing the possibilities for progress or connection that were ripe in that moment?

➜ Conversely, can you think of a time when you smiled and simply said, "Not bad. Tell me how things are going for you," shifting the emphasis quickly to your coworkers, clients, or customers and creating space for a conversation that would never have been possible if you had dominated all the "airtime" with self-absorption?

➜ What's the lesson for you here? How might you breathe and speak and pace yourself differently, allowing more space for others — allowing, as Goleman suggests — the chance for our own problems to drift to the periphery?

We have all witnessed how a self-absorbed leader, by his or her very nature, demonstrates a lack of empathy for others, which creates a lack of respect and trust and creates chaos within the organization.

Self-absorption becomes very apparent when a long-time CEO of an organization announces that they will be stepping down from their role. The others in the C-Suite start positioning themselves to be the new "heir apparent" and will throw people "under the bus" to remain a viable candidate. Yet their brand of leadership is often chaos — as a result of their self-absorption. And what happens to those who have been sacrificed and thrown under the bus? Ultimately, they leave the organization for greener pastures; they realize they deserve better and they go find leaders worthy of them (or they start their own companies and lead themselves). Self-absorption creates a toxic work environment; empathic leadership creates an empowered workplace. One person's behaviors and attitudes can impact many.

Self-absorption creates a toxic work environment; empathic leadership creates an empowered workplace.

Replacing Assumptions

A very effective way to increase empathy is by replacing assumptions with a sense of curiosity that opens us up to empathy. You achieve this through conversation and by questioning to reveal what lies beneath the surface of the other person's issue or perspectives. Curiosity is a good thing. It helps us to ask the questions and gather more facts and information, which leads to eliminating unfounded assumptions. The more questions we ask, the closer we get to the root of any issue and, once discovered, we can help devise a plan to help solve the problem at hand.

> Have you noticed that the word "improv" looks a lot like the word "improve?" More than a mere coincidence, it's a powerful reminder that when we master *improv* we *improve* relationships, teams, organizations, projects, and careers.

Improv Is All About Empathy

For business leaders, an improv background provides an excellent foundation for empathizing with others. First, as a leader, you need to be a great listener and fully present during every conversation — controlling your emotions and recognizing theirs. Leaders should take their ego, agenda (i.e., their tendency toward playing politics or steering a conversation to achieve their own personal outcomes), and excess emotion and put them to the periphery where they won't derail the conversation. When ego, agenda, and emotion are infused too strongly in a conversation, the conversation halts, and negativity is nearly always the immediate result.

ASK YOURSELF

➜ When was the last time you derailed a conversation because your ego, agenda, and/or emotion took over the conversation? How could you have taken a breath, listened with more empathy and genuine concern, and focused on the importance of the relationship or the organizational outcomes at stake? Did your self-absorbed approach to the conversation *create* its own set of problems when the ideal outcome for the meeting would have been the *solving* of the initial problem(s)?

➜ Leaders — great leaders — inspire and motivate through empathy …. not through ego, agenda, and emotion. Developing the kind of empathy to improve your leadership in this way can start with an improviser's mindset.

Empathy, Emotional Intelligence, and the Improviser's Mindset

If all this talk about empathy is ringing some bells and reminding you of professional development and personal work you have undertaken to improve your "emotional intelligence" (EI or EQ), that's great. That gives you some brainy "muscle memory" for the work we're doing here. If you're like most leaders, you have taken at least one EQ assessment (at work or maybe in college), you've attended professional development workshops or webinars on emotional intelligence, and your organization has even built standards for EQ into employee performance evaluations/metrics. Yet some people still find it difficult to understand that a leader's emotional intelligence (of which empathy is a key component) is more critical to the organization than a leader's technical knowledge. Why can Google figure this out, but other companies can't? A *Washington Post* article about the employee culture at Google reported that:

"In 2013, Google analyzed hiring, firing, and promotional data back to 1998, when the company was incorporated. The top ... characteristics for success at Google are: being a good coach; communicating and listening; possessing insights into others; having empathy toward and being supportive of one's colleagues; being a critical thinker and problem solver; being able to make connections across complex ideas."[4]

These characteristics are otherwise known as "soft skills" in modern-day business jargon. When I use the term *soft skills* in a conversation, I watch for the other person to roll their eyes. And when they do, I typically respond, "They call them *soft* skills but wouldn't you agree that they are *hard* to master?" Their eyes stop rolling and become wide open to the truth. The truth is that technical skills (e.g., like knowing how to apply debits and credits as an accountant or knowing how to write HTML for a website or knowing how to draw a patient's blood) are easier to learn than soft skills like effective listening or demonstrating empathy. And if you want to get promoted in today's business world, you have better mastered your interpersonal skills — those nebulous soft skills that are hard to master.

Mastering the soft skills is easier, thankfully, with an improviser's mindset. Just by the nature of the philosophy of "Yes, and ..." the leader is acting in a more empathic manner than responding with either "No, because ..." or "Yes, but ..." The words *no* and *but* have a negative implication and can create a negative response when they inevitably make others feel defensive, dismissed, and disrespected. "Yes, and ..." keeps conversations moving forward positively.

You might be wondering, however, isn't it possible for a truly self-absorbed leader to use "Yes, and ..." language and still do so in a way that is oppressive or disrespectful? Yes, and that's not very common. (See what I did there?) Imagine that a coworker presents an idea that you want to dismiss out of hand. So you say, "Yes, and .... I still expect you to do it my way." Even though you used "Yes, and ..." in constructing your sentence, you were not operating in the *spirit* of "Yes, and ..." You weren't truly acknowledging

---

4   Valerie Strauss, "The Surprising Thing Google Learned About Its Employees — and What It Means for Today's Students," *The Washington Post*, Dec. 20, 2017, https://www.washingtonpost.com/news/answer-sheet/wp/2017/12/20/the-surprising-thing-google-learned-about-its-employees-and-what-it-means-for-todays-students/.

the value of what was shared with or expressed to you. That kind of passive-aggressive communication style is a more overt use of the newly common American phrase "Yeah, no." (If you have teenage children, you likely know this term very well!)

> **The words *no* and *but* have a negative implication and can create a negative response when they inevitably make others feel defensive, dismissed, and disrespected.**

When used properly and genuinely, "Yes, and …" creates a more empathetic response by helping you to park your ego and listen to understand what the other person is trying to convey. "Yes, and …" often forces you to pause for a moment to process the information you've just heard, and then respond with a question or a positive comment. By the time the conversation has concluded, you as the leader will have a better understanding of others' wants and needs and, as a result, you can try to support those in more meaningful and impactful ways.

The Business of People

Let me ask you a simple question: What business are you in?

Before you answer with "the restaurant business" or "the business of higher education" or "the retail business," think about what makes your business (and your entire industry) tick. If you're a reader who has been listening to my podcast or reading my book or blogs, you know that this question is a bit of a "trick question" and a truly important one. The answer to the question "What business are you in?" is always "the people business!"

Without people, you have no one working with you, no customers, and no stakeholders. The better you treat and understand the people you serve (and I suggest you do so through improv leadership), the more empowered and loyal your stakeholders become. The ability to truly listen to another person and be able to empathize with them is an ability that positions you to genuinely show gratitude, respect, and support. That costs you nothing, except for your time.

> *"I think if you spend as much time listening as talking, that's time well spent."*
>
> **–ANNE MULCAHY, FORMER CEO, XEROX**

What steps are you willing to take to become a more empathetic leader? Take some time to think about it … because this is the number-one skill needed in our leaders today and into the future.

The ability to truly listen to another person and be able to empathize with them is an ability that positions you to genuinely show gratitude, respect, and support.

BONUS BITES!

A DISCUSSION WITH JAY SUKOW ABOUT EMPATHY

The incomparable Jay Sukow, who penned the Preface for this book, recently sat down with me to talk about empathy and its vital application in the workplace. What follows here are Jay's own words, prompted by my questions on the subject.

"The definition of empathy? It's the ability to put yourself in someone else's shoes and feel what they feel, not just a rough approximation of what you *think* they feel. If I'm asking a person to share with me their experiences so I can better understand, I'm also asking them to relive a lot of their past, which in some cases can be traumatic. I have many friends who have said that they're just tired of answering the same questions over and over. They've been asked by a lot of people to *explain* the situation. They're just thinking, 'I don't want to explain anymore, go out and learn.'

"They have a point. I *should* do my part to try to understand — to genuinely feel for them. So I go study and try to educate myself for the conversation. There are books, magazines, articles, etcetera. We have access to a free library, open 24/7, 365 days a year. We used to call it the 'worldwide web.' I can take it upon myself to learn more in order to understand. Or, I ask the person: 'What books should I read? What movies should I watch in order to gain a better understanding?' After reading the books and watching the films, I empathized with greater knowledge. The key is to dig into the information and go deep.

"That is part of the power of improv because as an improviser, I have a thirst for knowledge and I am very inquisitive. The more that I learn, the more that I educate myself, and the better person I can become.

"Now we need to look at ourselves and determine what path we are going to take with our knowledge and are we willing to change. That's not an easy thing to do. When you're talking about empathy, it's like, 'I can't change somebody else. I can listen to understand and be open to the conversation.' Of course, you don't have that same experience. Of course, you don't know what it's like. But you can take those situations and go, 'What am I going to do based on that? Now that I have the information, what am I choosing to do? I want to make this change. I know there are things I've said or thought or done in the past that don't align with how I think or feel or behave today. So I want to make a change moving forward. I can't change what I did, or didn't do, but I can now move forward. I can make an active change and be empathetic with them.'

"Now let's discuss empathy as it relates to *leadership*. A leader is someone who knows they don't have all the answers and trusts those around them to find those missing pieces versus someone who thinks they have all the answers. Those leaders who think they are the 'smartest person in the room' are only looking to surround themself with 'yes people.' Why? Because you're dealing with people who have big egos who need to have those egos satisfied. They're not looking for your opinions or your thoughts and this is definitely not some sort of a cooperative relationship. You see, it's all about *them* which equates to lack of listening to understand and the unwillingness to change. There are those leaders who lack empathy and sympathy, and those dysfunctional leaders end up creating or reinforcing dysfunctional organizations."

Once you put your own ego out of the way, you stop judging the ideas of others — instead, you consider them brilliant, and eagerly follow them!

CHAPTER 4

WAY OFF BASE:
THE DEATH OF THE EGO IN
MODERN LEADERSHIP

I learned early on — in my introduction to the art of improv — that I was a poor listener. This had a lot to do with my inflated ego; when I would have a leadership title, I believed that the title or position of power meant that I always had the right answer. In truth, the people reporting to me often had far better ideas, answers, and insights. One day, I came up with this personal proverb that I have come to truly believe in:

"The collective knowledge outside of your office far
exceeds the collective knowledge inside your office."

We all have an ego. Some egos are under-developed, others are well-developed, and yet others are over-developed. Over-developed egos can, in some cases, ultimately transform into full-blown narcissism. When a person's ego becomes over-developed, they can begin to operate from a perspective that the world revolves around them — that everything is all about them. They are the smartest people in the room; just ask them — they will answer with a resounding YES!

Many CEOs have well-developed egos, and organizations need that in their chief leader. The concern with those CEOs who have an over-developed ego, however, is that it leads to narcissism and, more often than not, narcissistic leaders stop listening to those around them. This can become very dangerous. Narcissism has cost many leaders their careers and has destroyed many companies because of the toxic culture it creates.

In 2019, *Inc. Magazine* published a powerful article exposing what they considered to be the failings of three big corporate CEOs who almost killed their companies by creating toxic workplace cultures. The three leaders under scrutiny: Uber CEO Travis Kalanick, Papa John's CEO John Schnatter, and Wells Fargo CEO John Stumpf.

Minda Zetlin, co-author of *The Geek Gap*, penned the article and argued:

> *"... it takes particular ineptitude to start with a perfectly successful company and drive it toward failure. That's especially true when the reason for the decline has nothing to do with the company's product or services, and everything to do with bad behavior by its executives."*[1]

This article demonstrates that CEOs who make everything about them and disregard the advice from their teams are doomed for failure. The ability to listen to understand is one of the key components of leadership, yet it's just thrown aside because of an over-developed ego. We see this in board rooms and we see this in our elected leaders. It is all about *them*.

Leaders who lead with an "improv leadership" style have a foundation of respect, trust, and support of their organization and their people. These

---

1   Minda Zetlin, "Here's How 3 of the World's Worst CEOs Almost Killed Their Companies by Creating a Toxic Culture: Their Behavior is a Master Class in How Not to be a Leader," *Inc. Magazine*, July 31, 2019, https://www.inc.com/minda-zetlin/worst-ceos-toxic-culture-uber-papa-johns-wells-fargo.html.

leaders know how to suspend their judgment, be active listeners, be present, and be adaptable. They also believe or intuitively understand that leadership is the positive effect you have on another person. The *positive* effect!

Leaders know how to suspend their judgment, be active listeners, be present, and be adaptable.

Leggo Your Ego

So how does mastering the art of improv help you to put the power of effective leadership into hyperdrive? It helps you to "leggo your ego."[2] Improv is all about the team and not about you. You are to make your teammates look good, not yourself. Rule number one, you never throw a teammate under the bus. Let me tell you a story about an NFL football game between the Arizona Cardinals and the Seattle Seahawks held on October 2016.[3] The story isn't about the game at all, but about how the coaches responded to the game's unfortunate end. The game ended in a tie when both kickers, Arizona kicker Chandler Catanzaro and Seattle kicker Stephen Hauschka, missed game-winning field goals in overtime. Ugh.

During the post-game press conferences, each team's coach had an opportunity to comment on the missed kicks. Arizona Coach Bruce Arians said this about his kicker: "Make it. This is professional, this ain't high school, baby. You get paid to make it."[4] Can you imagine how the Arizona kicker felt after hearing his coach pile on criticism and blame after an already heart-breaking moment?

During the Seattle press conference, on the other hand, the media (and the players) saw a very different type of leadership on display. Seattle Coach

---

2   With a nod to our friends at the Kellogg Company for their iconic "Leggo My Eggo" commercials for Eggo Waffles. A marketing slogan that burns bright in our memories.

3   Justin Bariso, "These 2 NFL Coaches Reacted Very Differently to Their Players Mistakes – and Taught Us a Major Lesson in Leadership," *Inc. Magazine,* October 24, 2016, https://www.inc.com/justin-bariso/a-lesson-in-leadership-2-football-coaches-2-player-mistakes-and-2-very-different.html.

4   Ibid.

Pete Carroll said this about his kicker: "[Hauschka] made his kicks to give us a chance and unfortunately he didn't make the last one. He's been making kicks for years around here ... but he's gonna hit a lot of winners as we go down the road here. I love him and he's our guy."[5]

And that, my friends, is proof that the very same situation, when handled by two different leaders with different levels of ego and empathy, can be handled in drastically different ways.

Coach Arians was demonstrating ego leadership by throwing his field goal kicker under the proverbial bus, whereas Coach Carroll was demonstrating improv leadership by not throwing his kicker under the bus and supporting him in public. Now that you're becoming versed in the foundations of improv, I'm betting you can practically hear Carroll saying: "*Yes*, he missed the final field goal. *And* ... he's still an amazing kicker." Carroll understood the power of "Yes, and ..." and the importance of empathy during a difficult moment.

Don't get me wrong. Professional sports, like all businesses, are about results, so the missed kicks were, I'm sure, addressed through feedback and training in the right way and during the right time and place. So, yes, I would imagine that Coach Carroll did have a discussion with his kicker (behind closed doors) about the misses. In improv leadership, you praise a teammate in public and only criticize (when appropriate) in private.

---

5   Justin Bariso, "These 2 NFL Coaches Reacted Very Differently to Their Players Mistakes – and Taught Us a Major Lesson in Leadership," *Inc. Magazine,* October 24, 2016, https://www.inc.com/justin-bariso/a-lesson-in-leadership-2-football-coaches-2-playe r-mistakes-and-2-very-different.html.

ASK YOURSELF

➜ When, in recent memory, did you "call out" an employee or peer (or student, intern, volunteer, etc.) — criticizing them, even if only slightly, in public when you had the distinct opportunity to have their back? If you could do it all over again, how would you have handled the situation differently? What can you commit to doing in future situations?

➜ For inspiration, check out the media and social media coverage of the #DearIntern moment in September 2021, when an HBO Max intern sent out an erroneous email to a huge number of HBO Max subscribers and the brand managers from HBO Max had his back and "helped him through it."

Listening and Presence

Vulnerability, empathy, and a willingness to let go of our ego — they all matter when it comes to developing the kind of leadership capacity our employees, peers, and other stakeholders deserve from us. Crucial to the development of dynamic, admirable leadership is learning to communicate in a way that doesn't negate the experiences of others — adopting the "yes, and …" approach instead of the "no, because …" or "yes, but …" habit. Let's now talk about some additional skills and attitudes that underscore these principles. I've long believed that listening and presence, when added to the "yes, and …" collaborative approach, are the fuel to kick your leadership into hyperdrive.

> **Vulnerability, empathy, and a willingness to let go of our ego — they all matter when it comes to developing the kind of leadership capacity our employees, peers, and other stakeholders deserve from us.**

You don't have to participate in the working world for very long before you discover the terrifying truth that you will — often — get asked questions that stump you. You'll be left speechless and "solution-less" in the face of queries and objections from bosses and peers and customers. You'll think that saying "I don't know" is somehow the worst thing you could possibly admit. Maybe you break into a cold sweat when asked a question during a presentation Q&A or your heart starts racing when find yourself in the board room or a meeting with the boss and you're blindsided with a question you were completely unprepared for. I've been there.

When asked a dreaded question or an unanticipated one, the true answer often is simply: "I don't know." But most of us are terrified to tell the truth in those moments — to say "I'm not sure" or "I don't know" and many of us are initially short on practice for what it feels like to go off script to say: "That's a great question, and I don't know the answer. Here's what I *do* know ..."

That sense of "not knowing" when someone is looking intently at us for an answer ... well, it's hard for all of us. But it's especially difficult for leaders with over-developed egos.

Thomas Koulopoulos, founder of Delphi Group has asserted that one of the biggest challenges in leadership is that — by and large — the perception of not knowing is a sign of weakness. This perception drives over-developed egos crazy! The ego-driven leader never wants to be seen as weak. So, instead of driving their egos crazy during these moments of ignorance, leaders should lean into the "not knowing;" they should stop talking, be quiet, and listen to their team for direction and vision. According to Koulopoulos:

> *"The essence of leadership is getting people to follow your lead and vision [— people] who inherently know more about the nuts and bolts of whatever it is you're leading better than you ever will. Think of it this way: You follow a manager because you have to, but you follow a leader because you want to."*[6]

---

6   Thomas Koulopoulos, "Here's How Great Leaders Listen to and Understand Their Team," *Inc.*, https://www.inc.com/thomas-koulopoulos/heres-how-great-leaders-listen-understand-their-team.html.

These next two improv exercises are designed to raise your awareness about whether your ego might be getting in the way and about how a better approach is to focus on the team and not yourself.

EXERCISE #2: Talking Without "I"

Talking Without "I" is an improv exercise that demonstrates how to park your ego. This exercise requires two people to have a conversation about anything. During the discussion, each player tries not to use the words "I," "me," "my," or "mine" and instead responds to the other person using "we" or "us."

Bracketed in italics are examples of how the improvisers are likely to want to default to "I" language, but you can see how "we/us" alternatives emerge when the participants really try.

> **Improviser 1:** It's a nice sunny day; let's go *[I'd love to go]* to the park.

> **Improviser 2:** That's a great idea and *[I think]* we should plan a picnic.

> **Improviser 1:** Let's bring *[I'll grab]* a blanket, some fruit, crackers, smoked sausage, and wine.

> **Improviser 2:** We can't *[I don't want to]* forget a small turkey sub with some Baked Lays chips.

> **Improviser 1:** Perfect! Now let's both *[let me]* run to the store and get what we need *[I have on my list]* and possibly more.

This exercise aims to help us park our egos so we can be collaborative with our partner, using the general philosophy of "Yes, and ..." There are several opportunities where the word "I" or "me" or "my" or "mine" could be used in that example above. It is more fun and exciting, however, when we can work as a team in accomplishing our goals versus being the "tell you what to do" person.

Next time you're making small plans at work — like scheduling a meeting or planning a lunch — practice doing so without the words "I," "me," "my," or "mine." It's apt to feel stilted and unnatural, and that's okay. The idea is to develop stronger self-awareness about the degree to which your everyday language and decision-making might be, by default, a little more self-centered than you realized (or that you'd like to admit). How might shifting to a "we" or "us" point of view open you up to new levels of empathy and collaboration with your coworkers?

How might shifting to a "we" or "us" point of view open you up to new levels of empathy and collaboration with your coworkers?

EXERCISE #3: Thank You

Thank You is another improv exercise that demonstrates how to park your ego *and* to show gratitude. This exercise requires two people to have a conversation about anything. Each time after the initial discussion, you will reply "thank you" and add on to the other person's response to deepen the conversation and the connection.

> **Improviser 1:** That was a great job you did on your presentation!

> **Improviser 2:** Thank you! What could I have done better?

> **Improviser 1:** Thank you for asking for my feedback. I've always admired your desire to grow and improve. I think if you paused periodically during the presentation, that would help the audience absorb and process your talk.

> **Improviser 2:** Thank you for that feedback. I will watch the video and look for those opportunities. What do you think I did well?

> **Improviser 1:** Thank you for asking. You did many things well, and I especially noticed that your vocal inflection was outstanding.

This exercise aims to show gratitude to the other person for the information they are providing. In today's corporate world, we seek information from others — other departments, other stakeholders, etc. — so we can provide the best report/analysis/ forecast possible. The more we offer appreciation, the more the other person appreciates our efforts. I use this "Thank You" exercise to demonstrate that when asking for feedback, it's vital that we don't become defensive. Instead, I encourage you to accept the feedback by saying "thank you." You can decide later what to do with that feedback but don't get defensive in the moment — that defensiveness is your ego getting in the way. In addition, learning to accept praise with a "thank you" is also valuable. While it can be a sign of humility to be inclined to respond to praise by diminishing yourself or giving credit elsewhere ("Well, it was really Paul who did all the hard work" or "It's no big deal — it only took me a few minutes" or "I probably could have done a better job if I'd had more time"). While humility is certainly preferable to ego, being too meek in the face of a compliment can hurt not only your credibility but the relationship. Not accepting praise implicitly says that the giver of the praise is wrong; and doing so doesn't help in the trust department.

When asking for feedback, it's vital that we don't become defensive. Instead, I encourage you to accept the feedback by saying "thank you."

Ego Leadership Is Outdated

In his book, *Bosses Are Hired … Leadership is Earned*, transformational leader Carson Sublett — who has enjoyed a storied career in the pharmaceutical industry — tells us: "Never underestimate the impact of ego, or the fear of change in some individuals. In difficult situations, sometimes good people with decision-making authority just make bad decisions."[7]

> **We are all, at least to some degree, guilty of ego leadership; we are, after all, humans. And when difficult situations arise, the ego can take center stage. But doing the work to minimize the role of our ego when we lead will ultimately take us to a place of more effective leadership for a modern age.**

I couldn't agree more. We are all, at least to some degree, guilty of ego leadership; we are, after all, humans. And when difficult situations arise, the ego can take center stage. But doing the work to minimize the role of our ego when we lead will ultimately take us to a place of more effective leadership for a modern age. "Ego leadership" is outdated because it generates behaviors that are no longer (thank goodness!) tolerated in today's workplace. With an ego-based leader at the helm, blowups or temper tantrums are bound to ensue — during meetings or in the execution of projects or general business operations — when it doesn't go the leader's way. Improv leadership, conversely, is a more collaborative leadership style that appreciates the contributions of the team. When the team fails, the leader takes responsibility for the failure. The leader doesn't throw his team under the bus, start shouting in the conference room, tweet out hurtful comments and insults about them, or say that they take no responsibility for the failure they led.

---

7   Carson Sublett, *Bosses Are Hired …. Leadership Is Earned: Experiences, Lessons, Decisions, Life*, 2019, Silver Tree Publishing, p. 64.

BONUS BITES!

Throughout your reading of this book, you may want to take breaks to watch some videos about the topics we're exploring (and, of course, to try out the exercises I've outlined for you and your team). One video that is not to be missed is the TEDxESCP presentation from Bob Davids entitled "The Rarest Commodity is Leadership Without Ego."

Find it at https://youtu.be/UQrPVmcgJJk or by scanning this QR code.

"*Real listening is a willingness to let the other person change you. When I'm willing to let them change me, something happens between us that's more interesting than a pair of dueling monologues.*"

—ALAN ALDA

CHAPTER 5

OFF KEY: LEARNING TO *LISTEN* TO AVOID TONE-DEAF LEADERSHIP

My biggest challenge during my early days as an amateur improviser — back when I was taking my first improv workshops — was the simple act of listening. I thought I was a good listener, and I wasn't. Perhaps you can relate.

There were several times during improv workshops when I would be participating in a scene and I wasn't really *listening* because I was too laser-focused on anticipating where the scene was *going*. When another improviser would call on me in the scene, 80% of the time I had no response back to them (or my response was weak or disconnected from the overall story) because I had been too distracted by trying to predict the direction of the scene. In my distraction and my focus on the future, I was lost in the present and was blindsided when I got called upon. Time and time again, I would hear the instructor say to me, "Pete, you aren't listening again. Try it again."

Leadership is all about becoming a better listener. *Excuse me, what did you say?* You heard me right (if you were listening!); leadership is all about listening to understand vs. listening to respond. Listening to *understand* means you really, genuinely want to understand what is being said (to you directly or in the room as you participate in a meeting or attend a presentation as an audience member). When you listen to understand, you "park" your ideas and your biases somewhere else, and you go out of your way to eliminate all distractions while you're listening (I'm looking at you, clock watcher or smartphone addict). When you are exhibiting the kind of listening skills worthy of a true leader, you suspend your judgment (i.e., set your ego aside) to focus on listening to what the other person is trying to communicate and you do so all the while managing your emotions. It is authentic.

Leadership is all about becoming a better listener.

Listening to *respond*, on the other hand, is having your agenda in the front of your mind when engaging in a conversation or a group discussion (or even when sitting in the audience during a presentation that will eventually have a Q&A session at the end). When you are listening to respond (rather than listening to understand), you aren't fully listening to what is being said — because, truth be told, you feel that what you have to say is much more profound and vital, and you are just waiting for the other person to stop talking. Or, even worse than listening half-heartedly while you wait for an appropriate moment to respond, you create such a moment by force — you interrupt the person who is speaking and start talking to get your thoughts out of your head (and, likely) to show how smart you are. If you're not a leader who is guilty of "listening to respond," I can pretty much guarantee that you have known some leaders whose communication style is dominated by the kind of ego-driven deficit in listening skills. Am I right?

ASK YOURSELF

➜ What could you do, starting immediately, to make it easier
  (or even fool-proof) to be a better listener at work and in your
  life? What reminders or tricks could you put into practice right
  away, and how might you hold yourself accountable for being
  the kind of leader who listens to understand instead of always
  listening to respond?

Listening to understand is a skill that needs ongoing practice and strengthening. During the past 20+ years, I have become a better listener, with plenty
of setbacks. In my book, *Improv Is No Joke: Using Improvisation to Create
Positive Results in Leadership and Life*, I share this story, which is relevant to
our conversation in this chapter.

> Let's say a CPA has a client across the table who is pouring out her
> angst about what's keeping her up at night. The client is making
> it clear what she needs and wants, but the CPA is thinking of the
> services that they came in to sell ... and he's waiting for his opening.
>
> "Well," the CPA tells the long-faced client, "we have this new
> product here that we've developed ..."
>
> The client wonders whether the CPA was listening to her — and he
> wasn't. *He was waiting to deliver a sales pitch.* Far better if he could
> have put those products and services to the side and truly heard his
> client's wants and needs and asked questions to learn more about
> them. A real conversation results in a meeting of minds. That's the
> way to a genuine sale — one that's a real fit.

We all can strengthen our listening skills if we work on them every single
day. And when you do this consistently over time, you might hear a client,
customer, or co-worker say, "I am not sure why I told you that." (As their way
of acknowledging their own surprise about how vulnerable they can be with
you because you are a genuine listener.) Or you might discover important

stakeholders coming to you specifically for the "service" of your listening skills, asking something like, "Do you mind if I rant about a situation that happened to me without judging, only listening? I need to vent."

When I am delivering a workshop, I will ask: "By the show of hands, how many of you are excellent listeners?" I usually see a hand or two. Then I ask, "And how many of you are excellent interrupters?" The hands go flying in the air and the uncomfortable, self-aware laughter begins.

To help them understand why it is essential to become better listeners, I typically engage them in two straightforward improv exercises: "One-Word Story" and "Last Word Spoken."

EXERCISE #4: One-Word Story

This exercise is typically undertaken in groups of 4-5 people.

Introduce the exercise by telling the participants/improvisers that they are going to create a story that's never been told before, and that this story will be created one word at a time. To create the story, each person will add one word at a time as the story progresses from one person to the next. After the first improviser says a word, the person to the right will add the second word. We will continue in this manner as each improviser contributes one word at a time to the story.

> **Improviser 1:** The
>
> **Improviser 2:** Dog
>
> **Improviser 3:** Stole
>
> **Improviser 4:** The
>
> **Improviser 5:** Sock

Keep going until everyone has had four (4) contributions, meaning you've told a story with 16-20 words.

The purpose of the exercise is to demonstrate being always in the moment, letting go of the need to figure out the ending or the desire to steer the outcome, and having trust that the end result will be correct (or interesting or meaningful or funny) however it turns out.

Think about ways that you can apply this in your daily business life. Those who are leaders of organizations tend to be "control enthusiasts" and the ability to let things go and see where the journey takes us can be more powerful. How can we become more comfortable letting others finish our sentences or allowing them to fill in the gaps in our thinking?

> **Those who are leaders of organizations tend to be "control enthusiasts" and the ability to let things go and see where the journey takes us can be more powerful.**

At the risk of unraveling the entire point of Exercise #4, let me share a truly funny story. In February 2017, I was the closing keynote at the White Castle Leadership Conference in Columbus, OH. The title of the keynote was "Improv is No Joke." During my 90-minute presentation, I asked for a volunteer to join me on stage to play One Word Story. A general manager from the Cincinnati area volunteered for the exercise and her name was Lisa. This is the dialogue that we had:

Peter: Are

Lisa: We

Peter: The

Lisa: Best

Peter: Employees

Lisa: Here

Peter: At

Lisa: White Castle

Peter: That is two words.

Lisa: Not when you work for White Castle! It is one word.

Peter: Let the record show that White Castle is one word. *(Yes! And)*

So, suffice it to say, every now and then, getting one word ahead of yourselves can help you stay "on brand" at your company. Far be it from me to slice your brand name in half! But be sure to keep listening to every single word your colleagues say … because they deserve your undivided attention in the present moment and "one word" thinking can help.

EXERCISE #5: Last Word Spoken

This game is played in pairs (i.e., two people).

The two participants/improvisers are going to have a conversation with one another (on any topic) and they are going to speak one sentence at a time. Improviser A will begin the conversation. The last word in his or her sentence becomes the first word in Improviser B's sentence.

Improviser A:	I like to fly kites.
Improviser B:	Kites are great fun.
Improviser A:	Fun times with kites is when it is windy.
Improviser B:	Windy conditions are the best time to fly a kite.
Improviser A:	Kite flying requires lots of string.

Continue this for 60 seconds.

The purpose of the exercise is to listen to the entire sentence when someone is speaking ... because the last word spoken may be the most important word in that sentence. When you interrupt or are not present, you will miss key pieces of the other person's thoughts.

Imagine how this new skill for "listening to the very end" (i.e., to that final word) might change everything at work. Let's say that your coworker Suzanne gives a detailed update on a critical project and gives you everything you were hoping to hear (e.g., it's on time and on budget) but ends with "All we have to do is figure out the shopping cart function. Right now, it's broken."

Say what? Broken?! I heard that!

Well, that final word (and business issue) perhaps needs your attention. Try, in situations like these, to fall back on your "yes, and ..." skill. After hearing that last word (broken), how might the conversation be advanced by affirming your colleague and building upon what she was saying?

"Okay (yes), it sounds like the project has come a long way since the last update. Nice work. And it also sounds like the shopping cart feature

might be something that needs our extra attention now. Would it help if we enlisted some troubleshooting support from Nathan in IT or does the current team have everything you need?"

More Than Just a Game

These exercises that I'm encouraging you to try with your teams are practical and applicable. In the moment, they might feel like games. That's good — have fun with them! Laughter and shared experiences bond us to our teammates. But, as you are probably beginning to suspect, the exercises teach us practical skills that can be applied in moments when "game play" is the furthest thing from our minds. Just as "wax on, wax off" became a critical skill in the iconic '80s movie *The Karate Kid*, improv exercises can teach you and your team to be better communicators and better leaders. Great learning is fun and sticky and creates skills that can be deployed during high-stakes moments. When practiced regularly, these improv games give you a sort of "muscle memory" for how to behave in real-world situations.

ASK YOURSELF

➜ When can you start practicing these skills at work? Could you and your team get started on strengthening your listening skills by starting to play this book's improv games weekly during staff meetings or over a group lunch? This book contains 16 exercises; in just 16 weeks, you could try them all out at least once and then make plans to practice them again.

Have you ever noticed that there are no shortage of courses, workshops, books, articles, and other resources about effective speaking .... but very few resources on effective listening? It's time we fixed that. Be sure to follow me on social media and join my mailing list at www.PeterMargaritis.com to learn about my new workshop on effective listening skills.

Another Example of Why Empathy is Important

We've previously established that empathy is vital to healthy relationships — that it allows us to connect more genuinely and to leave our egos behind. What we *haven't* established yet is that having empathy for the people around you (i.e., "feeling" it in your heart) isn't enough ... you must express and demonstrate it. One way to demonstrate empathy is to *listen* with empathy. I would argue that the most critical component of listening is an empathic mindset.

Empathy — if it is to be demonstrated in the workplace and in other important interactions — requires of us that we be fully present and that we listen deeply to understand what another person is saying from their perspective. In Chapter 3, we explored definitions of empathy from Michael Miller, Daniel Goleman, and Jay Sukow. Dr. Prudy Gourguechon, a psychiatrist with expertise in trauma, builds upon those definitions by suggesting that:

> *"Empathy is the ability to understand another person's experience, perspective, and feelings. Also called 'vicarious introspection,' it's commonly described as putting yourself in another person's shoes. But make sure you are assessing how they would feel in their shoes, not how you would feel in their shoes."*[1]

Learning how another person feels in their shoes is critical and challenging to becoming a better listener. We need to ask many questions — many of the right, appropriately timed and diplomatically delivered questions — to understand the other person's situation and feelings. We all come from different backgrounds — not just different hometowns or cultural or religious contexts, but different lifestyles, ethnicities, races, socioeconomic contexts, career journeys, and personal stories. As my friend Dino Tripodis once said, "We are the sum of our experiences." And while we'll never fully comprehend the sum of someone else's experiences, it would behoove us to try. When approaching a collaboration or important conversation with someone you might not know that well, take the time to understand their

---

1   Prudy Gourguechon, "Empathy Is an Essential Leadership Skill -- And There's Nothing Soft About It," *Forbes*, December 26, 2017, https://www.forbes.com/sites/prudygourguechon/2017/12/26/empathy-is-an-essential-leadership-skill-and-theres-nothing-soft-about-it/.

journey; listen and learn and think about how you may need to change your mindset based on the new information you have just received.

Active listening is HARD; it takes intention, time, effort, and continual practice. Sit back, breathe, smile, show that you are open to what is being said — that you are listening and learning, not just formulating a pithy response or a dismissive comment or angling to shift the conversation so it can be all about you. Start working on strengthening your listening every day. As each day passes, you will be closer to becoming a better listener, developing better relationships, and having a more significant impact on your world.

BONUS BITES!

It's admittedly exhausting when you're trying to communicate something important and you can tell that your boss or coworker (or spouse or child) simply isn't listening to you. It's frustrating, exhausting, infuriating. But can it also be adorable? Well, only sometimes.

Three-year-old Mateo earned internet fame and a trip to *The Ellen Degeneres Show* for his "Listen Linda" video in which he turned "failure to listen" into a sassy childhood art. Watch the now-infamous video at https://youtu.be/g5aBMtzJEIY. I dare you not to giggle and fall in love with this little stinker.

*Improv takes place in
the present tense.*

CHAPTER 6

MASTERING AUTHENTIC LEADERSHIP: THE ART OF MONOTASKING AND BEING PRESENT

So there I was, at The Second City in Chicago, during a workshop being held in one of their off-stage rehearsal rooms, and we were focusing on what is called "object work." The object was physical but invisible, and we needed to bring it to life. For example, if the phone rang, you picked it up with a slightly closed fist (like you are answering a landline with a corded or cordless handset) or with your hand cupped or in a claw position (for a cellphone). The idea is to make it seem that the object exists but is invisible to the audience. The idea is not to turn your hand into the phone (i.e., not to use your thumb as the earpiece and your pinky sticking out as the mouthpiece). Some skits involved several objects. If there was an invisible table in a certain spot, then you needed to walk *around* the table, not *through* the table.

Object work was — you guessed it — another area in the practice of improv in which I struggled at first. I walked through tables, chairs, kitchen counters, TV sets, fireplaces, etc. I was a bull in a china shop, but luckily my clumsiness with invisible objects didn't result in actual injury or destruction! The instructor would say: "Pete, do we need to take you to urgent care? Because you just walked through a closed front door!" I was lacking presence because I wasn't listening with both my eyes and ears; I had become distracted to the point of failure (which is how I learned).

> ## Being present is about monotasking, not multitasking. It's about being focused and thinking about one thing, one person, one place, one task at a time – free of distractions, full of mindfulness.

In this crazy world that we live in today, full of distractions and uncertainties — email, 24-hour news coverage, virtual meetings, social media notifications, etc. — are you finding it hard to stay present and to operate "in the moment?" I sure am! But what exactly does it mean to "be present" or "in the moment?" I'm glad you asked! Is being present the same as multitasking? No! We as humans can't multitask despite what we think. The more we do at once, the more poorly we do multiple things. Think about it this way: texting and driving, *or*, reading your email during a meeting — is that being *present?*

Being present is about monotasking, not multitasking. It's about being focused and thinking about one thing, one person, one place, one task at a time — free of distractions, full of mindfulness.

In improv, being present is critical to the success of the ensemble. You can't be thinking ahead and trying to predict the future nor can you be stuck in the past remembering what was. When you do this, you will miss what your teammate is trying to communicate, and the scene falls flat or falls apart (or both!).

ASK YOURSELF

➜ Take a moment and think about a time when you were not "present" — at work or in your personal life — and then think for a moment about the ramifications that ensued. What went sideways? Was anyone hurt or upset? What consequences did you suffer?

➜ If you're like most people, you have at least one story like this that involves the dreaded "reply all" in an email response, where you said something to the wrong people (sometimes *about* those people). What can you do, starting today, to reengineer your life and work such that you are more present and so that you can prevent these kinds of disasters in the future?

A New Kind of Mindfulness

You've heard talk about "mindfulness" — in fact, it's all the rage. Mindful people often practice yoga or tai chi, they "disconnect" from phones and other devices during important interactions, they even eat without the mindless distractions of television or driving a car. Being mindful has many benefits. And at work, those benefits are significant.

Research shows that people spend almost 47% of their waking hours thinking about something other than what they're doing. Thought leaders at the *Harvard Business Review* (*HBR*) suggest that "The ability to maintain focus and concentration is every bit as important as technical or management skills. And because leaders need to absorb and synthesize a growing flood of information in order to make good decisions, they're hit particularly hard by [not being present]."[1]

---

1   Rasmus Hougaard and Jacqueline Carter, "How to Practice Mindfulness Throughout Your Work Day," *Harvard Business Review*, March 4, 2016, https://hbr.org/2016/03/how-to-practice-mindfulness-throughout-your-work-day.

It is next to impossible to be present all the time. However, there are times in our workday when we need to be intensely focused on our essential work and eliminate all distractions. The one big distraction that requires elimination is the internal conversation we are having with ourselves.

The one big distraction that requires elimination is the internal conversation we are having with ourselves.

When we have constructive conversations with others, we're inevitably also having an internal conversation with ourselves. And it's nearly impossible to listen to two conversations at once. This internal dialogue derails us from truly listening and understanding what the other person is trying to convey. Even though we are physically present (i.e., in the same room with someone), we aren't always psychologically or intentionally present. We let ourselves become preoccupied with other activities or let our minds drift to other things. We listen to our inner voice when someone is talking. The ramifications of the lack of being present are that people feel unheard and become frustrated. The art of being present and listening to the other person is a sign of your appreciation for their thoughts and ideas.

But is presence something you're just born with the talent for? Or can you learn to be present? You can learn! In their *HBR* article entitled "If You Aspire to Be a Great Leader, Be Present," Rasmus Hougaard and Jacqueline Carter discuss making a plan for presence. They share a story about Doug Conant, CEO of Campbell Soup Company, where he "developed rituals for physically and psychologically connecting with people at all levels in the company." Here is an excerpt from the story:

> *"Every morning, Conant allocated a good chunk of his time to walking around the plant, greeting people, and getting to know them. He would memorize their names and the names of their family members. He would take a genuine interest in their lives. He also hand wrote letters of gratitude to recognize extraordinary efforts. And when people in the company were having tough times, he wrote them personal messages of encouragement. During his tenure, he sent more than 30,000 such letters. To*

Conant, these behaviors were not just strategies to enhance productivity; they were heartfelt efforts to support his people."[2]

That is an amazing story and what a powerful and motivating example of being present and showing appreciation. I'm not suggesting you write 30,000 letters but I *am* suggesting you find a way to be present — focused, attentive, in the moment — with the people who deserve to be seen and heard and appreciated.

And I'd also love to recommend that readers of this book begin to think of boardrooms, offices, and presentation podiums as if they were actual improv stages, and that you begin to think of your colleagues and audiences as improv "teammates." How might your "performance" improve if you finally thought of it as that — a performance? Improv performers never throw one another under the bus or lose sight of their imperative to build upon each others' strengths and serve the audience. On stage, there is no animosity or indifference, just focus and collaboration. I can't help but think that improv troupes treat one another better than most business colleagues treat one another because they have the right mindset. Improvisers are refreshingly collaborative and pleasant (as compared to most people you'll encounter in the board room) simply because improvisers respect the rules of engagement (i.e., the foundations of improv) and because they see one another as collaborators or teammates, not as adversaries.

ASK YOURSELF

➜ What kind of presence do you currently bring to your meetings or daily workplace interactions? What little things can you start doing to demonstrate that you're paying attention and that you care? Leave your smartphone/tablet/laptop computer in your office and not bringing it to your meeting? When you have an

---

2   Rasmus Hougaard and Jacqueline Carter, "If Your Aspire to Be a Great Leader, Be Present," *Harvard Business Review*, December 13, 2017, https://hbr.org/2017/12/if-you-aspire-to-be-a-great-leader-be-present.

associate sitting across from you at your desk, have you thought about moving from *your* side of the desk to the *other* side and sitting next to them (and out of eye range of your email inbox)?

➤ If you have only a dozen or so employees or contractors, could you include handwritten sticky notes when you send out paychecks? (My publisher does this with her team and when she sends out royalty checks!) Or could you send more "congratulations" and "thank you" and "I appreciate you" cards or even emails?

➤ Perhaps you could allow more space for personal commentary during Zoom meetings and face-to-face meetings to demonstrate that you are aware of what other people are dealing with in their lives and work — like saying "I heard about the wildfires you're having out there. What's it been like? How are you and your family holding up?" or "I noticed your department has brought back the candy bowl and redecorated the lobby — I love the vibe!" or "You're an avid runner, yes? Your commitment to fitness is an inspiration ... and puts some of us to shame."

➤ Do you know your employee's birthday? You should because nearly everyone loves to hear "Happy Birthday" on their birthday. Get a birthday card and make their day extra special. Do you know your largest customer's or client's birthday? Look it up, make note of it, and do something kind when their day rolls around. Being present takes many forms.

➤ Think about ways you can be "present" by making it a priority to offer public accolades (like mentioning in front of others that Jim did a great job on this week's Monday-morning report to investors). Atta-boys and atta-girls are nearly always appreciated.

➤ And don't forget that good old-fashioned eye contact and a pause, a smile, a nod — when you could have rushed to the next topic or kept walking down a hall instead — can go a long way. How can you be more present today?

Monotasking

Achieving any sort of mastering of the art of monotasking requires more than just quieting your internal dialogue and putting some "proof that I'm paying attention" practices into place. It also requires selectively eliminating some of the things that are sabotaging us — like our beloved devices. When it comes to distractions (at work and at home), the worst offenders are powered by semiconductors. Hundreds of times (or thousands of times!) each day, our attention is pulled to ringing phones, social media (through push notifications or a self-induced habit of doom-scrolling), text messages or other direct/instant messages, updates on workplace intranets and wikis, and oh-so-much email. And to be fair, not all distractions are technological in nature; if you have people constantly stopping by your office or cubicle unannounced, those distractions can add up to your inability to give your full attention to the task at hand or the person sitting across the desk or table from you. They deserve better.

There are times when we are participating in a meeting or are head-down on meaningful work — such as a project, an article, or a strategic plan — and we need to be 100% present. I admit that I am suffering from EADD — Entrepreneurial Attention Deficit Disorder[3] — and that being present is a considerable challenge for me. I'm always thinking about something else I could or should or want to do.

You may know that I host a podcast where I interview brilliant people who help me sharpen my own skills and change my mindset as we seek to improve and change the mindsets of our listeners. In Season 3, Episode 12 of the Change Your Mindset podcast, I interview Jake Kahana, co-founder of CaveDay, who has researched deep work and deep focus and has created (with his two co-founders) Caveday.org. CaveDay provides a platform where you can work on important items by monotasking, eliminating all distractions and being held accountable from a virtual group of Cave Dwellers. Since joining in July of 2020, my ability to monotask has increased 85% with this CaveDay community.

---

3   I did not coin this phase. I was introduced to the concept of EADD by Allison Maslan in her book *Scale or Fail: How to Build Your Dream Team, Explode Your Growth, and Let Your Business Soar.*

Another example of monotasking was when I was in Japan on business for the Victoria's Secret Catalogue as the International Circulation Manager. I was in a department meeting and witnessed brilliant monotasking firsthand via the Japanese leader who was soliciting comments and ideas on a topic during a meeting. He made his request and never said another word until everyone in the meeting spoke. The crazy thing was that he sat there, holding his hands over his chest, with his head bowed down. At first, I thought he had fallen asleep! After the last person spoke, he rose his head and looked at everyone in the room and summarized succinctly what everyone had said and incorporated their comments into his ultimate decision. I was blown away, and inspired.

On a side note, the conversations between this brilliant, truly "present" leader and his colleagues were translated to me in English by my assigned translator. The amount of active listening and focus that I needed to demonstrate was way off the charts because of the multiple voices in a sort of Japanese/English duet, and my need to stay focused on the content and energy of the overall conversation. I admit that when the meeting finished, I needed something for the massive headache I'd triggered from the excessive focus and listening, and I could have done with a nap too. Clearly, I didn't have the "muscle" yet for this kind of presence. I needed practice, and I was left feeling inspired to do so.

ASK YOURSELF

➔ What improv exercises can you and your team do to become better at being present in the moment? The two exercises in chapter five, "one word story" and "last word spoken" are good for improving your listening and being present and in the moment. This next exercise, repetition, is another way to work on being present and listening.

EXERCISE #6: Repetition

This exercise should be done with two people (i.e., in pairs). Have the two participants start a conversation, each speaking one sentence at a time. One participant
starts the conversation and before the other participant can answer, they must repeat
the sentence the other person said before adding on to it. If it feels more comfortable, participants can add a word like "Yes!" or "Sure ..." before repeating their
partner's sentence.

Improviser A: Let's go grab some dinner

Improviser B: *(Yes!)* Let's go grab some dinner. I know a Mexican restaurant
that's right around the corner.

Improviser A: (*Absolutely.*) I know a Mexican restaurant that is right around the
corner (*too*). They serve the best fish tacos.

Improviser B: They serve the *best* fish tacos! Along with the best margaritas.

Keep going for four or more rounds

The purpose of this exercise is to listen to the entire sentence to the end of the
person's thought before starting a response. The goal is to stay present and not to
re-live the past or predict the future.

Mastering Authentic Leadership

To be proficient in improv, you must be a good listener and be present
at those critical moments. Wait, let me state that another way. To be
a proficient *leader*, you must be a good listener and be present in those
crucial moments. The ability to eliminate all distractions and be focused
on the conversation is *hard* ... very hard. Not to sound like Allen Iverson —
whose media-interview rant during a Philadelphia 76ers press conference
included 22 mentions of the word practice — you might be wondering, "Are
we talkin' about practice?" Yes, we are talking about practice. Listening as
a leadership skill is something that you need to be cognizant about — and
practice — daily. The three improv exercises offered in this chapter —
One-Word Story, Last Word Spoken, and Repetition — are exercises that
will help you and your team become active listeners with more significant presence.

Leading with an "off script" mindset requires that we be mindful of those crucial times when we need to be present and in-the-moment, so we can eliminate all unnecessary distractions. It's increasingly vital that we can set aside the agenda, notes, script, slides, or other prepared minutia to immerse ourselves in the actual moment and deliver what the moment requires of us.

> **It's increasingly vital that we can set aside the agenda, notes, script, slides, or other prepared minutia to immerse ourselves in the actual moment and deliver what the moment requires of us.**

BONUS BITES!

For those of you who play golf, being present and focus (along with being adaptable) is essential in having a good round of golf. The reason is that we will not — no matter how hard we try — hit a perfect shot every single time. You can watch any golf tournament and see that even the pros have their struggles. For example, at THE PLAYERS Championship in 2021, Bryson DeChambeau topped his tee shot and the ball ended up in the water in front of him. He took a penalty drop. On his next shot, he sliced and ended up in a wasteland about 60 yards right of the green. It appeared to spectators like me that Bryson had lost his focus and that perhaps his inner critic was having his way in Bryson's head. I can only imagine what those thoughts were — "The ball went 50 yards and into the pond" and "You call yourself a professional golfer?" and "Millions of people saw you almost whiff your tee shot." Perhaps he didn't think any of these things, but he had a serious performance lapse that looked to be the result of a momentary lapse in presence and focus. Was he distracted? I don't know, but it sure looked like it.

Every golfer has had these moments — when your golf game reverts back to the first day you ever picked up a club because you aren't present and because you're distracted by living in the past of something you can't change. We start beating ourselves up instead of letting go of the past and just hitting the next shot that's in front of us. Mistakes beget more mistakes. We forget to improvise based on our well-honed skills. We forget to go "off script" when the moment calls for it.

For me, it was amazing to watch on May 23, 2021, when Phil Mickelson won the PGA Championship at the age of 50 years and 11 months old. In that moment, he became the oldest person to ever win a major golf championship. During the tournament, the commentators mentioned several times how Phil had been working on his focus and staying present in the moment. When he was interviewed after the win, Phil reflected on his mindset prior to the tournament, explaining: "I feel or believe that I'm playing well and I have an opportunity to contend for a major championship on Sunday, and I'm having so much fun that it's easier to stay in the present and not get ahead of myself [or live in the past]."

Throughout the PGA tournament, Mickelson was maintaining his focus through breathing exercises and visualization so he could stay in the present, which in his case meant focusing "only on this golf shot, not the one before and not the one after."

The following week, Mickelson was playing in the Charles Schwab Challenge where he didn't make the cut, shooting two over par. As I wonder about what went wrong, I can't help but think about the week he had after winning the PGA Championship as the oldest player ever to do so — the celebrations, the media interviews. Distractions everywhere.

> *"Psychological safety is fostering a climate of respect, trust, and openness in which people can raise concerns and suggestions without fear of reprisal."*
>
> **—ADAM GRANT**

CHAPTER 7

SCRIPTED FOR SAFETY: LETTING GO OF NEGATIVITY AND DISMISSAL

I can still hear my improv teachers saying:

- ➔ "This is a safe environment."

- ➔ "You will not be made fun of for something you have said, or an idea that you create."

- ➔ "Go ahead and try."

- ➔ "We learn when we make mistakes."

- ➔ "Don't beat yourself up. Reflect and learn."

➜   "Failure is good."

That last one took me a while to fully embrace: "Failure is good." For me, the only way I was going to embrace the principle was to see, feel, and experience it first-hand. That opportunity was coming for me.

In an Improv Cincinnati workshop, a group of us were conducting an exercise where everyone lined up against the wall and two people had to step forward and do a scene. Soon enough, it was my turn to step forward, alongside Merle. In our scene, Merle was driving a car, and he was on my right. During our dialogue, I never mentioned anything about where we were (i.e., I never feigned a British accent or mentioned Big Ben up ahead) nor did I think to ask him: "When did you learn to drive a car with the steering wheel on the right side?" I couldn't believe I missed it — that big, obvious sign that he wasn't driving a car designed for American roads — and I started beating myself up as soon as the scene was over.

The Improv Cincinnati instructor, Tone, recognized what I was doing because my negative body language was as obvious as a right-sided steering wheel. Tone asked me to quit beating myself up and to take more time reflecting on why I *didn't* bring up the obvious in the midst of the scene. He suggested that once I understand how I'd missed that opportunity, that I keep that lesson stored in my long-term memory. I was learning and that was okay. But in the moment, I felt like a failure; I was literally in an improv class and afraid to improvise. I was hesitating to go "off script" because it still felt unnatural to me to exercise that kind of courage. I had a lot yet to learn.

You might have a lot yet to learn too. Mastering the art of business improvisation takes time and intention. But here you are, reading this book and you're picking up some fresh ideas for how to bring your best self to work situations and to "real-life" interactions. And maybe it's not so scary because you're not alone.

> ## I felt like a failure; I was literally in an improv class and afraid to improvise. I was hesitating to go "off script" because it still felt unnatural to me to exercise that kind of courage. I had a lot yet to learn.

Horrible Bosses, Dismissive Peers

Imagine you're in a meeting and your boss asks you a question about your ideas on a particular subject. After you share your thoughts, your boss has that look of disgust on their face and says, "We can't do that because that's not the way we've always done this around here" or "No, we tried that in the past, and it didn't work." Or maybe they just squint and shake their head. Horrible bosses making us feel an inch tall.

Perhaps your biggest problem isn't horrible bosses but dismissive peers. When you bring up what you think is a viable and creative idea in a meeting, everyone starts laughing and someone says, "There he/she goes again ..." (referring to your reputation for presumably crazy ideas) while rolling their eyes. Negativity and dismissiveness hurt! It's that "Yes, but ..." or "No, because ..." dynamic that we've talked about so much together in this book. You don't deserve for anyone to do it to you, and you certainly shouldn't be doing it to others.

Negating our colleagues is a dead end. When a peer or boss responds this way, creativity stops; the fear of criticism or reprisal suddenly suppresses the rest of the group's creative thoughts and ideas. No one wants to be humiliated like this in front of others.

Then it gets even worse — you're in a meeting with the accounting and finance team, and they are reviewing your financial results for the past quarter. This is where the rubber meets the road, analyzing how the company is performing and living up to its mission and vision. But you've worked at this critical and dismissive organization long enough to know that if you open your mouth, you serve yourself up as a target. You are afraid to ask questions or make any comments because you don't want to look stupid. After all, you don't have an accounting or finance degree (or if you do, perhaps you aren't the CFO), so what do you do?

When you work with people who lack good listening skills, who have over-developed egos, and who don't have comfort going "off script" during respectful conversations, projects and relationships (and entire businesses) can go sideways. What is the real issue in these hypothetical scenarios? The "stick to the script" corporate culture doesn't allow you to speak your mind and ask questions without feeling insecure or embarrassed. In my 20+

years in the corporate world, I had experienced too many times when I was ridiculed because I said something that was perceived as stupid, or when I asked a question to which others thought I should have known the answer. Is this behavior motivating, inspiring, or productive? Of course not — and yet, we've all experienced it at one time or another.

> ## You can create a culture where all ideas have validity, where ideas are accepted and discussed, and where questions are asked without any judgment or the fear of embarrassment.

The good news is that you can create a culture where all ideas have validity, where ideas are accepted and discussed, and where questions are asked without any judgment or the fear of embarrassment. Okay, quit shaking your head and thinking *"that'll never happen"* or saying out loud, "There Peter goes again with his crazy ideas and comments." As you continue to read this book, do this — keep an open mind, and don't pass judgment until you hear me out. Deal? *DEAL!*

The New Corporate Culture

There is one critical element in creating this new corporate culture, and that element is psychological safety, a concept I introduced in this book's introduction. In her *Harvard Business Review* article titled, "High Performing Teams Need Psychological Safety and Here's How to Create It," Laura Delizonna defines psychological safety this way:

> *"[Psychological safety is] the belief that you won't be punished when you make a mistake. Studies show that psychological safety allows for moderate risk-taking, speaking your mind, creativity, and sticking your neck out without the fear of having it cut off."*[1]

---

1   Laura Delizonna, "High Performing Teams Need Psychological Safety and Here's How to Create It," *Harvard Business Review*, August 24, 2017, https://hbr.org/2017/08/high-performing-teams-need-psychological-safety-heres-how-to-create-it.

I know someone out there — one of you reading this book right now and thinking of me as that "improv-comedy guy" — thinks that I'm making this up and using *HBR* as a cover, but I am not. Psychological safety is a real thing. Google the term to learn more. And then dig deeper to imagine how your own organization and career could be improved with more psychological safety for yourself, your team, and everyone around you.

In a similar article by *re:work* titled "The Five Keys to a Successful Google Team," the authors begin by explaining that "Who is on a team matters less than how the team members interact, structure the work, and view their contributions."[2] In other words, the way the team collaborates is more important than who is on the team. In improv, the team is the sum of all its parts ... not just the individual contributions.

The Googlers go on to state that there are "five key dynamics that set successful teams apart from other teams at Google, and the number one dynamic is psychological safety." Psychological safety is defined as the ability to say "yes" to the question "Can we take risks on this team without feeling insecure or embarrassed?" The remaining four dynamics are: dependability, structure and clarity, meaning of work, and impact of work.[3]

So, the question becomes, how do you increase psychological safety on your team? Laura Delizonna suggests that we "approach conflict as a collaborator, not an adversary when conflicts come up, avoid triggering a fight-or-flight reaction by asking how we could achieve a mutually desirable outcome and be curious to hear the other person's point of view."[4]

Yes! And that's exactly what we've been exploring here in *Off Script*. Becoming an improv leader is all about letting go of control, going "off script" in conversations and negotiations, being present instead of rushing to the future, and by collaborating in authentic, empathetic ways.

---

2   Julie Rozovsky, "The Five Keys to a Successful Google Team," re:WORK, November 17, 2015, https://rework.withgoogle.com/blog/five-keys-to-a-successful-google-team/.

3   Ibid.

4   Laura Delizonna, "High Performing Teams Need Psychological Safety and Here's How to Create It," *Harvard Business Review*, August 24, 2017, https://hbr.org/2017/08/high-performing-teams-need-psychological-safety-heres-how-to-create-it.

I am no "brain expert," but what I do know is that when you are harassed by a boss or coworker with an over-developed ego or a dismissive, closed mind, your brain goes into fight-flight-or-freeze mode. We act first and think later. We lash out or turn away or sit frozen and expressionless. That has never happened to you, right? Of course it has. You're only human. When this happens at work, it debilitates our strategic thinking and kills our self-esteem. And, the truth is that no matter how dedicated and talented you are, when this happens at work, you can go from a productive member of the team to a disgruntled employee. It all falls apart.

Let's continue to explore the Delizonna article and the Google article because there's much there when it comes to improv leadership. Let's start with the definition of psychological safety as "the belief that you won't be punished when you make a mistake." In improv, we say: "There are no mistakes, only gifts, and happy accidents." No one is perfect and everyone makes mistakes — even the most confident and competent among us. We need to expect and embrace mistakes. So first, leaders and teammates need to respect each other, trust one another, and support each other when taking risks. Remember, there are risks in *everything* we do, so there must be grace at every turn. Don't punish — but instead praise — the person for taking the risk. There is another saying in improv: "*Bad ideas* are bridges to good ideas. *No ideas* lead to nothing." If everyone supports (and even endorses or justifies) everyone else's actions (or at least their right to take those actions), then we're fully and truly in this together, and there are no mistakes — just bridges.

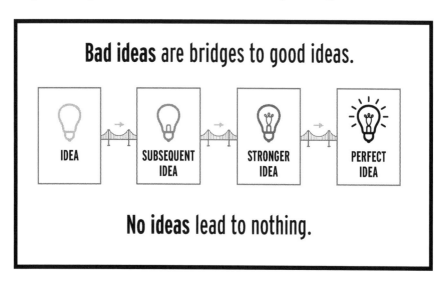

Now, let's talk about what's really on your mind. Perhaps you're thinking, "Okay, Peter. Logically, I see the value in abolishing criticism, condescension, summary dismissals, and other 'horrible boss' behaviors from our conference rooms and board rooms, and putting ourselves out there with bad ideas or untested hypotheses. But it's human to fear being embarrassed or feeling insecure in front of our colleagues." Yes! And if you are in a position of leadership, you can be the person on your team — or in your entire company — to shift the culture in the right direction by being the first leader to put their neck out there with your own fledgling ideas and to be the first to assure your employees and others that all ideas are welcomed and respected. The solution begins with you.

Check yourself to see what's getting in your way. Is it your ego? Once you put your ego aside, you'll inevitably find that you'll stop judging others' ideas so harshly — instead, you may consider them brilliant and eagerly follow them! Perspective and attitude in the face of a new idea are determined by your perspective and attitude *before* the idea is ever presented. You see that great improvisers accept the ideas of the other teammates without judging them to be "good" or "bad" — always thinking, "This is now our idea." (Pause for a moment to acknowledge that you have never seen an improviser on *Whose Line Is It Anyway?* or *Saturday Night Live* stop abruptly, shake their head, and say "That's a bad idea ... that will never work." They roll with the ideas, embracing them as the direction they will now take or the wave they are about to ride.) When we do this unilaterally throughout our team (not playing favorites but exercising an open mind to everyone) and when we give people the freedom to speak their mind, magic will happen almost immediately.

Perspective and attitude in the face of a new idea are determined by your perspective and attitude *before* the idea is ever presented.

As we say in improv:

> *"There are gems in every idea. Embrace and build.*
> *Treat every idea as though it has the potential to*
> *change the world and — at some point — one will."*

Psychological Safety in High-Stakes Meetings

Creating a safe place for the team to share their ideas under the umbrella of psychological safety may be relatively easy to achieve — at least within your distinct team, where you share a lot of talents and perhaps all have the same functional expertise (e.g., engineering, operations, marketing, IT, HR). But what about when you're out of your element and expertise, like when you're asking a question during a financial meeting and you don't have the financial foundation necessary to articulate a question? That fear crops back up, and we worry about sticking our necks out and looking foolish. To avoid being perceived as stupid, we are more inclined to nod our heads up and down and agree than to ask a question that will help us learn (and might help others learn as well).

There are many kinds of high-stakes conversations and meetings that take place in your organization, but I would argue that there might be nothing more important happening among the people in your business than the conversations surrounding the company's financials. And these conversations are not the sole realm of the accounting and finance team. No matter what you do or your level of leadership purview, your ability to participate meaningfully in financial conversations is vital to your company and your career. And if you're the chief executive, teaching your finance leaders to be *improv leaders* is up to you.

But at the outset, most accounting and finance people will come up short as it relates to collaborative, accessible conversations. When you ask the financial question, you will (more than likely) receive an answer full of accounting and finance jargon, leaving you even more confused. You'll get a lot of "well, that's before taxes" or "fully amortized" or "but that's not a capital expenditure." And you might be quite sure they didn't answer your question at all. So, what is the solution? *Knowledge* is the solution. Accounting and finance knowledge, to be exact. If you don't have some intermediate financial literacy because you're not an accountant, after all, it's time to learn some fundamentals of business finance. Because being a leader (no matter what your background or what industry you serve) requires being a leader who demonstrates financial leadership. Perhaps you're a university president; you better understand how the enrollment numbers this fall are lining up with financial aid packages, philanthropic donations, and operational expenses and what it all means for your campus. Perhaps you're the CEO of an e-retailer and your background is in the technology interfaces that make your online store more popular and profitable than others who sell similar products; you need to know how to recognize — in real time — the sales and profit trends that can belie problems ahead or opportunities waiting to be tapped.

> **If you don't have some intermediate financial literacy because you're not an accountant, it's time to learn some fundamentals of business finance. Because being a leader requires being a leader who demonstrates financial leadership.**

In the conclusion of this book, we'll go deeper on the concept of financial leadership to leave you with some perspectives that I think can impact your bottom line. For now, though, the answer to the fear and trepidation you feel when asking questions during financial conversations is taking the time to gain a more solid understanding of the fundamentals of accounting and finance so you can be a better steward to your organization. The more you know, the more quickly your questions and contributions can generate the "big ideas" and insights that drive your company and your teams in the right direction.

"We Could Save About $80K a Year" – A Case in Point

If you look closely, every organization (and every leader's career) has stories — for better or for worse — that illustrate the impact and business outcomes of learning (or failing to learn) the fundamentals of accounting and finance. In my consulting career, I've heard stories that made my heart race with possibility and made me heart*sick* over opportunities (and dollars) lost. Here's just one example I'll never forget.*

In the early 2000s, my colleague Mark Robilliard was facilitating a corporate workshop for team leaders and middle managers in a large multinational corporation with headquarters in Sydney, Australia. After becoming "accounting literate" using the Color Accounting System™, these Aussie leaders embarked on the final session of this particular workshop — a session during which the participants had a quick review of their own work area and then discussed their thoughts on generating additional revenue or incurring less expenses.

One of the participants (the team leader in the internal mail room) shyly raised his hand and nervously said: "I think we could save about $80,000 per year if we changed how we do this process" ... and proceeded to define the suboptimal process and the operational fix that could be pursued.

The CFO —who just happened to be in the room —almost fell off his chair at the news of this easy $80K cost-savings measure. When he recovered his composure, he asked the team leader: "How come you never brought this to us before?" The answer was simple: "I just do my job. I didn't know we should be thinking about the business too."

Story shared with permission from Color Accounting International co-founders Peter Frampton and Mark Robillard.

ASK YOURSELF

→ What value would these types of business conversations —
where you remind employees up, down, and across the organization that you're looking to them for ideas about cost-savings
initiatives or revenue-generating changes — have for your
organization?

→ Do you regularly solicit ideas that could change the balance
sheet at your organization?

→ Shouldn't everyone be "accounting literate" and develop a
"business-owner" or at least business-leader mindset? Imagine
how much money you might be wasting, or the sales you are
currently foregoing!

Low-Hanging Fruit: Creating Safety, Cashing in on New Ideas

Everyone in your organization should increase their accounting literacy
(including you!) because the entire point of being in business — even if
you run a nonprofit organization — is to *stay* in business. And nobody
stays in business with an empty bank account. But money-making and
money-savings ideas come from people, and people need to work within
a culture where they feel supported, empowered, and welcomed to bring
forth their financial ideas. As a leader, you can create that culture. Just
imagine how much money your organization could make or save if every
person in the organization did their job *and* thought about the business too.
Novel idea, right?

So be thinking about the related issues of psychological safety and financial/
accounting literacy within your organization. How effective are your senior
managers, managers, sales team, and back-office teams around finance?
Do they perform with psychological safety in your accounting and finance

meetings? Do they speak their mind and ask questions without feeling insecure or embarrassed? What can you do to improve their competence and comfort in both regards?

> **How effective are your senior managers, managers, sales team, and back-office teams around finance? Do they perform with psychological safety in your accounting and finance meetings? Do they speak their mind and ask questions without feeling insecure or embarrassed? What can you do to improve their competence and comfort in both regards?**

So what are we waiting for? I'll let Laura Delizonna and her HBR article have the last word on this important topic:

> *"If you create a sense of psychological safety on your team starting now, you can expect to see higher engagement levels, increased motivation to tackle difficult problems, more learning and development opportunities, and better performance."*[5]

---

5   Laura Delizonna, "High Performing Teams Need Psychological Safety and Here's How to Create It," *Harvard Business Review*, August 24, 2017, https://hbr.org/2017/08/high-performing-teams-need-psychological-safety-heres-how-to-create-it.

BONUS BITES!

When you have a moment, take a listen to my *Change Your Mindset Podcast*, Season 4, Episode 28, "Creating a Team of Psychological Safety with Steve Morris." Here are the show notes to get you excited. (I know, I know. I had you at "multi-million dollar racing yachts!")

> What type of work culture have you created? Does it provide the belief that you won't be punished when you make a mistake?
>
> Steve Morris started his career designing multi-million dollar racing yachts and building and coaching high-performing teams to help his clients win the most demanding races. He ran and grew a small business, then transitioned his career, becoming a certified project management professional in charge of million-dollar budgets and even helping the US Navy launch ships. Six years ago, he started his own business, Catylator, with a mission and passion to help business owners build better lives through creating better businesses, getting unstuck, fueling growth, achieving higher profits, and having more fun with their crew.
>
> In his work with leadership teams, Steve became aware of the concept of psychological safety. In a Google study that aimed to determine what was different about their highest performing teams, they discovered that the one trait the best teams all had in common was psychological safety.
>
> But what is psychological safety? It's about creating an atmosphere or environment within a team where members feel safe and comfortable asking questions, taking risks, and giving feedback.
>
> One of the techniques Steve uses to help teams facilitate psychological safety is something he picked up from the Lego Serious Play methodology. The first step is to level the playing field. No matter what your title is, everyone at the table is on equal footing. Then, people build models — with Lego blocks! — that represent their

ideas and they take turns explaining what their model means to them. The beauty of this is that nobody can say, "You're wrong." The meaning is personal. This creates an environment that allows people to feel safe sharing their stories.

When you're able to create the right environment, teams can operate at their best. No idea gets shut down and people feel safe to think outside the box or bring their best ideas to the table.

Find the full podcast here:
https://podcasts.apple.com/us/podcast/change-your-mindset/id1127514117?i=1000528616823

*Fear is interest paid on
a debt you may not owe.*

CHAPTER 8

TURNED OFF: WALKING AWAY FROM YOUR INNER CRITIC

I n the early days of my improv journey, my inner critic's voice was loud and obnoxious. I gave my inner critic a name – Nick. Nick was just trying to protect me by holding me back from risk. One day before an improv workshop, Nick and I had a long talk where I told him that I was placing industrial-strength duct tape over his mouth during every improv workshop. It was time to take risks and to fail because — as I had learned through this process — failure is expected and is part of the learning and growth process. Failure is often necessary and fear is often a conman. After a month or so, I didn't have to tape Nick's mouth because my inner critic saw the benefit of my risk taking. I was becoming brave and shedding my fear — that proverbial interest paid on a debt I didn't even owe.

Failure is expected and is part of the learning and growth process. Failure is often necessary and fear is often a conman.

Have you thought about that voice in your head? You know the one. The voice that keeps coming back with the warning, "Don't say that idea out loud because people will think you're stupid or crazy." Or, another favorite, "You have to be kidding me ... you know you can't speak in front of an audience – you will look like a fool." You know that voice; it has a lot more to say on any number of things — and none of it is good. This is the voice of your inner critic. We all have one.

So what exactly is an inner critic? It's the unconscious and self-conscious voice inside each of us that judges and demeans us at every turn. It diminishes our value or makes us second-guess ourselves. It criticizes and it's often cruel. And it rarely has a legitimate reason to do so. We are all far more competent than our inner critic would have us believe. The inner critic is a liar. My friend Cathy Fyock calls it "The Bitch." A highly active inner critic can be paralyzing — it can take a toll on one's emotional well-being and self-esteem — and in some cases, it can trigger dangerous or even life-threatening despair. Without realizing it, many people who seek support from a therapist or counselor to help balance thought patterns and change their mindset are looking for someone to help them silence their inner critic. The cruel and critical voice can sometimes be deafening.

Jerry Seinfeld has delivered a standup routine in which he joked that people's number-one fear is public speaking. Their number-two fear is death. So, they would rather be in a casket than giving the eulogy.

And it's sort of true. The National Social Anxiety Center reports that "public speaking anxiety affects about 73% of the population. The underlying fear is judgment or negative evaluation." Indeed, the vast majority of us are terrified of public speaking.[1]

---

1   John Montopoli, "Public Speaking Anxiety and Fear of Brain Freezes," National Society Anxiety Center, February 20, 2017, https://nationalsocialanxietycenter.com/2017/02/20/public-speaking-and-fear-of-brain-freezes/.

The Reliable Inner Critic

That inner critic of yours never goes on vacation — it's there continuously, giving opinions on anything and everything you do. And as the stakes get higher because you're about to go "on stage" at work (whether that means a real stage or a conference room or a board room or a lecture hall or an important meeting with your boss), the closer you get to "go time," the louder and more incessant the critic becomes. For many people, they can get physically sick — nauseated, sweaty, short of breath — from the stress that the critic brings their way. Whether you're in front of a big audience or sharing thoughts during a meeting, all you can see or think about are all those eyeballs leveled at you. It's terrifying.

You're competent and usually quite confident, but your inner critic is constantly telling you how you are going to fail. So what can you do? How do you overcome this fear? How do you silence the inner critic?

Improvisation!!! Yes! And by employing the foundations of improvisation, you will overcome the fear and effectively silence the critic every time!

Improv will help you change the conversation in your head and start programming your brain to use "yes, and ..." instead of "yes, but ..." or "no, because ..." Why does this matter? Think about the difference between "but" vs. "and." Using "but" introduces a contrasting thought and stops the other line of thought in its tracks. Using "and" instead connects one idea with the other — allowing both to be considered jointly and allowing you to build upon and strengthen your own ideas and mantras and internal pep talks. So, for instance, you could be saying to yourself, "Yes, you have been asked to give this presentation, but you'll do awful." Or, you could turn it into the following: "Yes, you have been asked to give this presentation, and you can do it." Just a slight change in words and tone from "but" to "and" has an immediate and positive impact on your confidence, self-esteem, and perception of your self-worth.

Just a slight change in words and tone from "but" to "and" has an immediate and positive impact on your confidence, self-esteem, and perception of your self-worth.

Consider the classic children's story, *The Little Engine That Could*. It teaches this very principle. Each of the different locomotives in the story was an external critic — each pointing out why the little engine couldn't accomplish the task at hand. And the little engine could easily have listened to all the negativity and let her own internal critic echo the doubts of everyone else. But eventually, the little engine — who had been told she wasn't fast enough, big enough, or powerful enough — was the best locomotive for an important job. Despite the doubts and criticism, the train (as we all know) repeatedly chanted to herself, "I think I can, I think I can, I think I can." And she did.

"You're not fast enough."

"You're not smart enough."

"You're not experienced enough."

"You're not interesting enough."

"You're simply not enough."

The inner critic needs to be reprimanded and corrected for this. And guess what? You have the power to do it. Tell yourself, "I can do this ... I *am* enough" and the more times you repeat it, the more likely you are to believe it. This positive programming of the brain is real and can be used to overcome your immediate fears. The more you say it, the more you will silence that droning voice of doom that cycles through all your fears: "You can't do this, you don't know what you're talking about, you're a fraud, you're going to fail, something will go wrong." STOP! Turn it off; it's time to walk away from your inner critic, once and for all.

The Perfect Inner Critic

As much as I despise the inner critic and encourage you to kick it to the curb, I'll be the first to admit that the inner critic sometimes speaks a tiny bit of truth. You see, this last part of the inner critic's diatribe — "something will go wrong ..." — is very likely to come true. Why? Because we expect ourselves to be perfect, and there is no such thing as perfection. Of course you will make a mistake! (Probably more than one. And that's okay!) Remember that most of the time, unless it's a real blooper, the only person who knows about "what went wrong" is you. Your listeners and audiences won't see it or hear it or care about it. Your colleagues and boss and customers and other stakeholders aren't particularly concerned about the little mistakes you make, and why would they be? They're too busy wrapped up in their own egos, worried about their *own* mistakes! Only you and your inner critic are preoccupied with the "what ifs" that keep you up at night. Because you and your inner critic are perfectionists who sometimes forget to look at the big picture.

When you're overly focused on perfection, you can go into a downward spiral if you make even a minor mistake, such as forgetting to make one of your less important points while giving a presentation or being interviewed on a podcast or talking to your boss. If you maintain your confidence, something like that won't trip you up. So what? They don't know what you *meant* to say so they're not at all concerned about what you *didn't* say. Cut yourself some slack for the errors and omissions that have zero impact on the people, projects, and organizations around you. It would be best if you accepted the fact that you *will* make some slips. Again, last I checked, you are human! Think of little gaffes or oversights or mistakes as opportunities to learn to do even better next time. And in the moment, roll with them ... this is what keeps us interesting and interested. Mistakes are unintended "off script" moments — nothing more and nothing less. And they're perfectly normal and acceptable.

ASK YOURSELF

➜ Do you think it's possible that the all-too-human tendency to be focused on ourselves — the same tendency that fuels the inner critic and makes us worry about "me, me, me" every time we step on a stage or into a conference room — also overwhelms our co-workers and audience members too .... And that it's possible that they're so focused on their own concerns and insecurities that the least of their concerns is the little "mistakes" *you* might make? Rather than focusing on your wrinkled outfit or your stumbled-over word or what others might think about you, focus instead on service to *your audience* — on sharing ideas and insights that will help others and make a difference for your organization or theirs.

➜ When you're focused on service, it's hard to be nervous. Worry and fear are nearly always useless emotions — they are interest paid on a debt you may not owe.

A Little Vulnerability Goes a Long Way

I like to think that remembering that we're human serves us in two ways: 1) It helps us dispense with unnecessary worry and fear because "we're only human" so we can't possibly be perfect. And 2) Remembering that we're all human — our bosses, peers, customers, and others — reminds us that we have a lot in common and that we have many ways to relate to and connect with one another. Vulnerability can be an ideal way to connect over that shared condition — the human condition. In fact, a certain amount of vulnerability goes a long way in winning over your audience. An excellent example of this is Australian singer/songwriter Megan Washington's 2014 TED Talk entitled "Why I Live in Mortal Dread of Public Speaking." When Megan opens her speech, you are immediately aware that Megan lives with a stutter. "I didn't know when I, uh, agreed to to-to-to do this whether I was expected to-to talk or to sing," she begins. She explains that, while she has no qualms about singing in front of people, she has a mortal dread of public speaking. And despite that dread, there she is ... on that big stage with all the cameras and with the possibility of millions of people listening to her speech someday. Throughout the presentation, the audience watches Megan struggle to get certain words out, but it doesn't matter to those of us watching and listening. She's human and she's amazing and she's — just like you and me — perfectly imperfect. Her vulnerability warmed the audience to her, keeping them engaged up until the moment she disclosed a deeply personal and fascinating fact: You can't stutter when you sing. At this point, she plays and sings a beautiful song superbly, ending with a roaring applause from the audience.[2]

A certain amount of vulnerability goes a long way in winning over your audience.

Maybe you don't have a stutter and maybe you aren't an award-winning singer or songwriter. But, like Megan, you're human and unique. And your ability to be vulnerable is a strength, not a weakness. It's important to remember: the inner critic will tell you scary things and have you musing with doom about far more than you need to know or explore, and none of it is true or relevant to your efforts. You will hear what you "can't" do or how you will "screw up." And here is what you can tell that naysayer: "*Yes*, I know I will make mistakes, *and* they will not hamper me. *Yes*, I will not be perfect in the way that I might practice or hope, *and* that means I can learn and feel the excitement of going 'off script' and perhaps get better in the future."

Here's my deeply personal secret and a fascinating fact about me: Even today, whenever I get up in front of people, I get butterflies, *and* I can control them now and make them flutter in the direction of my choice.

Even today, whenever I get up in front of people, I get butterflies, *and* I can control them now and make them flutter in the direction of my choice.

2   Megan Washington, "Why I Live in Mortal Dread of Public Speaking," TEDxSydney, 2014, https://www.ted.com/talks/megan_washington_why_i_live_in_mortal_dread_of_public_speaking,

Reasoning with the Inner Critic

With all this bad-mouthing of the inner critic, it's only fair that I take a moment to say something nice about the purpose and value of the inner critic. It's not *always* the bad guy. The inner critic does serve a purpose. If I were to consider delivering a speech on nuclear physics, I would hope that my inner critic would start screaming at me long before I stood at the podium because, well, I don't know the first thing about nuclear energy and my remarks on such a topic would be ludicrous at best and dangerous at worst. So the inner critic piping up to say, "Hey, Peter ... don't volunteer to speak at *that* conference. It's not for you," is a good thing. However, the critic doesn't know when to shut up; it always goes too far, from friendly constructive feedback to all-out unnecessary character assault. And that's where you need to train it. You might know enough about a topic to deliver a decent speech, but the critic keeps nagging: "Your nose hair is showing. Your tie is crooked. What a nitwit." If you pay too much attention, the prophecies of failure could come true. You get hung up on your shortcomings rather than focusing on your strengths. I understand; I've been there.

Sometimes the key is just to confront it: "Shut up! Shut up!" You can accomplish this through the "yes, and ..." approach of improv. "Yes, I hear what you're saying, And I'm going to do it anyway." A friend of mine recently took on a gig, speaking to the commercial real estate industry ... and she knew very little about multi-tenant office buildings or industrial complex when she signed the contract to deliver the keynote. She was nervous and a little out of her element. So she said, "*Yes*, I want to do this. *And* I have a lot of homework to do so that I can apply the lessons of my talk to the practical realities of the audience's industry." And then she did. Ultimately, she delivered the most well-attended and highly engaged presentation in this professional association's history. Because she didn't let the inner critic undermine her after she let it do its job in reminding her how much time to set aside to do her homework and be amply prepared. The critic can (and will) still try to undermine you — even as you grow as a leader — but the critic, over time, won't speak as loudly. You'll build up self-esteem. You'll feel confident. You'll control the critic, once and for all.

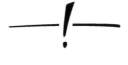

BONUS BITES!

MEET YOUR INNER CRITIC (AND TELL IT TO PIPE DOWN)

I have another great video for you to watch, thanks to Pam Victor and TEDxEasthamptonWomen. What's it all about? The video description from TEDx is below.

> *"In life, one of the most wonderful, albeit terrifying, facts is that there is no script outlining what will happen. We are simply left to improvise, often without being taught to do so. In her talk, improv comedian Pam Victor discusses what she learned from her own formal training to become a master of the art of improvisation, and how these skills can help us to conquer that critical little voice that tells us we aren't good enough to achieve our goals."*

View the TedX here:
https://www.ted.com/talks/meet_your_inner_critic_and_tell_it_to_pipe_down

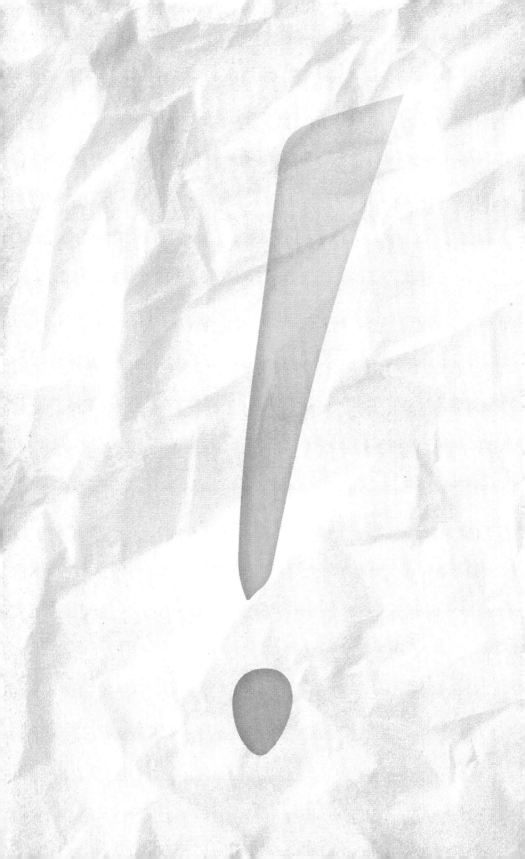

PART II

The Day-to-Day Realities
of Improv at Work

Listen, react, keep it simple.

CHAPTER 9

NEW SCRIPTS: COMMUNICATING AND COLLABORATING FOR BETTER RESULTS

As an icebreaker to my workshops on corporate communications, I use an exercise called "The Snowflake." I ask the attendees to pull out a blank sheet of paper and I inform them that they are to listen carefully and follow my instructions to the T but that they cannot ask any questions until the exercise is over. I start by saying, "Fold the paper in half," and I give them a moment to do so. Then: "Tear off the bottom right corner. Fold the paper in half again." I wait for them to comply. "Tear off the bottom right corner. Fold it in half one more time, and this time chew off the bottom left corner, if necessary."

Then I ask everyone to unfold their sheet of paper, and I walk around the room examining the resulting paper snowflakes. Whether I have a crowd of 20 or 100, I rarely find any two snowflakes alike. Like real snowflakes, each is unique. (Incidentally, I do the same exercise with virtual groups, but instead of walking around, I ask the attendees to show their snowflake using their webcam. Welcome to Generation Unmute!)

"People, help me understand something," I ask. "I gave you instructions for each step. So why isn't every snowflake the same?"

"Well," they often respond, "you didn't give us *detailed* instructions."

"You're right, I didn't," I agree. "Some of what I said was open to interpretation." I pause to let them think about it. How could I expect the same results, they wonder, if I didn't explain which direction to fold or how much to tear off or how big a bite to chew? Our ability to achieve consistent, predictable results fell apart at the level of effective communication.

What makes an organization great? What is it that makes them truly stand out among their competitors? Excellent, innovative, and effective communication. This kind of communication invites productivity, adaptability, stronger relationships, and successful negotiations, and it brings an end to tired, useless jargon that derails, distracts, and limits every situation.

> **Excellent, innovative, and effective communication invites productivity, adaptability, stronger relationships, and successful negotiations.**

What is needed in any organization (including your organization!) is an innovative approach — one that lays the groundwork for and then inspires excellent, open, and effective communication both internally and externally during the day-to-day inner workings of the organization. And that innovative approach is found in the foundations of (you guessed it!) improvisation. Yes, that's right, improv. Improv is a unique and powerful approach that promotes a simpler, more positive, and effective way to communicate, collaborate, and cooperate as a team — whether with your internal people or external constituents.

ASK YOURSELF

➜ When you give instructions to your employees or other team members — especially when you're in a rush — do you leave out details that are important? How could more clarity and detail improve the odds of consistent, desired results? And what simple processes could you put into place at your organization to hardwire this kind of detail when giving assignments?

➜ Perhaps you ought to have a "help desk" style ticket where key information is spelled out, or a "creative brief" like they use in advertising agencies to clarify goals and parameters. Or maybe a checklist or a sample would set your teammates up for success. Remember that time spent up front on clear communication will help ensure you get what you're asking for.

➜ And, if what you're asking for is something truly creative and innovative, and you don't want to stifle the possibilities, then maybe "paper snowflake" instructions are perfect. Just be sure to be unequivocal about the liberties that people should take. "Go ahead ... tear it as much or as little as you like. For the bite, go with a chomp or a nibble — whatever suits you. And for the folds, 'in half' is merely a suggestion. Make the snowflake *you* want to make."

At Its Foundation, Improv is Leadership in Motion

The foundation for effective leadership, as we established in Chapter 5, is active listening. When leaders are listening to their employees and engaging them using the skills learned from improv, growth happens.

Improvisation promotes cooperation and with greater cooperation, productivity goes up. The foundations of improv fundamentally create productive interactions because they force people to truly listen to one another — to think of themselves as a troupe or as teammates or as "players" in a very important performance or game. Many companies are discovering the powerful effect this has on the way teams work together. It also has a profound effect on the way your *customers* feel. When employees are cooperating and collaborating in admirable, productive ways, customers and other stakeholders feel it and benefit. Good interpersonal communication and effective leadership has an "inside out" effect as it shifts the atmosphere of the entire corporation to one that feels and looks more energized and in sync.

> **Good interpersonal communication and effective leadership has an "inside out" effect as it shifts the atmosphere of the entire corporation to one that feels and looks more energized and in sync.**

But it's not just about finding one way to communicate and sticking with it year after year. It's about being malleable and responsive, knowing that teams and marketplaces change. In today's dynamic market, companies need to be adaptable and — you know I'm going to say it — "improv leaders" are perhaps the most adaptable leaders among us. Indeed, learning improv is great for business, now and in the future. Gone are the days of punching the clock and demonstrating loyalty and submission in the workplace (putting our noses to the grindstone and expecting it all to be drudgery); our newer generations want to have fun and they want to be engaged. The art of business improv has really struck a good nerve with the younger generations who have been more exposed to improvisation classes (on college campuses, at community centers, and even in business schools) and the popular show *Whose Line Is It Anyway*. These fresh-faced, modern-day leaders are driving the face of corporate solutions by sparking creative thinking and ending the corporate jargon that has left innovation stale.

> **Fresh-faced, modern-day leaders are driving the face of corporate solutions by sparking creative thinking and ending the corporate jargon that has left innovation stale.**

You are now, by virtue of having read this far into this book, a bit of an expert in business improv and in the imperatives of improvisational thinking with concepts like "Yes, and ..." With luck, you have even begun to try out your "Yes, and ..." skills, knowing that "Yes, and ..." is the glue that holds it all together. So much is possible for you and your stakeholders when you make the internal commitment to operate in a way that feels as if you're not allowed to tell each other "no" — that your conversations must be collaborations and that even when someone has fledgling ideas that simply can't work, it's important to remember that *all* ideas give us a context in which to think and a foundation upon which to build.

Replacing the words "No, because ..." and "yes, but ..." with the improv phrase "yes, and ..." will invite active listening and valuable input and will teach you (and others) how to adapt in the moment for the greatest results. So much is communicated by that phrase, which is why I keep bringing it up — whether we're exploring vulnerability, ego, listening, being present, negativity, the inner critic, or any of the other key concepts explored in this book. "Yes, and ..." is the backbone to how I approach leading and communicating, and it's the cornerstone of the methods I'm hoping to teach you in this book. "Yes, and ..." is supportive and respectful. It *focuses* the conversation rather than shutting it down — it takes a conversation's participants deeper instead of pushing the people apart. It shows you are listening to the other person and that you trust what they have to offer. "Yes, and ..." ties all the fundamental principles of effective communication and adaptation into a practical and productive two-word tool that will cause companies and their leaders to stand up, stand out, and make a difference.

> **"Yes, and ..." is supportive and respectful. It focuses the conversation rather than shutting it down – it takes a conversation's participants deeper instead of pushing the people apart.**

One Idea at a Time

Have you ever watched preschoolers play with blocks? Whether playing alone or with others, they typically focus intently on one block at a time, selecting it for its color or its proximity, sometimes examining or admiring it before putting it to use, then stacking each block on top of another until the towering stack gets so high or so unstable that it just topples over. Or, sometimes it's so fun to watch it fall that excess height and instability aren't necessary, and our little block-stackers knock it all over on purpose. And when a game of blocks is played between more than one child (or with one child and an adult caregiver), both participants have an agenda. They each want to pick up a block and put it on the tower and each one probably has an idea about what the tower will look like when they're done, but they invariably keep building until they can't build anymore.

A successful workplace relationship is built in the same way – one block at a time — first collaborating, then sharing, observing and/or listening, and building on each new "block" with a shared vision in mind. That is how you connect with other people ... one block, one idea, one conversation at a time.

We are more likely to succeed in our relationships when both parties can envision a common goal. Improvisation teaches us to set aside our personal agendas and ego and openly collaborate with our teammates using the philosophy of, wait for it, "Yes! And." There's that glue again — "Yes, and ..." Successful people all intuitively do this in building strong relationships — they just don't realize they are doing it and using improvisation to make it happen. Indeed, many of the most successful "improv leaders" don't have any idea that they have mastered the art of business improv. And the best of the best are the ones — like you — who have actively chosen to apply the lessons of improv to their workplace interactions in a deliberate, strategic, generous way.

EXERCISE #7: Emotions

Emotional intelligence (EI or EQ) is one of the top five skills that leaders need to develop and *continually* develop. This kind of intelligence comprises self-awareness, social awareness, self-management, and relationship management. What follows is an emotions exercise that touches on all these topics and allows you to assess the emotions of others in a conversation and adapt to where they are (emotionally) in that present moment.

> The exercise begins with two people having a conversation about anything they choose. After about 15-20 seconds, the moderator (boss, coach, facilitator) randomly chooses an emotion (happy, sad, angry, enthusiastic, depressed, despondent, surprised, etc.), and asks the participants to take on that emotion's body language and tone until a new emotion is introduced.
>
> The original topic of the conversation should not change. If the pair started out talking about whether the company should introduce a "bring your dog to work day," they must explore and continue the conversation in the myriad emotions introduced, vacillating from one emotional state to another but never changing the subject (i.e., when the emotion changes to "sad," the participants *can't* suddenly start talking about their Grandma's funeral).
>
> The exercise lasts between three and five minutes with new emotions added, at the will of the moderator, and the conversation must stay the same — but the mood and tone must switch to the emotion introduced.

You can go to my YouTube page – The Accidental Accountant — to watch a demonstration of this exercise.

The purpose of the "Emotions" exercise is to help increase your emotional intelligence through the opportunity to see your colleagues demonstrating strong, defined emotions in a safe practice field without high stakes. We all need to be more self-aware of our emotions and become more socially aware of others' emotions. The best way to be prepared for this? Practice! A leader's responsibility is to assess the team's emotional context — addressing those emotions that might become detrimental to the team's success and harnessing those emotions that fuel innovation and morale — all the while managing his or her own response to others' emotions and maintaining or improving the cohesiveness of the team.

Before he became CEO of Second City Communications (the business solutions division of the world-renowned improv comedy company, The Second City), Tom Yorton worked in corporate America where the art of improv is often poorly mastered or even understood. He had this to say about the connection between the corporate trenches and the art of improv:

> *"My experience — and in fact, my scars — are from bumping up against the same organizational hurdles that improv is so effective at helping companies get over: challenges that include connecting with customers, engaging employees around change, moving into new markets, innovating new products and services, working without a script."*[1]

Business Buzz Words and Other White Noise

We all have some of our favorite "buzz words" we like to use (at work and at home), and some we can't stand when we hear others say them. Most buzz phrases are trendy analogies or memorable metaphors that don't mean much. They are great at creating imagery, but is it the kind of imagery that allows everyone to be "on the same page?" (I can't even talk about business buzz phrases without using one!)

Think about a few of these common corporate buzz words used in a lot of meetings and emails during the day-to-day operation of most businesses. Do they create a clear path or is there just a buzz in the room? Here are some common buzzwords and what I think of when I hear them:

➤ *Benchmarking*

I know I'm supposed to think about how our processes or people, or products or services measure up to others, but I literally think of a "marked bench" — my photo on a bench at a bus stop.

➤ *Back of the envelope* or *Back of the napkin*

I get it — it's about scribbling out a cool idea that's still rough and simple and doing so with such frenetic energy that we'll sketch it out on whatever we can find (like a torn envelope or a damp

---

1   Tom Yorton, "Improv for Business? Yes!," *The Business Innovation Factory,* September 20, 2012, https://www.businessinnovationfactory.com/video/tom-yorton-improv-business-yes/.

cocktail napkin). But I hear about colleagues working on business ideas on random scraps of paper, and I think we must need
more legal pads

➜ *Go the extra mile*

I'm picturing a sweaty dude, not a disciplined or dedicated
employee or business partner.

➜ *Best practices*

This reminds me of kindergarten, where we practiced being our
best selves. And it sounds a bit like a description of the things
we're supposed to do to demonstrate that we're polite, like "caring
enough" to send a Hallmark card.

None of these buzz words mean anything anymore. Put too many of them
in the conversation and the listeners, if they are even listening anymore,
tune out. They are empty words and provide very little clear direction and no
focus that employees can rally behind. With no clear direction for colleagues
to follow, stress increases and productivity goes down. It becomes everyone
doing what they think "best practices" means ... and I can pretty much guarantee that we're not all "on the same page" when it comes to the definition
of "best practices."

With no clear direction for colleagues to follow, stress increases and productivity goes down.

What if we replaced the jargon with simpler and more precise speech?
A company that states the customer service policy as "We strive to provide
top-notch service to all our customers" might consider a more clear and
actionable commitment of "We listen to the customers and meet their
expectations." Now take that a little further to layer on some processes and
planning: "Yes, and ... let's hold a quarterly brainstorming session with all
the employees to think of ways we can show the customers we are listening."

BONUS BITES!

This little thought-provocation is from my first book, *Improv Is No Joke*. I thought you might enjoy it. I rewrote the Gettysburg Address using corporate speak to demonstrate that we need to get back to plain English so our audiences can have a better understanding of what in the world we're trying to say.

Fourscore and seven years ago, our stakeholders brought forth on this continent a new nation, conceived in liberty and dedicated to the value proposition that all men are created on a net-net basis.

Now we are operating in the space of a great civil war, testing whether that nation, or any nation so conceived and so dedicated, can add value while moving forward in a results-driven way. We are met on a great battlefield of that war in a new paradigm. We have come to dedicate a portion of that field as a final resting place for those who here gave their lives that this nation might experience a game changer. It altogether is what it is. It is our new normal.

But, from the 30,000-foot view, we cannot dedicate, we cannot consecrate, we cannot hallow this ground. We do not have the bandwidth. The brave men, living and dead, who struggled here, have consecrated it far above our poor power to add or detract, our desire to think outside the box. In the big picture, people will little note and long misremember what we say here but can never literally forget what they did here; they were team players who stepped up to the plate when their nation needed them. It is for us the living, rather, to be robust about pushing the envelope for the unfinished new context which they who fought here have thus far so nobly advanced. At the end of the day, it is rather for us to be here dedicated to the great task remaining before us; that from these honored dead will come a win-win for that cause for which they gave 110 percent in their last full measure of devotion; that we here proactively resolve that these dead shall not have died in vain; that this nation, under God, going forward, shall see the glass as half full and have a new strategic freedom; and that the intellectual capital of the people, by the people, for the people shall not perish from the earth so long as we measure the appropriate KPIs, rely on best practices, and get our ducks in a row.

> "Preparation *is the key to success in negotiation. Not memorization.*"

> —RUSS RIDDLE, JD

CHAPTER 10

UNSCRIPTED GIVE-AND-TAKE: USING BUSINESS IMPROV TO RESOLVE DISPUTES AND NEGOTIATE DEALS

Most of us have experienced a negotiation gone bad. The car you paid too much for, the boss who talked you into more work when you stepped into her office for a raise, the spouse who got their way on a vacation destination that you hate. Negotiations can be scary and full of risk, but they can also create wonderful mutual opportunity. We've all had a negotiation fall apart, but have you ever been "negotiated up?" That's right — negotiated *up*. It happened to me.

In the early years of running my business, I wanted to work with a specific association because they were part of my target audience. In my initial conversation with a decision-maker in the association, she asked what my fee was. I replied, "What is your budget for this event?" The association leader responded by telling me her "speaker budget" for the entire year — the total amount she could spend on me, plus all the other speakers they might hire that fiscal year. And her annual budget was only $1,000 above my fee for the single event. Oh, boy — she couldn't afford me. I wanted the job, though, so I was willing to take a hit here. In the interest of getting in the door with an important player in my target market, I offered to deliver the presentation for a fee that was 75% less than my normal fee. Yikes! I was basically giving away my time and intellectual property.

Then came the awkward pause. After about what seemed like 30 minutes but was more likely about 30 seconds, my would-be client replied with a fee that was 50% *more* than what I had just offered. I got negotiated *up*! I learned a valuable lesson that day: Learn how to negotiate better! I got lucky in that moment that my new client understood the value I was bringing and was willing to be fair about compensating me as generously as she could afford. But he could have easily said "Deal!" when I offered the rock-bottom price. And I would have kicked myself, and maybe have come to resent the client for undervaluing my time and talent.

In the future, I wanted to value *myself* better. And I encourage you to do like-wise — whether you work inside a corporation or are a consultant or small business owner, you constantly have the chance to negotiate well or poorly. You can use the power of improv to have respect for yourself and your value. For example, a prospect once asked me how much I would charge for an hour keynote. I quoted an amount between $7,500 - $5,000. The prospect asked, "You want that much for an hour?" I said, "Yes, I am asking for that much for an hour *and* the 30 years of experience." There was a long pause and the prospect then said, "That's outside of our budget." So I improvised. I replied, "That's fine. If I agree to take the budgeted amount, would you be willing to provide me with the warm leads *and* if you are recording this session, I would like a copy of the video." The prospect replied, "Deal." Be willing to negotiate to a point of win-win. Take the view that a negotiation is a relationship-building exercise, not an adversarial battle. So, from that point forward, I have always started by offering my full fee. When a client can't or won't pay that fee, I work with them respectfully and creatively to find common ground where both parties *win* and walk away with value.

Give-and-Take for a Win-Win Result

Nearly every conversation in the workplace contains an element of negotiation — of give-and-take to help multiple parties arrive at a solution or new, amenable situation. So even if you don't think of yourself as a negotiator, it would benefit you to develop strong negotiation skills. Lucky for you, your "improv leadership" skills are putting you on the right path to being a truly adept negotiator.

To succeed in negotiations, we need to drop our agendas long enough to truly listen — and to do so with respect for all involved. This is true for formal negotiations around a conference table and is also the only way to achieve success in the daily negotiations of life and career — during a chat with the boss or with one's spouse, or even with a child. Respectful straight talk (not big confidence or the perfect business suit or the loudest voice) makes the biggest difference in conversations.

Six Skills for Successful Negotiation

1. HUMILITY — Take your ego off the table.
2. CONSIDERATION — Respect the other party.
3. FOCUS — Be in the moment, monotasking with no distractions.
4. LISTENING TO UNDERSTAND — Listen to the other party's needs, wants, and unique perspectives
5. ADAPTABILITY — Adapt to the situation.
6. COLLABORATIVE SPIRIT — "Yes, and ..." can guide you to additive solutions.

These skills — which can be approached as steps — help in removing unproductive emotions from the table. Anthony K. Tjan, a renowned venture capitalist and bestselling business author, once said: "Time and emotion — these are the two things most often wasted during a negotiation." And he's right. We tend to react emotionally and negatively to any points of a negotiation that oppose our own agenda, no matter how valid those points may be. And that emotional resistance wastes time. When our goals for a negotiation are so firmly anchored that we cannot budge, it becomes hard to see any common goal as a solution. Instead, emotions kick in and egos inflate — and we cease to listen. All we hear is our own voice in our head trying to find a way back to what we want.[1]

How Can Improvisation Make You a Better Negotiator?

What do you feel when you hear the word "negotiate?" Dread, anxiety, excitement? Do you believe that negotiation skills can be taught or do you believe some people are just born with a talent for negotiation? Do you agree with this statement: "We negotiate all the time?" And have you ever resorted to an internet search engine, asking one or more of these questions in preparation for an important negotiation in your career or life?

- ➤ "Most helpful skills for a negotiation"

- ➤ "Role of the ego in a negotiation"

- ➤ "How to be more confident as a negotiator"

- ➤ "How to use leverage in a negotiation"

It's easy to think of negotiation as something that only takes place between client and service provider or to think negotiations are only needed when approaching a contract or a big-ticket decision or sale. Not every negotiation table, however, has a client on the other end. Sometimes it's an employee. And when it is, it is often about negotiating to give them a voice in their role within the company and in the business's direction. These negotiations take success to a whole new level.

---

1   Anthony K. Tjan, "Keeping Time and Emotion from Killing a Negotiation," *Harvard Business Review*, July 21, 2014, https://hbr.org/2014/07/keep-time-and-emotion-from-killing-a-negotiation.

So what turns some negotiations into success stories and what leaves others dead in the water? Conducting a successful negotiation requires the use of six essential skills — humility, consideration, focus, active listening, adaptability, and collaborative spirit.

Negotiations can quickly come to a grinding halt when "yes, but ..." comes to the table. That's when emotions get heated and time gets wasted. Michael Wheeler, Harvard Business School Professor and Program on Negotiation (PON) faculty member, wrote a book entitled *The Art of Negotiation: How to Improvise Agreement in a Chaotic World*. In talking about the book, Wheeler explains that:

> *"My approach to negotiation takes into account real-world interactions between parties by looking at the uncertainty of negotiations and how to develop flexible strategy when you have incomplete information. Negotiation cannot be scripted. Your goals may change during the course of negotiation, a little or a lot. Unexpected opportunities and obstacles may pop up. Your across-the-table counterpart may be more or less cooperative than you expected."*[2]

Indeed. And because negotiations rarely go as we would ideally script them, we must be prepared to go "off script."

Because negotiations rarely go as we would ideally script them, we must be prepared to go "off script."

Remember to Go Off Script When Needed

Too many times we develop and practice a rigid strategy — a script or a plan — prior to going into a negotiation and because we think that plan is ironclad, we tell ourselves to stick to our guns. We often think deviation

---

2   Michael Wheeler, "Negotiation Skills from the World of Improv for Conflict Management: A Negotiations Skills Q&A with Michael Wheeler," Harvard Law School Program on Negotiation, Daily Blog, September 9, 2021, https://www.pon.harvard.edu/daily/ negotiation-skills-daily/negotiation-research-negotiation-techniques-from-the-world-of-improv-for-conflict-management/.

or changing our mind (i.e., "going off script") in a negotiation is a sign of weakness and a sure path to defeat. But flexibility is power and improvisation is opportunity. Having a strategy, mind you, is a good idea. Some of the best business schools in the U.S., in fact, teach their negotiators to develop "negotiation worksheets" in advance. These scripts or plans aren't a bad idea, per se, but by sticking too tightly to the script and being afraid to improvise, we can tank our negotiation from the beginning. When we are too rigid with our negotiation strategy or plan, we inevitably quit listening to the other party — because we are following (to a fault) the linear thought process we created and practiced. We miss out on key opportunities or threats by not being fully present. Michael Wheeler reminds us:

> *"There's a misperception that military strategy is very rigid. Yes, there's a chain of command, but there's also a military saying: 'Plans go out the window with first contact with the enemy.' In an uncertain situation, you have to think through your best-[case] and worst-case scenarios."*[3]

This military strategy can be witnessed back in 2011 when the U.S. Navy SEALs executed the raid on Osama bin Laden's compound in Pakistan. Improv expert Bob Kulhan recounted:

> *"The mission had been meticulously planned; the SEALs trained for it over months and several contingency plans were developed and put into place. When one of the Navy's Blackhawk helicopters crashed within the compound, a very specific kind of improvisation was required if the mission was to succeed."*[4]

Ultimately, the mission did succeed because these military service members went off script in the light of new circumstances. This is a very high-stakes example of adapting to a change in strategy to achieve a positive outcome.

As we have established, improvising is not "winging it" or making things up. Improvising is all about over-preparing and developing alternative plans so

---

3   Michael Wheeler, "Negotiation Skills from the World of Improv for Conflict Management: A Negotiations Skills Q&A with Michael Wheeler," Harvard Law School Program on Negotiation, Daily Blog, September 9, 2021, https://www.pon.harvard.edu/daily/negotiation-skills-daily/negotiation-research-negotiation-techniques-from-the-world-of-improv-for-conflict-management/.

4   Bob Kulhan, Getting to "Yes And:" The Art of Business Improv, Stanford Business Books, 2017, p. 3.

that when you enter the room, you can comfortably throw the script away — so you can listen and stay present in the negotiation and adapt in order to achieve success. The key points of the script will come back to you when (and if) you need them, so don't think that the preparation was for nothing. The preparation is important, but what is not important is that you say everything you initially planned to say, in precisely the way and timing you had planned. Remember, no plan withstands contact with the enemy (or, in this case, the other party in the negotiation).

When you step into that room (or log into Zoom or pick up the phone or say "come on in" when the other party approaches your doorway), go into the moment intent on listening to the other party's needs. What are they really saying when they block your proposal or articulate objections? Be adaptable by taking your ego off the table. Take a deep breath if you need to and then let the next words that come out of your mouth be "Yes, and …"

A successful negotiation is only possible if you are equal parts preparer and improviser — being able to rebound, to take the proverbial building blocks, and build with them. That is how you connect with other people. That, my friends, is how you get things done … one block at a time.

Unconventional Techniques

Let's take our discussion of negotiation and expand upon it with some unconventional techniques to help you achieve a win-win, not a win-lose, while you are negotiating. The win-win approach in negotiating is a give-and-take conversation, and each party will have to give up something (hopefully something small) to get something (hopefully something meaningful) in return.

Now some of you may be rolling your eyes and thinking, "Why would you take such an approach? Don't be a push-over! Go for the jugular and take everything." Going for the jugular is never a good idea if you're negotiating with someone with whom you're trying to build or maintain a relationship. (Even with the car salesman you think you may never see again. Always respect the other person you are negotiating with.) Odds are that — whoever you are negotiating with — there is a high probability that you will have to have another conversation on a different topic in the future. You don't want to appear to be an adversary because this present moment will impact future moments and the relationship as a whole. You want to be viewed as a partner, especially if they approach the situation in the same manner. It's almost never a good idea to be an aggressive jerk in a negotiation (unless it's literally a life-and-death situation). In 99% of negotiations, when you take the gloves off and go for the knock-out, you lose too; you just waste time and energy trying to get everything you want and often end up receiving nothing. Negotiation is not a fight — it's a collaboration.

So how, you might wonder, can you approach a meeting such that you will not be perceived as an adversary but instead be seen as a potential business partner? The approach of Russ Riddle, JD — a friend, colleague, my attorney, and also a member of the National Speakers Association — is to start with a smile. *What? Smile while you are negotiating?* Yes! He says:

> *"If you start with that smile, it's disarming. They let their defenses down a little bit, and it opens up the heart, mind, and ears to hear what you've got to say. They're not going to agree on everything that comes out of your mouth, but it opens them up to at least hear it. And you know, a smile does things inside of us too. We get to feeling better. And when we feel better, we're on our A-game. There's a law of likeability, and far too many people forget that when they go into a negotiation or go into a confrontation of any kind. They forget that the likeability factor is in their arsenal."[5]*

The only thing I would add is to make sure your smile is genuine — that is the only way this works. No smirks or sarcasm or condescension. And if you're a woman, please don't think this advice doesn't apply to you just because you have perhaps heard that when a woman leader smiles, it might make her appear vulnerable. I call bullshit on that. Women leaders — just like men who lead — benefit from the likeability and the approachability factor. Humanity matters, regardless of your gender.

So far, we've explored two unconventional techniques for effective negotiation: entering the experience with a "give-and-take" attitude and starting with a genuine smile. Now, let's examine another unique tactic — helping your negotiation counterpart to "save face." Joshua N. Weiss, in a 2020 *Harvard Business Review* article, suggests that it's important that we let the other person "save face" during a negotiation. He explains: "*face* can be thought of as how people want to be perceived and connected to identity

---

5   Peter A. Margaritis, the *Change Your Mindset Podcast*, Season 4, Episode 9, "How to be Persuasive, Not Abrasive" with Russ Riddle, https://petermargaritis.com/s4e9/.

and dignity. When it comes to negotiation, it is about both sides preserving their and their organizations' reputations."[6] This hits squarely upon one of the foundational principles of improv — respect, trust, and support. Respecting someone (and allowing them to save face) is about looking at the people across the table from you and thinking about them as *human beings* ... showing empathy and understanding. Allowing someone to save face does not, in any way, diminish you. Again, it's not about one party winning and another party losing. Demonstrating respect is not about being subordinate to the other person, allowing yourself to be manipulated, or letting them walk all over you. The point of purposefully looking for ways to respect the other party and help them save face is to humanize the conversation and work as hard as you can toward a win-win situation.

Weiss's instructive article describes an international business of tug-of-war:

> "Two international executives, one Brazilian, the other French, had become embroiled in a high-stakes dispute over a company in which they were both involved. Both men were spending many millions of dollars to try to beat the other in a tense and destructive negotiation, and neither would back down. Enter an advisor, William. After much digging and exploration, he found that each man also wanted freedom and respect beyond money and control. Each wanted to go back to his normal life of doing business and spending time with family and come out of the fight with his head held high.

> "William advised them both to focus on maximizing those metrics as their benchmark for success. When they did so, an agreement emerged where one man agreed to leave the company's board, giving his counterpart the ability to run it as he saw fit. In return, he released the departing executive from a three-year non-compete clause, giving him the freedom to conduct other business, and exchanged his voting shares for non-voting shares so they could be sold in the public equity market. In the end, both men were able to

---

6   Joshua N. Weiss, "To Succeed in a Negotiation, Help Your Counterpart Save Face," *Harvard Business Review*, October 2, 2020, https://hbr.org/2020/10/ to-succeed-in-a-negotiation-help-your-counterpart-save-face.

stand in front of their fellow executives and employees, share that they had a deal, and wish each other well."[7]

Recognizing that freedom and respect were essential to each man, William was able to leverage the good intentions of the two negotiators, allowing empathy to play a role in solving the dispute. Because of the shared goal of freedom and respect, each party effectively parked their egos and looked for a viable solution. Parking one's ego is a challenging thing to do, and, in this example, it proved to be very expensive at first. But it doesn't have to be.

In thinking about this case study, I wonder, what if they had brought William into the process much earlier? How much could they have saved, and how much sooner would they have achieved their ultimate goal of having both freedom and respect?

Ask Yourself

➡ Think back to your last major negotiation. Perhaps it was a conversation with an employee who was up for a promotion but ultimately got frustrated and resigned, causing your company serious challenges related to the talent loss and the cost to recruit a replacement. Or perhaps it was contract negotiation with a big service provider or client, and the process encountered delays, required attorneys, and left you feeling like you got the short end of the stick.

➡ Now Ask Yourself, how much — in actual currency — did the suboptimal negotiation cost you or your organization? Hundreds or thousands of dollars? Tens of thousands or hundreds of thousands? When we take time to reflect upon what it costs us to take the wrong mindset and the wrong strategy into a negotiation — when we're unwilling to practice a balanced give-and-take, when we don't even attempt empathy, when we stick to a script and forget everything we

---

7   Ibid.

know about improv, and when we are looking to "win" at the expense of someone else's "loss" — we can almost always see clearly (in hindsight) that the price we pay for poor negotiation skills is steep.

Persuasion vs. Manipulation

In thinking about your own "negotiations gone bad," or about the head-to-head battle outlined in the Joshua Weiss article mentioned above, we might find ourselves wondering: "Were we/they trying to manipulate one another to get to our/their desired outcomes?" If so, would persuasion have been a better option? The answer lies in understanding the difference between manipulation and persuasion.

My definition of persuasion is getting another person to see the situation from your perspective or vantage point through the "benefits lens" (i.e., what are the benefits of what you're proposing?). Manipulation, on the other hand, is just using somebody for your gain and then cutting them loose, never really caring about how a situation might benefit (or hurt) them. Russ Riddle shared with me his take on this subject:

> *"Persuasion is about persuading someone to do something that's in their best interest. Yeah, it may give you a benefit as well, but it's not all about you. It's about them. Manipulation, on the hand, is to get them to do something because it's good for you. It might be in their worst interest, but you want them to do it because of you."*[8]

I'd go so far as to say that we should never be attempting to "persuade" someone into something that's not at least partially in their best interests. "But Peter," you might be wondering, "Sometimes we need to get people to do things they don't want to do — to get our grandson to eat his vegetables or to get our front-line employees to arrive on time to work. What would 'benefit' them is eating cupcakes or getting to sleep in." Yes, I see your point and when we look at it more closely, it becomes clear that good nutrition *is* in the best interests of your grandson and that on-time starts and good

---

8   Peter A. Margaritis, the *Change Your Mindset Podcast*, Season 4, Episode 9, "How to be Persuasive, Not Abrasive" with Russ Riddle, https://petermargaritis.com/s4e9/.

workplace morale *is* in the best interests of your employees. They may not see it that way at first, and it's your job to help them understand the benefits by being persuasive — help them understand your logical argument and even appeal to their emotions (e.g., your grandson's love and respect for you or the employee's sense of pride in being a "team player").

This is one of the places where improv is so powerful in business. In improv, we always think about the other person more than ourselves. *What? Wait a minute!* You heard me correctly — it's about them, not about us. This is precisely what a leader is supposed to do: think about the people they lead and make decisions and choose their words in a way that conveys that it's all about them (the employees, customers, clients, or other stakeholders) and not about themselves (the leaders whom might hold most of the power in a negotiation or conversation). I believe the whole concept of "them before me" is lost when it comes to negotiating, and that flipping the script back to that mindset could change everything for you.

> **I believe the whole concept of "them before me" is lost when it comes to negotiating, and that flipping the script back to that mindset could change everything for you.**

In the end, nice guys finish first, contrary to popular belief. And that's because there's a difference between being persuasive and being abrasive. Many leaders think they are persuasive when they start talking louder, puffing out their chest or "leaning in" (across a table, etc.) to take up more space or look physically intimidating, talking over the other person, or interrupting because they think that's going to win the day, and yet, it's the exact opposite. Negotiation isn't about brute force or physical strength, volume or rudeness, nor is it about wearing down an opponent until they acquiesce. When emotion and ego enter the negotiation process, then it becomes abrasive. And, you guessed it, abrasive negotiations cost us more time and money, and can result in emotional wounds and career-limiting outcomes as well.

There's a difference between being persuasive and being abrasive.

Improvised Negotiations

I've said it before and I'll say it again: when it comes to negotiations, don't be scripted. I am not saying to show up and wing it — that is failure in the making. You should, as always, be prepared (and even practiced), but be ready to go "off script" entirely. If you chain yourself to a script during a negotiation, you are practically doomed to failure. If obsessively tied to a script, you won't be fully present, nor will you be listening to what anyone else is saying. When you *prepare*, rather than memorize, you don't need a script. And you have created the adaptability to react to the other party's response more freely and appropriately.

Improvised negotiations "require rapid learning, adapting, and influencing," according to Michael Wheeler's book, *The Art of Negotiation: How to Improvise an Agreement in a Chaotic World.*[9]

Learning, according to Wheeler, requires that you "keep an open mind, and be ready to change, and adapt to the situation. Don't ask reality to conform to your blueprint but transform your blueprint to adapt to reality."[10] When negotiating, you are learning from your interactions with the person with whom you're negotiating. When the negotiation takes a turn, you must adapt to the conversation. For example, let's say you propose a potential solution to a business problem. The other party does not accept your proposal and offers a version of their own solution. A third option is created by taking the two prior proposals and incorporating them into a sort of hybrid approach that is better than either of the two initial ideas alone.

But how do you get the other person to agree to building upon their idea with parts of your idea? You exercise your powers of influence and you acknowledge the value of their ideas through techniques like "Yes, and

---

9   Michael Wheeler, *The Art of Negotiation: How to Improvise an Agreement in a Chaotic World*, Kindle edition, Simon & Schuster, October 8, 2013.

10   Ibid.

..." There are many ways to influence others; Wheeler describes influencing this way:

> *"You seek to influence those on the other side, to convince them of the value of what you're offering. What they say in response — and how they say it — speaks to that particular point, but it is also feedback on how effectively you're engaging your counterpart. Maybe your style suits them. If not, you'll need to change your approach."*[11]

In other words, you have to be present and listening (i.e., paying attention) — to the words, context, and body language of the other party. "Cookie-cutter strategies crumble in the turbulence of real-world negotiation."[12]

When Negotiation Helps Nurture Relationships

Have you ever considered the art of negotiation to be a strategy in building sustainable relationships? I will be honest; I never considered this a strategy until it was brought to my attention in my podcast interview with Russ. As I thought about it, it made sense to me — most negotiations are with people with whom I already have or want to create a relationship. Except for those perceived one-and-done scenarios, like negotiating with car salespeople, and if I could go back 30+ years, I would have looked at this process as an opportunity versus dread. Approaching this type of negotiating as a stereotype — and by therefore not wanting to have a long-term relationship with my salesperson — was the wrong strategy. I should have approached the negotiations in more thoughtful and fruitful ways. Because, as it turns out, I have bought and sold several cars over the years and I always worked with a new salesperson each time — even with family members. Imagine how much easier it would have been to form meaningful relationships with salespeople who I could have called upon, car after car.

When it come to negotiating to nurture relationships, the key is developing trust throughout the process on both sides, which takes time. What is the benefit? In buying future cars, you will go see your person at the dealer

---

11   Michael Wheeler, The Art of Negotiation: How to Improvise an Agreement in a Chaotic World, Kindle edition, Simon & Schuster, October 8, 2013.

12   Ibid.

(assuming you want to buy your next car from the same auto dealer), and they will already know your likes and dislikes. This should reduce the amount of time you spend at the dealership and improve your chances of getting the car you want and need, at a fair price and without too much haggle or hassle. Your time is not wasted trying to reestablish a new relationship with a new salesperson.

> **If we negotiate well — with an eye toward establishing and/or nurturing relationships (not just on "winning" a particular argument or getting what we want on this single negotiation) — we set ourselves up for future success and harmony.**

In life and in work, though, most negotiations are conducted between two parties who maintain a far more important and long-lasting relationship than the one you might create (and possibly maintain) with your car salesperson. We negotiate with business partners and key vendors, with family and friends and significant others. And if we negotiate well — with an eye toward establishing and/or nurturing relationships (not just on "winning" a particular argument or getting what we want on this single negotiation) — we set ourselves up for future success and harmony. Critical relationships (in our careers and in our lives) are those that we must constantly nurture. The first step toward solidifying the relationships that matter is making a decision to treat the conversations with respect, trust, and support.

Is it time to view negotiating through a different lens? I think so.

BONUS BITES!

WHEN AN IMPROV ATTITUDE TURNS A NEGOTIATION INTO A BIG CAREER OPPORTUNITY

An Interview with Roxanne Kaufman

CEO of Prolaureate, Inc.; Executive Coach; and Certified Master in i3° Transformational Leadership, The Leadership Challenge°, and The Five Practices of Exemplary Leadership°

One of the best parts about writing a book is the fact that it allows you to deepen relationships with colleagues and peers who you admire and respect. I was honored to interview my friend and business associate Roxanne Kaufman about how the art of negotiation (and "the art of improv") has figured into her life and her company. Below is what she told me, in her own words.

> *"Before founding and starting my leadership development firm, ProLaureate, I had spent the previous 14 years in a most unlikely (but very successful) corporate career. I got there without really knowing what I was doing, but as it turned out, it was a life-changing negotiation that started it all. It changed the trajectory of my career and my life. It's why I now include negotiation within the leadership programs ProLaureate offers. Negotiation is a game-changer. Effective and successful negotiation is a huge part of effective and successful leadership — and improv is an integral part of both.*

Effective and successful negotiation is a huge part of effective and successful leadership — and improv is an integral part of both.

"It all began when I decided to leave the non-profit performing arts world and join the for-profit corporate world. I was interviewing for a position with a global construction-products company. Senior leadership was comprised of three men: from construction, finance, and chemical/structural engineering. So what did I have in common with any of their backgrounds or their business? Nothing. What did they have in common with me? Nothing. So why did the interviews continue? Because the first conversation was not an interview — it was a relationship-building conversation about an opportunity, about a different way of thinking about their company, a different way of thinking about how they developed client relationships, and where they wanted to go with all of it. They were interested in continuing the conversation, and so was I. I prepared for these conversations through the lens of vision, values, goals, actions, strategy ... and heart.

"It was a process of preparation, gathering information, and influencing — in the most genuine and authentic way. It became a dance of left-brain, data-driven analysis and right-brain intuition and heart — a process. You need to know what you want the outcome to be (what makes up a win/win, what are the component parts, what are the actions that need to be taken for success, what are the major things that need to be addressed in the short and long term and how do we make that happen).

"Once you have done the preparation and information-gathering, and you know the outcomes that will create a win/win for both parties, you are in the zone. You get your head, brain, and heart in a place where you know the value you can bring to the other party ... and what they can bring to you. You know what they want, what's important to them, and what part of their heart is on the line. As well as their money, reputation, success, and everything else.

"The magic of negotiation and improv is to overprepare, and then go in with confidence and leave your notes and your ego behind. You are in the zone. Your body language changes, your voice changes, everything changes because now you are fully present, fully yourself, genuinely, authentically present, completely prepared. You've done your homework, you have studied who they are, where they've been, and where they want to go. You've had those conversations already, you've collected all the data, and you measure the impact that this conversation could have on you and them.

> ## The magic of negotiation and improv is to overprepare, and then go in with confidence and leave your notes and your ego behind. You are in the zone.

"That's what happened. I didn't realize that I was improvising. I just knew that this was an opportunity that had limitless potential and would be a great experience for all of us. I wanted this to happen. So we sat down for a final 'conversation' (that is to say 'negotiation') and at the end I said, "Let's try it for 90 days and see how it goes. If we love each other after 90 days, we'll continue, and if we don't, we'll part friends.'

"They agreed. And then they wrote a number down on a piece of paper and handed it to me. This was the salary they were proposing should we go forward after the 90-day mark. I smiled, thanked them, and told them how much I appreciated their offer. Then, I crossed out their number, and I wrote down another number and said, 'Here's what it will take for us to move forward at the 90-day mark.' Silence. This is one of those tactics that really is important in these kinds of conversations. Go silent. Make your face soft. Your face should not be sad or hard or ugly. It should be your dance face, not your fight face. I just smiled and looked them in the eye. They looked at each other, looked at me, and said, 'Okay." I was there for 14 years.

"The 90-day plan worked. Yeah, it *worked*, and the 90-day plan turned into 14 years. And for 12 of those years, I sat at the executive table. At that time, I was the only woman who had ever held that role.

"All I did to get there? Just three important things: I prepared, I studied and learned, and I got to know them. Before our conversations, I did my research. And then I just let it all go and essentially said: 'This is who I am, and this is my style. This is my brand. This is who I am, and I'm just going to go with that, and let these gentlemen be themselves. And if that works, then there's some chemistry here that will rise up, and something's going to happen.' And it did. And if that isn't improv, I don't know what is. I didn't know what I was doing at the time, but it has become — or perhaps emerged — as second nature. It's simply who I am — its authentic and real. The result of this amazing improv lesson was a shift in my career mindset; now my work isn't what I do, it's who I am. I don't have clients, I have evergreen partners, lifelong friends, and extended family members. And that's just the way it works. Improv in business. Pretty darn cool."

> *"No one will ever follow you down the street if you're carrying a banner that says, 'Onward toward mediocrity.'"*
>
> —MARTIN DEMAAT

CHAPTER 11

OFF COURSE: MASTERING CHANGE MANAGEMENT WITH A NEW MINDSET

O ne of the things I do and love, when I'm not delivering presentations on stages and in classrooms (and when I'm not writing books!), is coach organizational leaders on how to be effective "improv leaders." Among my many respected and adored improv-coaching clients is a client, Tyler, who is a certified public accountant (CPA). Tyler's boss instructed him to find an improv coach because it would help him to improve his presentations and communication. And I appeared to be just the guy. (I, too, am a CPA who worked really hard to "take the numb out of numbers" and eventually wrote an entire book on the subject.) Tyler and I had a lot in common, so I knew that our work together would be meaningful and that I could help him.

During one of our coaching calls, we did an improv exercise called "That's Not True." This exercise is about one person telling a story and being constantly interrupted by a listener who says "that's not true." Each time the listener, interrupts with "that's not true," the storyteller has to come up with a new choice (or story direction) ... on the spot. When we began, I gave Tyler the suggestion that he is going on a vacation. So, he started: "My wife and I got in the car and were driving to Chicago. I replied, "That's not true." Instead of replying, as I expected him to, with something like, "We were driving to Orlando," he replied with the longer explanation, "We wanted to drive to Chicago but we changed our minds and decided to drive to Orlando." I coached him on dropping the original idea and choosing a new location without mentioning the original destination. In other words, I wanted him to say, "We were driving to Orlando" and to continue his story. Chicago was no longer relevant. The purpose of the exercise is during times of change, we have to be willing to adapt to a changing landscape and let go of the past.

There are only a few things in life that we are certain of: death, taxes, and change. Do you look at change as an opportunity or something you would rather not experience? Do you expect that the new enterprise resource planning (ERP) system that is being installed at your company will go smoothly or that there will be several bumps in the road? How many times did you have to change course — at work or in your life — during the COVID-19 pandemic? Change is everywhere and change is constant. As a leader, how do you manage change?

Change is everywhere and change is constant. As a leader, how do you manage change?

I have always, for as long as I can remember, looked at change as an opportunity. I embrace change — even during a pandemic. (It did take me a couple of days at first, during which I pulled the covers over my head and then my improviser mindset kicked in. I am fortunate not to have gotten too "stuck" in 2020 when my sense of normalcy disappeared and I had to change everything if my business was going to survive. So I embraced the chaos and the change. It wasn't easy but it was okay.) For me, change is opportunity, and most of it is good. I have no desire, for example, to undo the changes that caused the big evolutions in my life and work. I don't want to go back to the way things were in the 1970s, 1980s, 1990s, or 2000s. Do you want to go back to the introduction of the World Wide Web as an internet service? Back to "you've got mail" and snail-slow dial-up internet speeds? For those of you who have purchased a new car during the past few years, are you willing to give up the new technology (Apple CarPlay! Lane assist!) and go back to rolling up your own windows with a crank, or not having the blindspot warning system in your side mirrors, or no longer having the ability to parallel-park hands-free? For most of us the answer is a resounding "NO!" Change is good in many ways.

There Are Two Types of Change

Change comes at us in two ways — designed or imposed. Designed change is when we know that change is going to happen and might have even chosen or engineered the change ourselves. Imposed change, on the other hand, is when we have no control over the change, no "say" in the decisions or circumstances that prompted it. But did you know that when change occurs, it can be both designed *and* imposed? How could that be?

Change comes at us in two ways — designed or imposed.

The perspectives of the creator of the change and the receiver of the change are very different. When you have top-down decision-making from the C-Suite, their perspective is that they have designed this change for the good of the organization. For example, the C-Suite team has decided to restructure the organization because of poor performance and loss of significant market share. When the restructure is announced to the organization, the rest of the organization has no prior knowledge because they were not consulted; this now is "imposed change." What was designed in a conference room is imposed upon the front lines. Imposed change pushed down on the organization leads to employees feeling stress, anxiety, and fear. They wonder and worry: *Will they have a job? Will their pay be cut? Will they have to relocate to keep their job?* Obviously, this kind of imposed change can be a real negative in many ways and rarely creates a highly productive workforce.

Would the above situation be better if those in the C-Suite consulted with all departments, along with talking to their key customers, key suppliers, and other stakeholders? Hold on! They would do what? I hear you laughing, and I can see you rolling your eyes. But yes, some leadership teams would, in fact, do that. Take, for example, the Xerox story.

The Xerox Story

Have you ever heard of Xerox? Yes, Xerox. In 2000, the CEO, Richard Thomas, resigned from the position that he had held for less than a year. According to the May 11, 2000, *CNN Money* article titled "Xerox CEO Steps Down," the share price of Xerox at the time was $25.50, down from its 12-month high of $62.63. During Thomas's tenure, he had restructured the sales organization unsuccessfully and the company was losing market share to their competitors.[1]

In 2001, Anne Mulcahy was named the new CEO of Xerox and was tasked with turning the organization around quickly. Mulcahy had worked for Xerox for 24 years; for 16 of those years, she was in sales. When Thomas resigned, she was promoted to president and COO, and then eventually elevated to the CEO role.[2]

Mulcahy inherited a company on the verge of Chapter 11 bankruptcy. The company had more than $17 billion in debt and had recorded losses in each of the preceding six years. A recent reorganization of the company's sales force had not gone according to plan. Customers were unhappy and the economy had started to falter. On top of all that, Xerox found itself in the middle of a protracted investigation by the Securities and Exchange Commission (SEC) of accounting improprieties in its Mexico unit. Mulcahy, as the new CEO, was under a lot of pressure from the board to turn this company around quickly.[3]

---

1   "Xerox CEO Steps Down," *CNN Money*, May 11, 2000, https://money.cnn. com/2000/05/11/companies/xerox/.

2   Ibid.

3   Ibid.

It has been reported that Mulcahy viewed her position as CEO through the lens of being a "chief communications officer," emphasizing the importance of listening to customers and employees"

> *"When I became CEO, I spent the first 90 days on planes traveling to various offices and listening to anyone who had a perspective on what was wrong with the company. I think if you spend as much time listening as talking, that's time well spent."*[4]

Mulcahy believes that effective communication consists of honesty and confidence, especially during a corporate crisis. She told *Insights at Stanford Business*, during an interview about her turnaround efforts, that: "When your organization is struggling, you have to give people the sense that you know what's happening and that you have a strategy to fix it. Beyond that, you have to tell people what they can do to help." She gave people a choice — "Either roll up your sleeves and go to work or leave Xerox." That simple.[5]

Mulcahy was asked by an employee to describe what Xerox would look like when it was restored under her plan. Most CEOs would have crafted a new vision statement for the new Xerox. Not her! She created a fictitious *Wall Street Journal* article describing Xerox in the year 2005. "We outlined the things we hoped to accomplish as though we had already achieved them," said Mulcahy. "We included performance metrics — even quotes from Wall Street analysts. It was really our vision of what we wanted the company to become."[6]

When the plan was developed and was being rolled out, Mulcahy spent a lot of time boarding airplanes to visit those who provided her with feedback, along with visiting and communicating with all the stakeholders on how the turnaround would be implemented. This was her way of getting buy-in — she told her stakeholders, "this what you shared with me and here is how your feedback is going to change the path of our company."[7] This is effective, 360-degree communication.

---

4   "Anne Mulcahy: The Keys to Turnaround at Xerox" https://www.gsb.stanford.edu/insights/anne-mulcahy-keys-turnaround-xerox

5   Ibid.

6   Ibid.

7   Ibid.

The purpose of sharing this story of Mulcahy's Xerox turnaround is to demonstrate how improv leadership — even during crisis or high-stakes moments — can involve collaborative, inclusive, engineered change instead of "imposed" change on hundreds or thousands of employees. Many leaders would have imposed massive changes quickly and hoped for the best, while employees felt gut-punched by all the change. Instead, Mulcahy invited everyone to help craft the change based on their own perspectives and expertise. She listened to ideas and built upon them. I can't be sure whether she actually used the words "Yes, and …" during all those idea-generating meetings, but I definitely think her behaviors are a strong example of improv leadership in action — demonstrating respect, trust, support, active listening, focus, adaptation, and the philosophy of "Yes, and …"

By asking the questions, listening to different perspectives, not getting defensive, and being focused and present in each conversation, something magical happened. The respect and trust for Mulcahy from those being interviewed grew exponentially because when you listen to understand (not just respond) in a conversation, parking your ego and agenda, and being focused on the other person's thoughts and ideas — without inter-rupting — respect and trust is the result. From all reports I've read about Mulcahy's leadership during this crucial juncture in the company's history, she wasn't just announcing her ideas about how she was going to fix the problem. She went to the employees because she wanted to know *their* thoughts and by doing so, she empowered them.

Listening, Collaborating, and Co-Creating

The Xerox story is an instructive one and it's relevant no matter where you work — regardless of your industry or the size of your organization. In Chapter 5, we talked about listening and now we're going deeper on that topic to talk about listening during organizational change. So let's think about the two topics in tandem, shall we?

When was the last time you listened to *understand* when you were soliciting thoughts and ideas from another person? When you do this, you are gath-ering bits and pieces of critical information to solve the problem at hand. Too many C-Suite leaders are afraid to solicit thoughts and ideas from others on the team or in the organization because of the myth that you, as a leader, need to have all the answers and solve all the problems. People are, after all, "looking up to you." I have always said, "The collective knowledge outside of your office far exceeds the collective knowledge inside your office." And at the risk of applauding my own thoughts here, it's true. Yes? Collaborating with others and working as a group solves problems. Issuing edicts from the C-suite often causes more problems.

Collaborating with others and working as a group solves problems. Issuing edicts from the C-suite often causes more problems.

When you collaborate, you are essentially co-creating with the team and/or the organization. By doing so, you have adopted the "Yes, and ..." principle of improv and will keep conversations moving forward in a positive manner, all the while adapting to whatever is being thrown at you and the team. Your role as a leader in the organization is to continually develop the people, their talent and their potential, and their ability to adapt to change. This is empowerment of others. This is effective communication. This is thriving amidst change and rising to even greater success and achievement. This is improv leadership!

Adaptability is essential in any change-management situation, as is divergent thinking; both skillsets and mindsets will help us in solving the problems before us. This next improv exercise, "New Choices," illustrates how we can make new choices by letting go of the past and accepting the new idea and seeing where the journey may take us. New Choices is like "That's Not True" except the bell works faster and is more effective ... *and* the exercise can be played either way.

EXERCISE #8: New Choices

This exercise should be conducted in pairs.

Improviser 1 tells a story and when improviser 2 rings the bell, improviser 1 needs to make a new choice. Improviser 2 should use the bell frequently.

Improviser 1: "I was driving to Cleveland."

Improviser 2: DING

Improviser 1: "I was driving to Akron."

Improviser 2: DING

Improviser 1: "I was driving to Pittsburgh [not hearing a ding, so continuing their story] to go see a Steelers football game."

Improviser 2: DING

Improviser 1: "To go see a Penguins hockey game [not hearing a ding] when I stopped for lunch at McDonalds."

Improviser 2: DING

Improviser 1: "I stopped for lunch at Arby's."

Improviser 2: DING

Improviser 1: "I stopped for lunch at Primanti Brothers."

The objective of this exercise is to listen actively, accept your "gifts" (i.e., accept the new suggestion), let go of the prior suggestion or line of thought, continue to move forward, and get comfortable with the uncomfortable. This exercise is hard and it's a little jarring, and that's the point. It helps us let go and change course quickly, without having time to get wrapped up in a particular storyline or outcome and without getting emotionally attached to where you were initially headed.

You can see a video of this exercise by going to https://petermargaritis.com/improv-video-exercises.

BONUS BITES!

We sometimes get stuck doing things "the way they have always been done," even when we don't know if there's a good reason for continuing to do so. If you aren't familiar with The Gorilla Story — about the five gorillas, the bunch of bananas, and the cold spray of water — head over to Google and read about this change management story.

My takeaways from the fabled gorilla story (which invariably is about monkeys or other primates and sometimes involves electrical shocks instead of cold water) are:

1. If you and your team are consistently punished for trying to get to the bananas (i.e., exploring a new idea or a new process, or changing a policy or procedure) at some point you will simply stop trying.

2. If you are losing and adding new staff to your team and they try to grab at the bananas, the other teammates will shut them down and say: "This is the way we have always done this *and* don't try because you will be met with resistance, ridicule, and it will be punitive."

3. This is ego leadership — which is outdated, non-collaborative, and stifles creativity, morale, productivity, and ultimately profits.

> *"Taking an improv workshop is one of the best ways to laugh, learn, and reduce your stress level."*
>
> —PETER A. MARGARITIS

CHAPTER 12

TAKING A LOAD OFF: STRESS RELIEVERS FOR OVERWROUGHT LEADERS

n April of 2020, I was approached by my improv coach, Jay Sukow, about conducting a "test" to see if a virtual improv workshop would be doable. Many would have said, "No. You can't conduct an improv workshop virtually. This can only be done live in a face-to-face environment." I, however, said, "YES! And let's give it a try." What we discovered is that a virtual improv workshop is very doable. Now came the questions:

- ➔ Was there a marketplace of interested participants?

- ➔ Could it be engaging and impactful?

- ➔ Could it be profitable?

So I decided to create my own virtual improv workshop and test it during the summer with a launch date in the fall of 2020. I invited 15-20 friends to participate for 90 minutes in this beta test. On average, we would have 8-10 participants at each gathering. After the test, I launched a six-week series of 90-minute workshops beginning in November 2020 and a second series that kicked off in February 2021.[1] The consistent dynamic and the feedback from participants through the beta test and the two subsequent offerings was that "it was such a great time." What was educational in nature was entertaining and enjoyable at its essence. Everyone laughed, bonded with each other, and learned. Everyone commented on how they looked forward each week to the class. They were able to escape the hectic nature of their work and lives each week for 90 minutes and that helped with their overall mood and attitude.

I can't say that the primary purpose of the workshops was happiness, but I'm thrilled that it was the result. So let me ask you: What makes *you* happy? Happiness could be walking on the beach, spending time with friends and family, traveling, attending a sporting event, meeting colleagues at a conference, or going out to your favorite restaurant. There are many ways to capture happiness. Unfortunately, there are many ways for that joy to be stolen or deferred.

So let's take a minute to discuss the opposite of happiness — the dreaded S-word. STRESS!

Stress is part of our everyday lives — it can come from so many sources. Some of our stress is the result of the daily frustrations of life, including our jobs or our busy schedules or our chronic health concerns. And other stress comes from unexpected challenges, such as a global pandemic, a personal medical crisis, job loss, family emergencies, work-related drama, or other tragedy or disruption.

Stress even comes from the "good stuff" — like starting a new job or having a baby or planning a wedding or moving into your dream home. On the way to good things, we can feel anxious and overwhelmed, we can second-guess ourselves and wish we were somewhere else doing something different.

---

1   Learn more about my virtual improv workshops at https://petermargaritis.com/virtual-workshop/.

Stress is everywhere, all the time. And here's the thing: Stress isn't always bad — it can sometimes motivate us into positive, meaningful action. And even in those situations that might initially seem like the negative kind of stress, you have the power to turn the experience into something positive (or at least into something with silver linings). Many millions of people realized this during the COVID-19 pandemic, suddenly realizing all the options and opportunities available to them:

- ➔ I can redo my business plan!

- ➔ I can write a book!

- ➔ I can rest and heal!

- ➔ I can learn to play the guitar!

- ➔ I can take an online photography class!

- ➔ I can reorganize my closets and cabinets!

The stress of the pandemic was significant for everyone who endured it. And many people found ways to immerse themselves in new routines, habits, activities, and projects instead of worrying about all the things they had no control over (like local mask mandates or when their company was going to re-open or whether a vaccine would be introduced quickly). The stress was, no doubt, rough for many people (maybe even most people). It took a toll. And it also brought so much into clearer perspective, especially for people who were previously overworked and overscheduled, feeling pressure to keep up with the Joneses and to climb corporate ladders or break their own personal records on the half-marathon course. Stress can cause us to reassess, and that's a good thing. Stress — when you deal with it right away or let things go as soon as you can — can have value in your life. Not all stress is bad stress (even the stuff that *looks* like bad stress can be okay!).

I have found that the following six "life tools" can help you take on the stress that comes with your job, family, and just the day-to-day responsibilities of life. Think of these tools as stress relievers for overwrought leaders. How can these tools help *you*?

Communication

Some of the greatest comedic films and plays revolve around communication (or the lack thereof). Think about classic movies like *Birdcage*, *Caddyshack*, and *Airplane* — movies that are full of comedic sequences based on confusion and miscommunication. This confusion turns into the frustration that the characters feel and express, causing us to laugh as an audience. Why? Because we know better, and it's funny when you're not the one experiencing it! The hilarious outcomes of other people's stress — in comedic films or in plays like Shakespeare's farcical and iconic *The Comedy of Errors* — can teach us much about how *good* communication can *prevent* stress (just as *poor* communication can *create* it).

> ## The problem created by poor communication is confusion and, unfortunately, lack of communication or rampant miscommunication exists in our lives and our work every day.

The problem created by poor communication is confusion and, unfortunately, lack of communication or rampant miscommunication exists in our lives and our work every day. Adapting to the new normal of Zoom meetings, virtual learning, and a large remote workforce adds to the confusion. And, when we're the ones experiencing it (rather than watching it on a cinema screen), it's not that funny.

Paying attention to improving our communication skills can reduce our stress and the stress of others. When people feel disrespected or discounted, stress intensifies. When they feel unheard, they shut down or respond with cynicism, distrust, or anger — and the situation becomes exponentially worse. Communication in today's modern environment extends to having a good microphone, a strong internet connection, remembering to unmute yourself when speaking, being aware of your nonverbal messaging, and making sure you are sending a positive message. Effective communication validates and motivates.

**Effective communication
validates and motivates.**

Adaptability

Adaptability is a *huge* part of improv – it *is* improv. And adaptability is one of the six helpful tools for stress management. Many things in life can be stressful, but we can choose to "go with the flow." Adapting is simply the ability to readjust as you experience things — whether that readjusts your sales pitch to a potential customer or the time in the morning you give a presentation or having to work primarily from home during a global pandemic. No matter the situation, it takes flexibility and confidence to address change head-on; and let's face it, things are always changing and things rarely go as planned.

**No matter the situation, it takes flexibility
and confidence to address change head-on;
and let's face it, things are always changing
and things rarely go as planned.**

Want to practice adaptability? Here's a game you can try — at work or with your family and friends. Start by soliciting three volunteers to sit up front and face the audience. Together, these three people up front or on stage are "Dr. Know-It-All." They can answer any question — but just one word at a time. To demonstrate the three-way skill, first have the three-person Dr. Know-It-All answer something like: "Why is the sky blue?" Each person should provide a word (starting with one person as the beginning of the line and going one person at a time) as they attempt to construct a sentence to answer the question. Inevitably, you will find that each volunteer has quickly formed some plan or agenda in their mind for how they want to answer. (You are likely doing that right now, deciding whether you want to craft an answer that's whimsical and based on mythology or whether you want to get the word "refraction" or "sunlight" into your answer.) However, when the player before the scheming improviser doesn't say something that fits their agenda, they get flustered and must scramble for a response. That scrambling is "adaptability" ... and it's not always easy.

This, incidentally, is what happens in real life — we come up with scripts or ideas before the person has even finished or started. Why? Because we don't want to look stupid or unprepared or less than eloquent. And yet, we don't respond appropriately with our scripted responses either because we're not really paying attention to the person whose words or remarks precede us and, therefore, we are unable to adapt based on what was said. When you start to focus, you can adapt and reduce your stress at the same time. Adaptable leaders are less stressed leaders.

Awareness

Another important tool for reducing stress when you're a leader is aware-ness. Being *aware* of your environment can help you *control* your involve-ment in whatever situation you find yourself. When you assess your surroundings, your team, those around you, yourself, and other factors, the observations add up to a kind of awareness that will help you develop confi-dence and overcome the stress.

Another way of looking at what some people call "situational awareness" is to examine how well developed your emotional intelligence (EI or EQ) is. Are you in control of your emotions right now? If you take a moment to consider how you're expressing your emotions and reacting to others around you, would you say that you're being respectful, thoughtful, or empathetic? Being self-aware about our emotions, socially aware of those around us, and having the ability to manage our emotions optimally helps build relationships and ease our levels of stress.

> **Being self-aware about our emotions, socially aware of those around us, and having the ability to manage our emotions optimally helps build relationships and ease our levels of stress.**

Awareness is presented here as the third stress-busting tool for leaders because it's the bridge between communication and adaptability. Awareness goes hand-in-hand with being a better listener and communicator, which results in adapting to situations more quickly and more effectively.

Do you know what else can help you be more aware and stress-free? Being prepared. (You saw that coming because you read that early in the book. You are evolving into a business improviser!) Well, being as prepared as you can be in any given situation is important (and yes, even though I want you to be able to confidently go "off script" in any moment, I still strongly encourage you first to be prepared). The more you understand the environment and the variables in the environment you may be going into (or the environment you are frequently in — like the board room), the more comfortable you will be when focusing on what is happening now. Without preparation, you're more concerned about your anxieties — including the stress that comes from not being prepared! You can't foresee the unexpected, but you can be ready for it with preparation and the confidence it brings — allowing you to be more aware of changing dynamics and allowing you to respond in the best way possible.

Attitude

All the stress-management tools in the world aren't going to help if you attempt to apply them with the wrong attitude. As they say, "attitude is everything." There is a vast difference between "I will do the best I can" and "This is going to fail." If you adopt a better attitude (one that doesn't broadcast defeat or incompetence), you might find that you are doing well. I have learned that this "positive attitude" impact is equally powerful at work and on the improv stage. No matter your source of stress, your success in overcoming that stress depends on your ability to perceive things positively. You either can see your situation as a challenge and make the most of it, or you can succumb to it and let the stress win.

No matter your source of stress, your success in overcoming that stress depends on your ability to perceive things positively.

One of the most significant ways to achieve the kind of attitude that will yield success is learning to shift your perspective from "yes, but ..." to "yes, and ..." Let me explain this again, because it's such a vital mindset shift that it bears repeating. "But" is a conjunction used to introduce something contrasting with what has already been mentioned. "And" is a conjunction used to connect words of the same part of speech, clauses, or sentences that are to be taken jointly. One stops a thought in its tracks and introduces something else. The other connects an additional idea to be considered jointly. It's eye-opening to think about how often we use the phrase "Yes, but ..." (or simply "But ...") and the dramatic effect that happens when you replace "but" with "and."

> Try it. Think about a conversation you just had with a colleague or friend. Where did one of you say "but" when you could have said "and." How would that have changed the tone or even the outcome of the conversation? "And" continues the conversation, gives hope, and makes room for new perspectives. "And" is a gift.

Take a positive attitude into your next meeting. Even if you don't ultimately agree on what's being proposed, you're at least allowing for the possibility of something positive happening — thereby showing respect and support for your associate. This works when talking to your inner critic as well! Doing this small (yet significant) shift in language promotes positive attitudes from all and encourages an atmosphere of acceptance and possibilities, not rejection and defeat. As a result, the workplace culture thrives. *And*, your leadership stress is reduced.

Calm in Chaos

"Don't panic." If you ever hear someone, say "don't panic," it's almost a sure-fire trigger that tells you to go ahead and start panicking. You don't have to, though — it certainly won't help you. When you're staring chaos in the face, you must refuse to tell yourself that you can't do it — that you can't overcome it or face it. The fact is, you can — and communication, adaptability, awareness, and all the improvisational techniques can help you operate clearly without panicking. You'll always know you can figure a way out. Being calm in the midst of chaos or crisis is the fifth stress-busting tool for leaders.

A big part of staying calm in chaotic moments is learning to manage your inner critic.

A big part of staying calm in chaotic moments is learning to manage your inner critic. We're all familiar with it — the voice that tells you you're not good enough, not smart enough, that you shouldn't be here. (That voice we spent a lot of time examining and silencing in Chapter 8!) What can you do when you start to hear the inner critic? You must flip the script, change the lines, and start programming your brain to use "yes, and …" instead of "yes, but …" When you do, you develop confidence. You tell yourself, "I can do this," and the more times you repeat it, the more you will believe it. Here are a few examples of how to incorporate this line of thinking:

➜ "Yes, I know I will make mistakes, and they will not hamper me."

➜ "Yes, I won't be perfect, and that means I can only get better."

➜ "Yes, my boss likes to ask 'gotcha questions,' and his aggressive management style doesn't say anything about my competence."

➜ "Yes, this is a high-stakes project, and I'm the best person for the job."

Humor

The final tool for managing stress in the workplace is a fun one. Yes! *Fun.* Far too many workplaces seem devoid of humor. I often ask my audiences, "When was the last time your coworkers burst out into laughter, and it wasn't at your expense?" The answer depends on your culture and your colleagues. A regular dose of laughter, however, reduces stress, and it's desirable. We should all be laughing more at work.

We should all be laughing more at work.

I'm an improv guy, so of course I think humor is important. But do the leadership experts agree? Yes, yes they do! In fact, a survey from Robert Half Talent Solutions found that 91% of executives believe a sense of humor is important for career advancement, and 84% feel that people with a good sense of humor do a better job.[2] Another study by Bell Leadership Institute found that leaders' two most desirable traits were a good sense of humor and a strong work ethic.[3]

A regular dose of laughter reduces stress — it is the best medicine. It loosens us up and bolsters the immune system. Stress, on the other hand, can make us sick, causing productivity to plummet. So, start laughing and get your coworkers to chuckle as well. (Trying out some of the improv exercises from this book is a great way to get started with the giggles in a safe space where you'll be developing useful skills along the way!)

Whether your stress in life results from personal challenges, trouble with family and home, or the demands of your job, so much of your future success in overcoming these challenges might depend upon your ability to perceive things positively and to maintain a sense of humor.

Stress is hard and it's everywhere. And you can free yourself from its clutches by assembling a toolbox with new approaches to communication, adaptability, awareness, attitude, calm in chaos, and humor. Try a few of them out (and ideally, try *all* of them out!).

Either you win, or you let the stress win. And, frankly, I think you're a winner. Choose to beat the stress through the art of improvisation.

---

2   Robert Half Talent Solutions, "Is a Sense of Humour in the Workplace Good for Your Career?," March 27, 2017, https://www.roberthalf.com.au/blog/jobseekers/sense-humour-workplace-good-your-career.

3   Bell Leadership Institute, "Bell Leadership Study Finds Humor Gives Leaders the Edge," March 2012, https://www.bellleadership.com/humor-gives-leaders-edge/.

BONUS BITES!

I find the best way to beat stress is through laughter. When you need a to laugh, here are some ideas that can help:

- **Watch a funny movie:** *Caddyshack* is one of my go-to favorites.

- **Watch a standup comedy special:** *Robin Williams at the Met* will have you doubled over in hysterics.

- **Watch a funny YouTube video:** Check out *Best of AFV - Winners Edition | America's Funniest Home Videos.*

- **Watch a sitcom:** Binge-watch several episodes of *The Big Bang Theory.*

- **Go to a comedy club:** I love The Funny Bone.

- **Go watch an improv comedy show:** The Second City offers shows across the nation.

- **Go to a public place "people watch:"** Wander the aisles at Walmart or grab a bench at the local park. Funny, smile-worthy moments are all around us.

*If everyone justifies everyone
else's actions, there are no bad ideas.*

CHAPTER 13

THE ART OF INNOVATION: DEPLOYING IMPROV TECHNIQUES TO ARRIVE AT CREATIVE SOLUTIONS

What am I most proud of in this life? Tackling the fear that cripples most of us — speaking in front of a live audience (and improvising on the spot!). The ability to step up onto a stage with another person (or team) without a script — armed just with my knowledge and life experiences — and ask the audience for a suggestion and then create a story "in the moment" is one among the most exhilarating things I have ever done in my life. I have discovered a freedom in improv. I have embraced that freedom to create, to test, to fail, to make the words and ideas of others even better through an additive process, and to laugh. It's all so fulfilling. Better yet, maybe by chance we create something so special that it can change the world and enrich lives.

You might be thinking, "But improv such as you describe above is about entertainment." Yes, and … it's also about creating something new — revolutions, ideas, movements, innovations. When we improvise — on stage and at work — we become collaborative creators and strategic problem-solvers. We get stuff done and we do so in a way that eclipses the kind of solutions we might surface if we weren't being improv-minded.

So what, exactly, is innovation? We know it when we see it, right? The iPhone, self-driving cars, artificial intelligence, virtual interactive platforms, and VR headsets all come to mind. When we think about innovation, we might think of Tesla or NASA or all the companies dotting the horizon in Silicon Valley. Innovation isn't always about technology, though. It's about fresh ideas and breakthrough approaches to solving our stakeholders' problems. Maybe it's a product that makes someone's life easier or maybe it's a recipe for a dinner entrée that has people raving. Maybe it's a new use for an old process or product, or maybe it's a service that clients and customers are suddenly clamoring for. And no matter what it is, that innovation started with an idea (maybe even a weak or downright bad idea!).

Innovation is about building, one idea at a time. (Sound familiar?) During my improv-world journey, I have come across many quotes about how we should be innovating, and one of my favorites is "Bring a brick, don't bring a cathedral." This expression reminds us that a leader (of a meeting, project, team, or organization), should not bring a final solution (i.e., the cathedral) to the problem, challenge, or goal being addressed, but rather they should solicit ideas (i.e., bricks) from the group to build a viable solution. And they should make clear to everyone else that their own ideas are just individual bricks too.

Innovation is about building, one idea at a time.

In Chapters 3, 4, and 5, we explored the role of the ego in the workplace. And when it comes to innovation, ego is the wrecking ball that knocks down the pile of bricks and destroys any nearly finished cathedrals. Ego-driven leaders who approach their team with *"the answer"* — projecting an attitude of "I am the smartest person in the room" — only serve to shoot down ideas from the team and stop innovation in its tracks. Innovation is fueled by the former, not the latter, approach.

Don't get me wrong ... As a leader, you sometimes will have the best idea during a brainstorming session. And heck, sometimes maybe you'll even be the smartest person in the room. But leadership is not about gloating or hogging the spotlight. It's about shining the light on everyone around you to see how the ideas and talents of others — by themselves or when added to your own — can create something greater than the sum of its parts.

Don't Criticize During Divergent Thinking

I love the saying: "You can't create and criticize in the same space." (You might be saying, "I have heard that one before" and you are right. We talked about this very issue in Chapter 1 and revisited it in Chapter 11. Now, it's time to go deeper.) Criticizing (ego-led) during creation is a hindrance to the creative process. Ego-less facilitation of brainstorming and problem solving, on the other hand, creates a safe space in which all ideas are welcome. And that safe space is where creativity flourishes.

Different leaders think in different ways, and the way *they* think becomes the way the entire team (or even company) is allowed to think. There are two kinds of thinking that might characterize the culture during the innovation process: divergent thinking and convergent thinking.

Divergent thinking is the process of coming up with as many ideas as possible and not censoring yourself or others — not criticizing or qualifying the concepts as they are presented. Divergent thinking is all about *quantity* and not about quality. And it looks a lot like improv, with lots of "Yes! And ..."

Convergent thinking, on the other hand, is the process of analyzing and critiquing the ideas to see which ones are viable. With convergent thinking, the goal is to get everyone to come together in the end, having "arrived" at one solution.

You may be wondering what's wrong with criticizing an idea during the divergent thinking process. It would seem we are using our time more effectively, right? Not really. When we say "we can't do that" or "we tried that last year" or "we don't have the resources to accomplish that," the idea-generating machine is killed. The incentive to volunteer your idea with the high probability of it being shot down before putting any thought into the concept makes the risk not worth taking. So, when you're running a divergent-thinking brainstorming session, be sure to nod and smile and write down all the ideas. Keep asking, "Excellent. What else?" (A way to say, "Yes, and ...") Keep the ideas flowing.

There is a 2020 Dilbert cartoon that is a perfect example of this killing of the idea-generating machine. It's called "Wally Makes a Suggestion" and, at the risk of underselling it by explaining it in my own words, Wally asks the pointy-haired boss if he saw the "brilliant idea" he had emailed over. The boss tells him that he's already "debunked it" in his mind, going on to tell Wally that if it was such a great idea, someone else would already be doing it, and insulting his intelligence and how he looks along the way. It's downright brutal. And when the boss asks if anyone else has any ideas to share, guess how everyone responds? You guessed it: "Nope. Never. Nope. Nope." Killing one idea killed them all.[1]

Most of you have experienced this, right? When one person in the room gets dismissed (a topic we explored in Chapter 7), we all clam up. We've seen what happens when good people present their ideas, and we don't want to get ridiculed or ignored so we just go silent. So, let's think about this differently and employ one of the foundations of improv that is profoundly simple and powerful. You guessed it! "Yes, and ..." The philosophy of "Yes, and ..." — as you now know by virtue of reading this book and becoming an improv expert yourself — is to accept another person's idea as valid and then add on to it (despite whether you think the idea is weak or unlikely to reap results or downright crazy or impossible to execute). When we accept an idea and add to it, we are actually increasing our collective confidence to take risks. And taking risks without the fear of being punished is where amazing creativity is generated! There is a name for this — it is called psychological safety, a concept we explored in Chapter 7 and which bears reiteration here in the context of our conversation on innovation. Psychological safety during divergent thinking creates a culture of all ideas being accepted without

---

1   Scott Adams, "Wally Makes a Suggestion," *Dilbert*, December 20, 2020, https://dilbert.com/strip/2020-12-20.

criticism or punishment. And when you're just swimming in ideas, a few of them are bound to become the big innovations your organization needs for sustainable, profitable growth.

Easier Said Than Done: Breaking the Impulse to Criticize

Here is the challenge. How do you *not* criticize an idea during divergent (idea-generating) thinking? Maybe to you it sounds simple — just don't do it, right? Not so simple! At least not for most of us. When lots of ideas are coming our way, and some of them are weak or irrelevant or downright crazy, it's only natural to chime in with "That won't work. Who else has an idea?" Divergent thinking without criticism is — for most of us — a whole new way of thinking and behaving and it takes time to master it. Changing our mindset takes time because we are hard-wired from our career histories to criticize during the ideation process. However, there are ways to change this pattern. The best way I've found to begin breaking this pattern is to set a timer for 10 minutes, and then see how many ideas you and your team can develop without any additional dialogue. Have someone write them all on a physical or digital whiteboard or flip chart. Or do an additive brainstorming process whereby everyone in the room takes out a piece of paper and writes two ideas on it then passes the paper to the person to their right. You must then take the sheet of paper that was just handed to you and come up with two more ideas that aren't already on that piece of paper. You repeat this process until your own piece of paper comes back to you and you collectively have dozens or hundreds (depending on the number of people in the meeting) of ideas to consider.

What I have learned from not criticizing while in an idea-generating setting is that the rules of engagement for the brainstorming session need to be discussed days before the actual process begins. I did a creativity workshop for a client of mine not too long ago. I thought I had clearly explained and defined the divergent thinking process — only to find out I had not! During the discussion, almost everyone participating would throw out an idea, would attach some qualifier to it (e.g., "maybe this is lame but ..." or "I'm not sure if we can afford this but ..."), and then someone would shoot it down. It was painful. I stopped the process and re-explained divergent thinking again and moved the process along. And again, it was only a moment before they reverted to their old ways.

With perfect 20/20 hindsight, I spoke with my client afterward and explained that what I should have done was to create a document outlining the divergent process. That document should have been sent to all participants two weeks before the program. Then, the client would have called a group meeting to review the information at least a week before the program and walked everyone through the process. Then, on the workshop day, I would have reviewed the document again and answered any questions to get everyone's buy-in. They would have been primed — aware of the "rules of engagement" and ready to do their best to follow the prescribed process. With that kind of prior instruction and buy-in, I could have facilitated the session differently. During the session, if some participants weren't following the rules, we would have taken a pause, reviewed the process, acknowledged how difficult this is, and started in again.

Success with this takes time because old habits are hard to break. It goes to the culture you are trying to create by recognizing that this is a process and not an event. Patience and tolerance by the leader are critical for the team to begin to change their mindset. The ultimate goal is to create a culture where crazy ideas are accepted and supported, and they are done so with patience and encouragement.

Ask for the Crazy Idea

In a recent creativity workshop with a Fortune 500 leadership conference for emerging leaders from the United States and Latin America, I explained the process this way: "The leadership of this company wants us to come up with new ideas on how to increase profitability. They want us to go deeper than raising prices and cutting costs. I want you to give me your ideas, preferably *crazy* ideas. What is said in this room stays in this room, *and* no one can criticize any ideas until all the ideas are documented." I did explain that crazy ideas provide us with bandwidth in coming up with the ultimate not-so-crazy idea, and what may seem crazy at first could be doable when considered more fully. When delivering your concept, I suggested to them, don't qualify or try to explain your thoughts about the idea — just put forth the idea with the goal of quantity, not quality. The more ideas, the better.

Crazy ideas provide us with bandwidth in coming up with the ultimate not-so-crazy idea, and what may seem crazy at first could be doable when considered more fully.

Once everyone agreed and had "bought into" the process, we began. In the first five minutes, the ideas were very safe and nothing crazy. A couple of participants wanted to add dialogue, responding to the ideas they were hearing. I politely stopped them and reminded them of the process, and then asked for more ideas.

In the following five minutes, ideas were being stretched further from those safe zones. Then one person from Latin America stated, "I know how we can increase profitability in our company. Let's kill our competition's salespeople." He said it with obvious humor and not a bit of diabolical intention, smirking all the while. Everyone in the room laughed. I paused for a moment, thinking *"That is a really bad (and murderous) idea and that leads me to a better idea."* I said nothing out loud, because he had momentarily stumped me — this took "crazy idea" to a new level. *How do I take an idea about mass murder and build upon it?* I needed to improvise. I was committed to the rules and I knew we could use this crazy idea to get us closer to a truly *good* idea. After my pause, I replied, "Okay. Yes, we could kill all of your competition's salespeople, AND none of us look good in an orange jumpsuit." I paused and twisted my mouth a bit, trying to think on my feet. "*And*, instead of killing all those salespeople, let's identify our competition's top salespeople and offer them a position with *our* company … with a 20% increase in salary and a bonus. And we get to stay out of jail." Everyone in the room had this look of "wow, this crazy idea process does work," and yes, it does.

Now granted, it would still be unethical to poach all the employees from the competitors (and maybe even illegal depending upon any non-solicitation agreements in place), yet the commitment to build upon each other's ideas got us thinking about the value of top salespeople, how to attract and retain the right ones, and how to grow through outstanding sales strategies. The attendees had come with bricks and not cathedrals, and together we were building something that just might be beautiful, unique, and strong.

Sticky Notes Give Everyone a Voice

Here is another approach to the divergent-thinking process. During ideation, stronger personalities begin to dominate the process. Those who may be more introverted often never get a chance to contribute. In these cases, sticky notes are the solution. Have everyone write their idea on a sticky note and then everyone can submit the idea and remain anonymous. For example, in one creativity workshop for a client, I ask the group to develop ideas for increasing morale in the department. Each person was to write down an idea on a sticky note and give it to me. There were approximately 35 participants or, as I like to say, 35 *ideas* suddenly to choose from among — 35 more ideas than the one idea I had in my head. Here are some of the ideas that appeared on the sticky notes:

- ➤   4-day work week

- ➤   Pizza on Fridays

- ➤   Happy hours

- ➤   Being recognized for their hard work

- ➤   More concise feedback

- ➤   Summer hours

As I collected the sticky notes and organized them on the whiteboard (sticking them up where everyone could see them), I noticed that the chief financial officer (CFO) had not turned in a sticky note. I approached the CFO, and he handed me his sticky note. I looked at it and handed it back to him, saying, "You need to share this one with the group. Hold onto this for a minute."

The 35 people in the room helped me group all the notes into clusters on the whiteboard, organized by general themes, and we debriefed what we were seeing emerge as the top, most-popular types of ideas. I then turned to the CFO and asked him to share his idea. He stood up and said that on his sticky note, he wrote: "thank you." He held it up for everyone to see. It was a powerful and almost solemn moment. He looked at his team and said, "I am quick to criticize and slow to praise, and that stops now. I will make a point of thanking you *first* more often and criticizing less because we all make mistakes." Jaws went slack with disbelief, and people started to smile. The overall mood of the room changed in a split second. They felt heard and seen, respected, and understood. For this team, little yellow pieces of paper changed not only the way they solved problems or developed innovations, but it changed the way they felt about one another. Saying "thank you" was one of the most important things they could do to improve morale, and thanks to the CFO's humility, they were on their way.

Ask Yourself

➜ How can you and your team begin to change how you innovate, adopting a more robust and engaging way that allows risk-taking, respect of others, patience, vulnerability, and giving everyone a say in the process? Start immediately and work on the process and, over time, your team's abilities to solve problems will drastically improve.

BONUS BITES!

One of the most popular TED Talks of all time (with nearly 21 million views as of fall 2021) was delivered by the late Sir Ken Robinson and it was entitled, "Do Schools Kills Creativity?"[2] There are so many reasons why I love this presentation (including Robinson's comedic timing and improv skills) *and* the number one reason I love this talk is Ken's well-reasoned argument about how our creativity gets stifled once we enter the education system. It is worth the 19 minutes to watch and if you'll indulge me, I'll tell you why this video (which I have watched 40+ times!) has resonated so much with me. I am most drawn to three things he says:

1. **"If you are not prepared to be wrong, you will never come up with anything original."** We all know leaders who refuse to be wrong — in the eyes of others and by their own estimation. What they say is always right. If an idea or approach or process isn't his or her way, then it must be wrong. These leaders choose "certainty" over creativity and, often, when think they are coming up with something original, they are in fact repackaging the idea as "new and improved." An unwillingness to risk being wrong holds us (and our organizations) back.

2. **"We run companies like this where we stigmatize mistakes."** Because we are so caught up at work in pointing out when an employee makes a mistake (instead of looking at those "failures" as what I call First Attempts in Learning [FAIL]), companies and leaders inevitably kill creativity in the people who work for them.

3. **"As we grow up, we don't grow into creativity; we grow out of it."** Stop for a moment and think about yourself — as a child who then spent years working for corporations, non-profits, higher education, and/or governments. Does this apply to you? Have you grown

---

2   Sir Ken Robinson, "Do Schools Kill Creativity?," TED, January 6, 2007, https://www.youtube.com/watch?v=iG9CE55wbtY&t=227s.

out of creativity? If so, how can you overcome your current condition to find your way back to a creative spirit? Or does the organizational culture in which you work kill your creativity no matter how hard you try? I believe that this is one of the main reasons why I could never go back to working for someone else. Many of us who "escaped" corporate America or other types of organizations did so because being an entrepreneur can sometimes bring back our creativity.

Creativity is a great way to talk about some of the principles we've addressed in this book, like good ideas and outrageous ideas and demonstrating a lack of ego or fear when communicating with others and brainstorming solutions to important problems. Creativity is key. Watch Sir Ken Robinson's presentation at https://www.youtube.com/watch?v=iG9CE55wbtY&t=227s.

*Great improvisers always accept
the ideas of the other players
without judging them to be
"good" or "bad," always thinking,
"This is now our idea."*

CHAPTER 14

BETTER OFF TOGETHER: INSPIRING A CREATIVE, IDEA-GENERATING WORKPLACE

Being creative in the workplace takes practice. It takes safety and supportive processes. And it also takes confidence. David Kelley, CEO of legendary design firm IDEO, spoke about the importance of building creative confidence in a 2012 TED Talk. When Kelley was in elementary school, one of his classmates was being ridiculed by a peer about the project he was trying to create. As a result, his classmate immediately shut down and quit the project, feeling discouraged about his peer's opinion. All these years later, the adult Kelley remembers that moment with specificity and emotion. Kelley went on to talk about how we can often "opt out" of being creative due to this kind of experience — we tell ourselves that we're not creative or that our ideas are not worthy, so therefore it's somehow true.

In creative workshops with left-brained business leaders, I always stress the need to think about more than just facts. Left-brained business leaders (like finance professionals, engineers, IT professionals, scientists, and physicians) are typically very facts-oriented people. The challenge is to get them to see that there is more to their leadership style than just the facts and figures. Many of them feel just as Kelley described, that they somehow aren't cut out to be creative, or that they aren't capable.[1]

The important thing for all of us who are leaders in technical professions (and a few other professions that are generally considered "not creative") to realize is that we are, indeed, creative! Creativity is, simply put, your ability to generate ideas. And we all certainly do that. If we remember and embrace the fact that we are innately creative, think about the number of ideas we can generate! So, never forget, your involvement in the creative process — regardless of your role, your seniority, your amount of extroversion, or your position of power — is just as real and just as important as anyone else's.

Improv Beyond the Stage

Business schools across America have taken note of the importance of idea generation and creative thinking in the business world. For the past several years, programs have started offering courses that help students not only learn ways to promote free thinking and brainstorming, but to adopt principles of improvisation in order to facilitate this creativity. One of the most powerful principles of improv, as you know, is found in the practice of the "yes, and ..." approach.

Bob Kulhan, an influential promoter of getting improvisation into business schools across America, summed up the idea of "yes, and ..." when he said: "When they're collaborating onstage, improv performers never reject one another's ideas — they say 'yes, and' to accept and build upon each new contribution." Fellow believer that improv belongs in business schools and in businesses — not just on stages in front of audiences — Holly Mandel (founder of the performance school Improvolution and its

---

1   David Kelley, "How to Build Your Creative Confidence," TED 2012, May 16, 2012, https://www.ted.com/talks/david_kelley_how_to_build_your_creative_confidence#t-76208.

corporate-targeted offshoot Imergence), says: "It's a total philosophy of creativity. 'Yes, and' creates; while 'no' stops the flow."[2]

It's this "yes, and ..." principle of improv that gets ideas churning up and out of people's heads so they can be built upon, enjoyed, and put into action. This virtue of "getting it all out" applies not just to others (to our employees, our peers, our kids, our friends); we ought to apply it to ourselves too. We, too, have brilliant ideas just waiting to be mined. We need to give them voice; we need to "think out loud" and get the creative juices flowing. We are, unfortunately, often our own harshest critic — a critic who is quick to dismiss our ideas as "stupid" and who sometimes, therefore, keeps us quiet. But it's not us who need to be quiet; we need to silence that internal *critic* for creativity to surface!

> **"Yes, and ..." gets ideas churning up and out of people's heads so they can be built upon, enjoyed, and put into action.**

There are no stupid ideas — every one of them leads somewhere (and even dead ends give us a chance to turn around and reassess!), and it's especially important in brainstorming to let all ideas rise. In creativity workshops, I stress the importance of truly believing that no idea is a bad idea. All ideas lead to a better idea. Don't just nod and smile when you hear me say that again and again. *Believe* it. And start acting on that belief. Yes, indeed ... all ideas are important. So, whatever is in your head, let it out! Even if the inner critic is shouting at you, dig your heels in and shout louder; shout it down and let the idea out! Remember that ideas lead to better ideas. No ideas lead to nothing.

EXERCISE #9: Outrageous Opposites

There are many exercises that you can employ in your brainstorming process. One of my favorites is an exercise called "Outrageous Opposites." If

2   Seth Stevenson, "Getting to 'Yes, And': How Improv Comedy Skills Became a Must-Have for Entrepreneurs," *Slate*, March 30, 2014, https://slate.com/business/2014/03/ improv-comedy-and-business-getting-to-yes-and.html.

you have a problem to solve, step 1 is to brainstorm *traditional* approaches in solving the problem. Step 2 is to brainstorm *outrageous* ideas for how to solve the problem. When you are finished, look at the outrageous ideas and see if there is anything you can expand upon. Very often, when you merge elements of a traditional approach with some outrageous flavor, you discover the perfect solution to your problem.

This exercise can be conducted in groups of up to perhaps 20 people. And yes, if you are a solopreneur or want to come up with some great solutions on your own, this is a game you can play by yourself. Below is an example of how it might play out at your office or in your conference room.

THE PROBLEM

Recruiting seasoned staff for our company. You need more talent and you need them to have valuable experience before they arrive.

THE EXERCISE

First, brainstorm some *traditional approaches* to recruiting seasoned staff. Maybe you could place some Indeed or ZipRecruiter ads, you could hire a headhunter, you could put up a poster at a professional conference where the ideal candidates might be attending, or you could offer a referral bonus to current staff.

Once you've come up with as many ideas as you can — ideas that feel comfortable, traditional, or acceptable (the kind of stuff your boss or colleagues wouldn't raise an eyebrow about) — put on your thinking caps to get more creative. Now, it's time to think of *outrageous approaches* to finding seasoned staff. Maybe you could hire a blimp to fly over a sporting event where you think qualified prospects might be enjoying some leisure time. Maybe you could place ads in restrooms at public places that attract your target audience. Maybe you could invite qualified prospects to an open house. Or maybe you could create a fun and surprising video about your company, then post it on all of your company's existing social media channels and then the ones where you've never had a presence too.

Review your outrageous approaches and see which ones might actually work for your organization. Can you push an outrageous idea even *further*? Are there elements of a traditional approach that should be married with an outrageous idea? Open your minds and discover creative solutions to important problems.

Want to see such a solution in action? Check out what the accounting firm Withum Smith + Brown did with fun YouTube videos designed to increase the morale in the company and entertain and engage clients. Their videos were actually so good that seasoned staffed from *other* accounting firms applied for positions with Withum firm. Win-win! Check out one of my favorite videos they produced. What's not to love? https://youtu.be/ZCs7O6cJgiQ

EXERCISE #10: Kill the Business

Another one of my favorite brainstorming exercises is called "Kill the Business." Instead of thinking of ways to *grow* your business, this is an exercise that focuses on ways to put your company *out* of business. Your team is looking at the company's weaknesses and listing them as a small, medium, or large threat. Once these weaknesses have been identified and categorized, then you and your coworkers (if you have them! this exercise works equally well for solopreneurs) should answer a couple of questions:

1. "I never thought about it that way!" What did we *not* think about before, which we can appreciate and address only now because of the "kill the business" mindset we adopted for this exercise?

2. "We ought to get on top of that!" What (or who) could attack us now and how can we quickly eliminate the threat?

3. "That's a no-brainer!" Which weakness is the most important one for us to fix?

This is an eye-opening exercise that will uncover opportunities you may not have discovered using conventional thinking.

Implementing a Creative Workplace

In the end, the workplace needs leaders who inspire and encourage the expression of creativity. And I believe that deploying improv techniques at work is often the best way to arrive at creative solutions.

In the end, the workplace needs leaders who inspire and encourage the expression of creativity.

John Dragoon — who serves as senior vice president, chief marketing officer, and channel chief at publicly traded Novell (an infrastructure software company) — understands that creativity is at the core of marketplace competitiveness. He shares wise words about the role of leaders in inspiring creativity:

> *"Truly creative leaders invite disruptive innovation, encourage others to drop outdated approaches and take balanced risks. They are open minded and inventive in expanding their management and communication styles, particularly to engage with a new generation of employees, partners and customers."*[3]

This doesn't happen overnight, but if the leadership of an organization encourages the generation of ideas, some of those ideas are bound to produce impressive results. Not all the ideas are going to work, no matter how much product testing or field work a company conducts. Some ideas will go nowhere; that's true. But if you have no ideas at all, *you* will go nowhere; your organization will stagnate and eventually even fail.

When it comes to creativity and generating ideas, all are needed, and all are wanted — at least in organization with leaders who are "improv minded." Don't be afraid to share and solicit ideas that are rough around the edges at first — all great ideas start out that way. With a little polishing and fine tuning, the results can be quite extraordinary.

---

3   John Dragoon, "What Is Creativity's Value -- In Marketing, In Business?," *Forbes*, October 4, 2010, https://www.forbes.com/2010/10/04/ facebook-zuckerberg-twitter-wendy-kopp-creativity-advertising-cmo-network.html.

BONUS BITES!

There are several resources where you can find excellent brainstorming exercises. Here are two that I recommend:

- *SmartStorming: The Game-Changing Process for Generating Bigger, Better Ideas* by Keith Harmeyer and Mitchell Rigie

- *Improvisation for the Theater*, Third Edition, Viola Spolin (these exercises, though written for the theater, can be debriefed from a business perspective)

> *"A player who makes a team great is more valuable than a great player."*
>
> —JOHN WOODEN

CHAPTER 15

THE ULTIMATE PAY-OFF: LEVERAGING YOUR LEADERSHIP TO BUILD THE BEST TEAM

n one of The Second City workshops, we played the exercise "Human Knot," which is a great teambuilding and problem-solving exercise. And yes, it's a little bit like Twister (the party game, not the movie!). The Human Knot is played with a minimum of six people and anything over six must be an even number. The maximum number is 10 participants per knot. You start the game by getting the team in a circle, shoulder to shoulder and facing inward. At The Second City, our facilitator had each person reach out their right hand and grab another person's right hand across from them (you know, like "shaking hands"— that time-honored tradition in the pre-COVID days of yore). Unlike a handshake, the grip was not to be dropped after a moment of polite recognition. We held on. She then told us to repeat this process with our left hands.

Already, we looked like a "huddle" — a football team ready to shout something motivating before throwing our arms up in the air and running back onto the field. And we were starting to giggle nervously about what was shaping up to be a predicament. We were, as promised, a human knot. Now came the hard part. Our facilitator told us that we, as a group of improvisers working together, must untangle our circle *without releasing hands*. And .... we only had 10 minutes to get ourselves into an unknotted circle. Oh boy! Once we started, we realized we had to take turns talking or nothing got better. And everyone had to participate, each of us communicating with the team what our strategy to success would be. As we tried to untangle, we were put in very close proximity with each other — our shoulders were pressed together and invariably we ended up "cheek to cheek" (both kinds). It was funny and it was frustrating, and it required 100% concentration and coordination. The cool part was that we were all taking turns communicating (and laughing) to try as a team to solve our dilemma. Luckily, we did untangle with (if my memory serves me correctly) about 45 seconds left on our 10-minute timer. Whew!

"Teamwork makes the dream work," as they say — and the human knot exercise is a great example of that. Together, we are better, yet when we *don't* operate as a team, we're a jumbled, tangled mess of opportunity that can't be realized. The work we do at our organizations — regardless of our industry or our business size — is constantly in flux. And the players — the teammates — often come and go at a dizzying pace. What works — for our customers in terms of our offerings and for ourselves in terms of our culture and organizational behavior — continues to change rapidly. What works one year will not be as effective the following year and certainly not 5-10 years down the road.

> ## What works – for our customers in terms of our offerings and for ourselves in terms of our culture and organizational behavior – will not be as effective the following year and certainly not 5-10 years down the road.

The right team — with the right leader — is the solution to every workplace challenge. Having the best team to accomplish the fast-paced demands of marketing, productivity, and customer service requires leaders who attract and embody more than just the technical and operations mindset. What's needed is inspiration, motivation, and creativity. Enter the "Improvisation Mindset." The elements of improv give your leadership the power to engage at levels beyond where you have ever been, amplifying your reach and impact to others and allowing your organization to attract the best and brightest talent. Organizations that put people ahead of projects — and even profit — ultimately accomplish everything they are trying to achieve. Merle Heckman, one of my editorial board members for this book, shared this quote with me: "I will not use the people to build the work; I will use the work to build the people."

Cultivate a Group Mindset

When your focus at work (deliberately or inadvertently) emphasizes "task accomplishment" to get through the day, that is all you will accomplish: tasks. Your team members will get the job done, but are they following you for the long run? Do they feel led and inspired, supported and motivated? What separates the *best* team from a merely *good* team is inspiration and motivation. It takes a bold leader to shift the focus in a creative direction, to harness the power of a shared vision, and to energize the team to see beyond the tasks to the bigger company goals and purpose.

> **It takes a bold leader to shift the focus in a creative direction, to harness the power of a shared vision, and to energize the team to see beyond the tasks to the bigger company goals and purpose.**

Throughout this book, I've shared many stories about improv workshops and have even mentioned the kind of improv that exists for the sole purpose of entertaining audiences — like public shows at The Second City or like the television show *Whose Line Is It Anyway?* And it's probably safe for me to assume that you've watched an improvisation skit at one point in your life. Think back to that skit (or those skits) and remember what the group dynamic looked like. Did you notice that when the skit began, the improvisers seemed disjointed in their approach at first and were trying to quickly "get on the same page" with their partner or the rest of the group? That's how it always works — in improv and in group dynamics at our jobs. During an improv skit on a stage or on TV, it may take a couple of lines before the group mindset forms, but when it does, the performance becomes energetic and fun and productive. The same concept is at play behind interpersonal communications on the job. A group mindset is achieved through inspiration (think improv skills) by introducing new ideas into the scene. We should always be endeavoring to think differently and bring in a fresh or even "outside" perspective. A group mindset can only be adapted by parking individual agendas and changing the conversation by putting into practice the principles of improvisation.

Let me offer another pop-culture reference, this time from the big screen instead of from the theater or the television studios. Most everyone has seen the movie *Braveheart*[1] with its famous scene: Mel Gibson's character, William Wallace, is about to lead the ragtag army — of different clans who don't always get along — into battle. He delivers one of the most inspiring speeches in all movie history in the face of a flooded field of opposition ready to wipe them out. At first, the army assembled before him is not "on the same page" with him — most of them want to go home and give up. He starts with honesty, and then offers some humor. And then he asks them what they care about, identifying "freedom" as the value that binds them. Then he builds upon their idea of being free by being alive, safe at home, and suggests that leaving now will sentence them not to death but to a lifetime of regret. With a "team mindset" stirring, he delivers the now-infamous line: "They may take our lives, but they'll never take our freedom!"

It's a fictional example and an extreme example, but's in an instructional example. While you may not show up to the office next week with blue face paint and a kilt to leverage your leadership, you can shift the focus, as William Wallace did, from the task of swinging an ax or spreadsheet to creating the group mindset needed to achieve the grander vision. Wallace

---

1   *Braveheart*, Directed by Mel Gibson, 1995, Icon Entertainment International, The Ladd Company, B.H. Finance C.V., Icon Productions.

did so by using the elements of improvisation. He listened to what the members of the crowd/army (i.e., his new "team") were saying and he went beyond their words to focus on their lives and the values that were most important to them. He respected their willingness to be there and trusted their ability to wield their "technical skills."

Mel Gibson's character adapted to the situation by using the "Yes, and ..." concept. One fighter pointed out that rather than going forward, they could turn and run and live. Rather than say *"No, because* we don't do that here" or *"Yes, but* that's a horrible plan," Wallace acknowledged the soldier's idea as valid and then continued the conversation by pointing out that (yes!) they *would* live, and only for a while — likely with devastating regret about turning away from the battlefield. He renewed the vision of Scotland's freedom, and everyone was motivated to fight ... and fight passionately.

> **If you don't have a clear vision for everyone on the team, you need one quickly. You may not be fighting for your lives, but you are fighting for your organization's place in a cut-throat market (and your own career opportunities in a competitive workforce).**

If you don't have a clear vision for everyone on the team, you need one quickly. You may not be fighting for your lives, but you are fighting for your organization's place in a cut-throat market (and your own career opportunities in a competitive workforce). Take time up front to get to know everyone on your team. Bonding is important, but you won't have time to waste for bonding in the middle of a crisis. Do it now.

Approaching Your Team

So how, exactly, do you bond with your team — getting to know them and connecting with them across a shared vision and a shared humanity? You start listening and you start talking. A strong leader is not afraid to consult with those around them to expand conversations. As for opinions and input, "pick the brains" of the people around you (especially the introverted colleagues who might not proactively offer their perspectives). Even if it is a bit intimidating to go "off script" at work, start practicing and using improvisation elements with your teams in regular brainstorming sessions, office surveys, and soft-skill/power-skill training for all members. And do so in a way that incorporates fun team-building games because doing so is an incredibly effective way to build the *best* teams for the long run.

Another way to understand your team more fully is with personality tests — assessments and personality/style profiles like Gallup's StrengthsFinder test or the DiSC profile. These types of "tests" are a great resource and can help you open conversations and adjust your style to the preferences of others. But keep in mind, they cannot replace getting to know your team members through your interpersonal and improvisational skills and having them do the same with one another. Let me offer a caveat and a clarification — when I talk about bonding and connecting at work, I'm not talking about deep friendships or going out for drinks every week (not that there's anything wrong with that!). Team building is not about "liking" each other, although that's great when it happens. Whether or not you and your co-workers think of each other as friends, you need to establish a base level of mutual respect and trust to build and engage the best team possible.

In addition, the team needs a diverse set of personalities to avoid "group think." When I was on faculty at THE [pause] Ohio Dominican University (that joke only works in Columbus, OH), I was asked to be on the faculty search committee for the math department. The reason they asked me was not the obvious reason you might be assuming. It wasn't because "well, he's an accountant and therefore he knows a little something about mathematics so this could be a good fit." I was asked to be on the math department search committee because I *didn't* think like anyone in the math department; the committee chair was hopeful that my different way of thinking would allow me to ask questions that the math faculty might never think of asking. Diversity of *thought* is an important kind of diversity on every team.

Diversity of *thought* is an important kind of diversity on every team.

Managing Conflict

Every year between January and April, accounting professionals are looking forward to (or dreading) another busy tax-filing season, and the business leaders they serve are expecting fiscal reports and/or tax returns. Stress increases during these times, and so does the opportunity for conflict to arise — potentially derailing even the best of teams. Otis D. Gibson, a specialist in creative conflicts, had this to say in a 2015 *Fast Company* article: "The crucial part of dealing with conflict is learning to deal with your emotions. Screaming something at someone doesn't make it truer." How true is that?[2]

But screaming at things (and people) does happen at work. And harsh, critical words are commonly spoken in many workplaces — up, down, and across the organization. We all have been on a dysfunctional team — where one or more members (and even leaders) is sabotaging success at every turn. And, when we're punching the clock for a dysfunctional team or organization, we dread driving to work or "Zooming" in; we dread being part of the team meeting because everyone is talking over each other; we dread dealing with members of the team who are disengaged. There is always one person who thinks they're the smartest person in the room, and they continuously tell everyone (in one way or the other). Because even the best employees can't thrive in this kind of environment, team members begin missing deadlines, making excuses, exhibiting negative body language, and are ultimately abundantly clear with their "I don't care" attitude. No one is being held accountable in a low-expectations culture, and everyone is doing what they think is right, despite what they have been asked or told to do.

We need to find ways to build stronger teams — virtually, in-person, and in a hybrid of both. The following are powerful improv exercises you can use to build stronger teams. I encourage you to try one out at a team meeting soon.

---

2   Sudhir Venkatesh, "How to Use Conflict to Unlock Creativity," *Fast Company*, June 15, 2015, https://www.fastcompany.com/1682575/how-to-use-conflict-to-unlock-creativity.

EXERCISE #11: Conducted Story

This exercise should be used with groups of 2-6 participants/improvisers. The leader will get a suggestion from the audience (which might be another group of employees who are waiting their turn to be part of the improv exercise) for a story theme, location, genre, setting, or situation (e.g., birthday party, campground, horror movie, church wedding, or the birth of a baby). The participants will line up and then be tasked with telling a story together. The leader will choose one player to start the story and will point at them with their finger. For the entire time that the person is being pointed at (i.e., "conducted" like a musician by a conductor), the player will continue to tell the story. Without warning, the leader will switch to another player and that subsequent player will seamlessly pick up the story.

Suggestion for a story location: Your spare bathroom

Improviser A: "I was in my spare bathroom the other day and ..."

The conductor points to Improviser C

Improviser C: " ... and I started to look at the toilet paper roll holder on the wall ..."

The conductor points to Improviser E

Improviser E: " ... and I started to wonder, 'why is that thing bolted to the wall?'"

The conductor points to Improviser B

Improviser B: " ... and I thought 'there must be a simpler way.'"

The conductor points to Improviser D

Improviser D: "So I tried to rip the holder off the wall ..."

The conductor points to Improviser C

Improviser C: " ... and found out that it wasn't bolted but super-glued to the wall!"

You would continue in a haphazard way, with improvisers getting multiple opportunities to contribute, until the story has been completed (or until you're all exhausted!).

The goal of the Conducted Story exercise is to have the improvisers seamlessly continue to tell the story, working as one voice and one repository of information and creativity. If the conductor moves from one improviser to another mid-sentence, the next improviser will pick up mid-sentence; if the conductor moves from person-to-person mid-word, the next person will pick up mid-word. If it is working well and if your team is operating in a true spirit of teamwork, the exercise will sound like one person telling a relatively cohesive story.

This exercise requires the improvisers to be actively listening, to be present and committed to the moment, and they must accept the offers that have gone before.

The business application of the exercise above? They serve to strengthen the team's creativity, collaboration, and developing the "thinking on your feet" skill, which is critical in today's business world.

EXERCISE #12: Beach Ball, Bouncy Ball, Frog, and More

This exercise should be played with 5-7 participants.

Items needed:

- → Inflated lightweight beach ball

- → Medium-sized ball that can be bounced (think kickball, soccer ball, etc.)

- → Three other small items or balls that can be thrown, such as:
    - □ Squishy ball or stress ball
    - □ Whiffle soft ball
    - □ Stuffed or squeaky toy frog

You will need one more item than you have participants (e.g., if you have six participants, you need a total of seven items).

The participants form a circle. The first step is introducing a beach ball to the team. The group's instructions are to pass the beach ball to another person by tossing the beach ball over their head.

When they start to throw the beach ball, they announce "beach ball," make eye contact with a participant, and throw it to that person. When the person catches the beach ball, they reply, "thank you." Then they look for another teammate to whom they'll pass the beach ball by announcing "beach ball," making eye contact, and throwing the beach ball to the participant. When caught, the participant announces, "thank you," and the sequence starts over.

After about a minute, you stop the exercise and introduce into the exercise a bouncy ball. The first participant passes the bouncy ball to another person by bouncing it on the floor. The same methodology used with the beach ball is to pass and receive the bouncy ball — announcing the bouncy ball, making eye contact, and passing. When receiving the bouncy ball, the participant replies, "thank you," and the sequence starts again.

Here is the challenge — the beach ball and bouncy ball are in the exercise simultaneously. After about a minute with both balls being passed, stop the activity, and introduce the toy frog. Instruct the group that the frog prefers to be tossed underhanded using the same general process: announcing, eye contact, passing the object, and saying thanks.

There are three objects in the exercise at the same time. Now watch the chaos begin. After about a minute or so, introduce another object (passed underhanded like the frog) and using the same rules.

Four objects are in the exercise at the same time. The chaos heightens. After about a minute or so, go ahead and introduce another object (passed underhanded like the frog and using the same rules).

Five objects are in the exercise at the same time. The chaos is out of control, *and* the audience is laughing out loud. After about a minute or so (you know the drill!), introduce another object passed underhanded like the others and use the same rules.

Keep adding objects as you see fit depending on the size of the team. Typically, a group of seven people will reach their capacity for attention at or before item eight.

At some point, call the game to an end and debrief the audience on what they just witnessed and experienced.

The business purpose of the exercise is to demonstrate the need for eye contact when distributing or communicating with a teammate to ensure they understand. Also, it reinforces a practice of saying "thank you" when receiving information from someone else. More importantly, we as leaders should see which teammates have much more on their plate and distribute the work more evenly amongst the team (i.e., if you see that someone is already busy bouncing a ball or catching a frog, you're more apt to send the beach ball elsewhere).

I have used this exercise when working with my clients and have deployed it during conference keynotes and breakout sessions. People will be nervous to volunteer, so I offer some incentive (like a free copy of one of my books, $5-10 gift cards, or something fun). Learning is important, and it should also be welcoming and rewarded.

EXERCISE #13: "Yes! And ..." to Solve a Problem

We've talked a lot in this book about the philosophy of "Yes, and ..." So how do you practice and model it in a safe place? By doing an exercise!

Gather 5-7 participants for this exercise, which provides a practice field for helping the team solve problems quickly when they arise. The key here, and in all improv exercises, is to park your ego at the door, suspend your judgment, listen to understand, accept what a teammate says as a possibility, *and* add on to those possibilities. It's important to accept the idea as if it is true and then imagine what else can be true. Through this exercise, you can create a culture of psychological safety where the team is able to speak their minds and feel safe taking risks in front of each other.

Here's how the game is played!

- ➡ Decide on a problem that needs to be resolved sooner rather than later (it can be a real problem that your organization is facing or a fictitious problem, like mice in the cafeteria).

- ➡ Have the team find a conference room, Zoom/virtual room, or someplace where they can work and not be interrupted.

→ Once the team is assembled, set a timer for 15 minutes.

→ The leader will state the problem at hand and ask for ideas. Participants can simply offer ideas in any order, or you can call on people or go around a circle.

→ Another teammate will be the scribe, capturing all this information on paper or on a computer. (Better yet, use the artificial intelligence app Otter to capture the conversation!)

→ When an idea is introduced, agree with the idea — no matter how crazy it is — and then add on to it. Remember that in improv, we say: "bad ideas are bridges to good ideas, and no ideas lead to nothing."

→ Explore and add to everyone's idea. Every time someone shares an idea, someone else must chime in with "Yes! And …" followed by some additional thoughts that build upon the previous idea.

→ After 15 minutes, look at what you have come up with and decide what is worthy of exploring further.

The purpose of the "Yes! And …" exercise is to reduce the time it takes to solve a problem through divergent thinking. You are looking for quantity, not quality. Remember, you can't create and criticize in the same space.

The best teams are built deliberately, with respect and kindness, over time and through educational experiences (like improv exercises!) that bond us to one another and give us a shared vocabulary and a common set of tools. The best teams come from leveraging leadership in a way that creatively confronts conflict and uses improvisation techniques to unlock the gems in every idea. Technical skills and managing the business operations are not enough in a competitive market flooded with younger adults searching for a more inspiring experience. The greater you develop your personal leadership, the greater your *team* will become.

The best teams are built deliberately, with respect and kindness, over time and through educational experiences (like improv exercises!) that bond us to one another and give us a shared vocabulary and a common set of tools.

BONUS BITES!

"Build a Tower, Build a Team" — TED Talk with Tom Wujec.

Check out this fascinating presentation about teamwork, in which Tom Wujec presents some surprisingly deep research into the "marshmallow problem"— a simple team-building exercise that involves dry spaghetti, one yard of tape, and a marshmallow. Who can build the tallest tower with these ingredients? And why does a surprising group always beat the average?

https://www.ted.com/talks/tom_wujec_build_a_tower_build_a_team#t-387998

I am inclined to answer both questions posed in the description of this TED Talk. However, this is a six minute and 35-second video, and the answers are revealed quite early. The key message in this video? That collaboration and facilitation are the keys to success versus being the CEO of the spaghetti tower. Enjoy!

There are no mistakes, only
gifts and happy accidents.

CHAPTER 16

FACING OFF: YOU, THE AUDIENCE, AND THE ART OF THE IMPERFECT PRESENTATION

I mprov has taught me to be mindful of preparation and practice — the two ingredients that are crucial if we want to be able to successfully go "off script" as Dr. Martin Luther King, Jr., and other inspiring leaders have done. Prepare and practice (the science of communication), then go off script (the art of improvisation). The more prepared you are and the more practice you have put in, the more likely you can handle anything that comes your way. On October 1, 2016, I was the officiant for my goddaughter's wedding. She is very special to me and leading up to the wedding there were parts of the proposed ceremony that would bring me to tears. I am talking full-blown "13-year-old boy crying because a girl dumped him" kind of tears. The day of the wedding, I went to the location where the outdoor ceremony was to be held; I got there seven hours in advance. I spent 3-4 hours in the space where the ceremony was to be held, rehearsing. I practiced getting past the tears (or just draining all the fluid out of them) so my goddaughter would have the day that she envisioned; I wanted this to be about the bride and groom, not about the crying officiant. When the time came, I didn't have to worry about my "performance" at all. Instead, I needed to remind the groom to breathe during every moment of the ceremony, right up to the pivotal moment when his bride came walking down the aisle. I got through the entire ceremony without any tears and I only choked up slightly a few times. There is a lot to be said about preparation and practice.

The more prepared you are and the more practice you have put in, the more likely you can handle anything that comes your way.

Have you ever given a presentation and realized afterward that you left out a critical part, mispronounced a couple of words, lost your train of thought, or (worst yet) totally blanked out at one point? These, among other presentation "snafus," have happened to most of us at one time or another. What causes it? It could be the result of lack of practice, or our nerves operating in overdrive, or both. And it might be acceptable in a staff meeting, but not in a board meeting, an all-company meeting, an analyst call, or a keynote address. Leaders need to articulate — and deliver — their thoughts and ideas in a way that inspires and motivates others (without the snafus) but they often come up short. Why? Because most leaders articulate their thoughts and ideas to paper (they write scripts) and then fail at the delivery because they have never practiced the words out loud. Preparation without practice rarely leads to an outstanding presentation.

Preparation without practice rarely leads to an outstanding presentation.

Apple founder, Steve Jobs, was well known for his extensive preparation prior to the launch of any new product. He rehearsed for hours and hours, weeks at a time, prior to every launch. He painstakingly studied every detail of his presentation — and then practiced it again and again. This kind of preparation is what leads to a flawless presentation, right? Well, let's think about that for a moment. A "flawless" presentation is one that is 100% perfect without any errors or mistakes and, depending upon how you define "flawless," perhaps without any changes or omissions. Maybe Steve Jobs was able to pull that off, but for most people, mistakes do happen during a presentation no matter how well they have prepared! But with excellent preparation, those shifts and changes (and "mistakes") are rarely even noted by the audience.

There Are Two Challenges

Here's the thing — there are two challenges when it comes to delivering a nearly perfect presentation:

1. Mistakes made by the presenter

2. Unexpected and unanticipated "derailers" that come out of nowhere!

Let's begin with those "mistakes" made by the presenter. I previously mentioned three common mistakes: mispronunciation, loss of thought, and blanking out. When these types of mistakes occur, 99% of the time, the audience has no idea a mistake has been made (the only person aware of the mistake is the presenter!). If you take away nothing else from this discussion about presentation mistakes, remember this: It's not about the mistake that has been made during a presentation; it's about how the leader *handles* the mistake — this is the critical part.

> **It's not about the mistake that has been made during a presentation; it's about how the leader *handles* the mistake – this is the critical part.**

One way to handle a goof-up during a presentation is to become so fixated on the mistake that it derails your train of thought and your presentation. You become so frustrated that you freeze or you just walk off the stage. In

2014 at the Consumer Electronics Show, film director Michael Bay was to be interviewed about Samsung's new curved 4K TV. When he walked on stage, he said that he "gets paid to dream" and then he stopped talking and began to stumble around his words. The interviewer says, "Let's just wing it" but by then, Bay was completely flustered and walked off the stage. When asked about what happened, Bay blamed the teleprompter. And I can imagine that having the teleprompter fail to deliver your script on time, accurately, or at all would really throw a presenter off their game. However, if Bay had been sufficiently prepared, rehearsed, and practiced, perhaps he would have been able to adapt to the problem of a misbehaving teleprompter.

If you would like to see the video, Google "Michael Bay walks off the stage at the CES show." The Michael Bay "CES show" story is instructive to us all. It reminds us that things can and will go wrong, and that how we respond is what makes the headline. The key is to not become fixated on the error — but instead to be adequately prepared prior to any mistakes so you will be able to adapt in the moment and carry on. And when you do, remember that you need to survive not just the momentary stumble but the entire presentation, conversation, speech, or performance. Just keep moving forward and reflect on the rest *after* you are done.

This is where improvisation strengths come out in full force. What I have learned from my many years of applying improv techniques to my presentations is that you can't plan for a perfect presentation. Even the best presentation is perfectly *imperfect*. You must let go of your desire for perfection to adapt to the new reality if things don't go quite as planned. Except for factual missteps (like saying "$500" instead of "$5,000" and then clarifying the correction to your audience), you can't typically go back and fix a mistake in the middle of a presentation. All this does is derail your pace. Silence your inner critic that is saying, "you forgot to say" or "you shouldn't have said that." The inner critic isn't helpful at this moment, so it needs to be marginalized. Maintain your confidence. Stay present and in the moment throughout your entire presentation. Adapt. Accept. Move on. Let the mistake go and move forward.

Perhaps you are thinking, however, "But what happens when I make a major, obvious mistake that everyone sees?" In this case, you should stop and own up to the mistake and make the correction. If you choose to move forward without addressing the major mistake, the audience will still be fixated on the huge error and will stop listening to you. As someone once told me, "If you lay an egg, step back and admire it and move forward." We all hate to make mistakes, but we need to own up to the ones that the audience has a visible reaction to, correct the error, and move forward. You know why? Because we are human beings and humans make mistakes. Own up to the big ones and let the little ones go to the wayside. A mistake or two during an outstanding presentation (or book!) isn't going to keep your stakeholders from appreciating your content and your energy. You and your message are what matter — a perfectly chosen word or impeccably timed joke are just icing on the cake. You can survive without them (and so can your audience).

> **A mistake or two during an outstanding presentation (or book!) isn't going to keep your stakeholders from appreciating your content and your energy. You and your message are what matter – a perfectly chosen word or impeccably timed joke are just icing on the cake. You can survive without them (and so can your audience).**

For the most part, mistakes made by you as the presenter can be prevented and managed. But what about the second challenge I outlined above? What if people or circumstances threaten to take you off course? Well, there can and will be unexpected and unanticipated "derailers" that come out of nowhere and potentially up-end your presentation: for example, your laptop freezes up, the LCD projector light bulb burns out, your microphone isn't working, you lose power two hours before your virtual presentation, an audience member in the front row won't stop coughing, or people coming in and out of your session keep letting the door slam. There are many more instances, but these are some of the ones that I have experienced. How you handle the distractions and disruptions is critically important. In the world of improv, we have been trained to be comfortable with the uncomfortable. We thrive in these situations.

These next three improv exercises are used to help you become more comfortable in your role as "Chief Communication Officer" even if your organization has an actual person in this role. Leaders must be able to articulate their thoughts, ideas, and vision to a variety of stakeholders. These exercises are designed to help you to become different in a way that draws people in and captures their imagination.

EXERCISE #14: One Minute Off-the-Cuff

For this exercise, you'll set a timer on your phone (or your computer or via Alexa or on a good-old-fashioned egg timer) for one minute and record yourself giving an impromptu speech on any topic that interests you. The only rule is that you can't prepare for it in any way. Remember to breathe during this exercise. Listen to the recording and celebrate what you did well and take note of where you stumbled or came up short. Then try it again. The more you do this, the easier it becomes.

This exercise is designed to get you more comfortable speaking off-the-cuff and to help you minimize the anxiety that comes from being afraid you won't have anything to say. You're brilliant and insightful and you *always* have something interesting to say!

EXERCISE #15: Gibberish

In her book *Improvisation for the Theater*, 3rd Edition, improv legend Viola Spolin describes gibberish as, "the substitution of shaped sounds for recognizable words. Gibberish is a vocal utterance accompanying an action, not the translation of an English phrase. The meaning of the sound in gibberish should not be understood unless the [person] conveys it by action, expressions, or tone of voice."[1]

Once you have your presentation somewhat memorized, it is now time to work on your non-verbal communication by using gibberish. When doing this exercise, use sounds to substitute for the actual words and focus on your body language. Or, you can focus on a specific word (cucumber) or a specific number (4) and use those as your gibberish words. For example, "cucumber, cucumber, cucumber." This may seem very silly at first. However, if you keep in mind that we need to use our non-verbal expression while delivering our message, you'll see that this kind of practice is essential in mastering the art of getting our message across. And, there are times when our non-verbal expression is a better substitute for the actual words. Here is the key to making this a success: while you are speaking in a form of gibberish, the actual words of your presentation are running through your head.

---

1   Viola Spolin, *Improvisation for the Theater: A Handbook of Teaching and Directing Techniques*, 3rd edition, Northwestern University Press, 1999, pg 114.

I teach this exercise to all my coaching clients, and they all are very uncomfortable at first. However, the more you try this exercise (just like anything new), the more you will get the hang of it.

This exercise is designed to not focus on the exact words that are being delivered and to focus on your body language. Many times, there is greater meaning to what you are trying to convey using your body language than the words. Just think of John Belushi in *Animal House*.

EXERCISE #16: Gush About Something You Don't Love

Enthusiasm is contagious. If you want your audience to be excited about your topic, then *you* need to show enthusiasm for it. Choose something that you don't love — like cooked liver, body hair, horror movies, pineapple on pizzas, running, or anything that you just don't love. Now, practice speaking about it enthusiastically. Use your voice, emphasis, and body language to make it seem like the most exciting thing in the universe. Do this for a few minutes, with or without an audience, a mirror, a timer, or a video camera.

This exercise is designed to prepare you for those times when you might not be as enthusiastic about the topic you are delivering and when you know that, despite how you really feel, you will get more people to buy in to your idea (project, presentation, proposal) if you can deliver the information with enthusiasm and confidence. Remember to fluctuate your voice and pay attention to your body language.

In preparing for very exciting topics like "revenue recognition" or "how to account for leases on your balance sheet" or a brand-new presentation, I practice "gush about something you don't love" along with gibberish because it is MY responsibility as the presenter to keep the audience engaged and these two exercises accomplish that goal. Period!

Never Lose Your Cool

All these fictional circumstances examined in the exercises above — the moments when words fail you and you have to settle for something akin to gibberish, the moments when you're asked to speak "off the cuff" with no notice, and the moments you have to summon up the energy and enthusiasm to "sell" something you don't really love — are derived from common, real-world circumstances that can and will happen to us all. So how do you get through them without losing your cool? I have witnessed leaders losing their composure when confronted with any of these challenges. Ordering people around, yelling at staff, making demands, and casting threats. Is that how you want people to remember you? How do you handle yourself under pressure in dealing with the unknown? Panic is not an option. Showing poise and control, assessing the situation, and finding a viable solution is the only professional option.

Here are the solutions that I have used when confronted with some of the above-mentioned challenges:

1. **Laptop freezing up:** Close your laptop and start your presentation. Break the tension with "Well, we don't need technology anyway, right? Let's take a break from it!" You will be successful if you have prepared and rehearsed/practiced your presentation to the point that you have an accuracy rate between 90-95%. You probably will make a minor mistake or two *and* you are not going to let that derail you.

2. **LCD projector light bulb burns out:** No one I know carries around a spare LCD projector light bulb. However, they do burn out at the most inopportune times. This should not completely halt your presentation. If you are delivering a keynote address or a company-wide meeting, use the same tactic as if your laptop froze on you. If your presentation is longer than an hour, take a quick break and find the meeting planner or the AV support staff and inform them of the situation. I always bring a printed copy of my presentation for anything over an hour and use that document as a reminder of the structure of the presentation. (And if I need to pull that document out of my bag, I don't read from the document. I only use it for reference.)

    On one occasion, the LCD projector quit working about 10 minutes into my full-day presentation. This particular LCD projector was one of those extremely large machines on a cart. It looked like it weighed a thousand pounds. When the light went out, I wasn't sure if the light had burned out or if the projector had died. I paused and then announced to the group that, sadly, the LCD projector had just passed away. We took a moment of silence for the projector and then I found the meeting planner and explained what had happened. I went back the room and said,

"We may need a few pallbearers to help wheel this projector out of here." Everyone started laughing and then I said that this will be taken care of in a few minutes and let's get back to the material. We carried on.

3. **Microphone not working:** If there is an AV person in the room, they will realize the problem and bring you another microphone. Go ahead and use your voice without a microphone until the situation has been corrected. It may take a couple of microphones to get it right and that's okay. Unless the room is a sports arena and you don't have a strong enough voice to "project" your voice to be heard without a microphone, you'll be just fine. Some audiences prefer the more natural volume and timbre of an un-amplified voice.

I was once delivering a four-hour preconference workshop in Las Vegas and the session started at 7:30 a.m. There were two other preconference workshops going on at the same time and I expected the AV support team to be busy with all the setup for the big day. I arrived early and we tested all the AV equipment. "All systems were go." When the session started, however, my lavalier microphone wasn't working. There was a dedicated AV person for the room and he was trying to figure out what was going on. While he was doing that, I just raised my voice to a level at which everyone could hear me. The AV person walked up and handed me a hand-held microphone and told me to use that. Well, that one didn't work either .... to the horror of the AV staff. I raised my voice and kept moving forward with my session. Then another handheld microphone was supplied and this time it worked. Third time was the charm! I was told later on that there was a "frequency channel issue" (outside my paygrade, otherwise I'd explain it to you) and that was causing the microphones not to work properly.

I received my participant evaluations a few weeks later. There were a few of comments about how I kept my cool during this challenge and adapted to the change seamlessly. I was glad to hear that the disruption wasn't particularly disruptive at all.

4. **You lose power two hours before your virtual program:** Gather up all your materials and laptop and go to a hotel and rent a room for the day. The Hyatt is renting rooms as an "office for the day" program. Or go to one of those shared office spaces and rent a private office. Be mobile, be adaptable, be flexible.

5. **An audience member in the front row won't stop coughing:** Normally, I keep two or three bottles of water at the podium or table in the front for my own consumption during a presentation. If someone is coughing, I will grab an unopened bottle and give it to the person coughing. This normally get the person to realize and to take the bottle of water and exit the class until the coughing stops.

6. **People coming in and out of your session keep letting the door slam:** I will stop briefly and request that when you are leaving or entering the room, if you could close the door gently or wedge the door open so not to distract other in the class. And "thank you!"

Improv is always about being comfortable with the unknown and I take that approach every time I do any type of presentation. No matter how much I prepare, there will be things that go differently from how I planned. And when I'm stepping onto someone else's stage, everything looks and feels different and nearly everything is out of my control. Accepting that it's okay to be a little uncomfortable helps me keep control over my emotions. The one thing you never ever want to do is to lose your cool in front of an audience. You are there to serve them — keep focused on delighting them, come what may, and everything is bound to turn out well.

BONUS BITES!

AN INTERVIEW WITH AMANDA ROSELLI, STRATEGY DIRECTOR, ACCENTURE INTERACTIVE

Amanda Roselli, a coaching client with whom I have been honored to work, is employed by a global marketing company as a strategist and growth consultant. She works in close proximity to executive leadership and is dedicated to improving her presentation skills so she can best serve her business and its stakeholders. We have worked together in group settings and one-on-one. What follows is the transcript of an interview I recently conducted with Amanda.

> **Peter:** What was your mindset, going into that very first class?

> **Amanda:** I didn't have a lot of expectations. I knew that I wanted to embrace everything fully. And also be uncomfortable because I think that growth always happens when there are moments of discomfort. It was beneficial for me to have the group workshop with my colleagues first, and then the individual coaching next. I also felt that I organized the whole program with my team and that I was a little more confident going into it. And then from that, I was able to focus with you a little more specifically on the things that you saw maybe in those first couple sessions that I could dig deeper on and work on.

> **Peter:** What was the one exercise that you felt that was the most beneficial to you?

> **Amanda:** The most beneficial exercise was "Presentation Improv"[2] because I do so much presenting from slide material and use storytelling with visual aids to get the point across. I found that the Presentation Improv exercise was the hardest for me. And I think

---

2   Presentation Improv is an exercise where a volunteer is going to give a presentation on a topic that the audience will determine. The presenter must use five PowerPoint slides (each of which contains only a picture) and the slides are a complete surprise to them in the moment they are clicking through and improvising their presentation.

because of that, it was also the most fun. For example, your topic could be "why Brussels sprouts should be considered a breakfast food." The first slide/picture you see could be five grandmothers in a rock band and you are trying not to laugh, as you're seeing just the absurdity of what's coming on the screen. You are also trying to be mindful of how you're portraying the shock and kind of panic of what you are viewing. And then third, the logic and the mental effort with which you need to tell the story (why Brussels sprouts should be considered a breakfast food) and have it have it have a semblance of flow through the presentation.

Peter: What changes have you been doing in your presentations based on what came out of the coaching?

Amanda: I have a standing time on Friday mornings where I practice some of the exercises. The ones that are a little easier, like "connect two things." I'll visit a random word generator website and then do my best to tell a story around those things. So just forcing myself to go along with prompts thrown my way has been helpful. So that helps me with the maintenance of my learning and continuing to practice. I've also tried to find ways to infuse some of those exercises into things like brainstorms or group discussions that are a little more free-flowing and designed with creativity in mind.

In terms of how I am delivering information, I find that I am calmer going into presentations than before. Now, I am always erring on the side of assuming things are *not* going to be perfect and knowing that I'm capable of handling anything that comes my way. I'll give you an example. Last week, I got pulled into a new opportunity with this client. We are developing a proposal for being more impactful across different business areas, from marketing and other operational standpoints.

The day we delivered the proposal to the client, the individual who was supposed to be doing the presentation production had technical issues. She joined the call from her phone and therefore couldn't advance the slides, which meant that I had taken on that role too. Because of that, I couldn't look at my notes that I had written in all the slides. So immediately, while we're on the call, I had to adjust my strategy for how I was planning to deliver that material. I had practiced before, and I had talked through it, and I knew the sequence of everything and what the high points were. So I didn't let it startle me or freak me out or make me panic too much. I just leaned into it and embraced it as one of those moments of things not going exactly as I planned it.

Peter: Well, I applaud you, standing ovation. I applaud you for doing the work after the class. Often, we're in the class, we're having fun, and then we'll need to start applying it after the class is over. And the world gets in the way. You taking scheduled time on a Friday to play these games, these exercises, means you will continue to get better. That's the key right there.

If you think you must *do well,*
you will have fear.

CHAPTER 17

OFF SITE: MAKING SURE YOUR VIRTUAL PRESENTATIONS AND MEETINGS DON'T SUCK

We were all thrown into this virtual world kicking and screaming — virtual meetings, virtual presentations, and virtual "happy hours" suddenly becoming the norm. Before the pandemic, most of us were conducting a portion of our meetings and events via WebEx or Zoom or conference call, but suddenly it was 8-10 hours a day ... every day. And while most of us had a certain amount of comfort sitting in front of a webcam or wearing a headset, almost none of us were prepared for doing our most important work — the boardroom presentations or the keynotes or the crucial conversations with employees — without the familiar trappings of office furniture, coffee and donuts, and shared space.

We've learned as we've gone along and now it's time to be more deliberate in ensuring that your virtual presentations and meetings don't suck. So here I am, with a few things to keep in mind when you're facilitating virtual meetings or presentations *and* when you are "just" part of the audience.

Let me start with some tips for good participation. Say that you're a team member or client logging into an online meeting. You might have little or no expectation that you're going to be speaking much or at all, but your camera is going to be on ... and everyone is going to see you. If I'm the leader or the meeting/event presenter, I have a few expectations of the virtual attendees.

I don't want to:

➤ Look up your nose

➤ See you walking around your house

➤ See a dark silhouette of you because you are sitting with a window behind you and no lighting on your face

➤ See you disappear into your virtual wallpaper — or watch various body parts appear and disappear

I don't think it's asking so much. Just as leaders and presenters deserved focused attention and respect during face-to-face presentations and meetings, they deserve it in a virtual world too. Get acquainted with your buttons for muting and for shutting off your camera. Set up your camera, microphone, workspace, and lighting so that you're bringing your best to the experience. You don't even need to put on shoes, but you should be prepared to be an attentive, ready participant.

I spend a lot of time on camera, coaching or presenting, and I hate to criticize audiences for their participation behaviors. I understand that many things can cause audience members to convey a sense of disconnection (and, in some cases, disrespect), however unintended. So I offer these observations and tips in the spirit of "here's how we can all be better and enjoy our work even more."

Three ways we inadvertently "disconnect" during virtual presentations and meetings:

1. **As audience members, we don't turn our cameras on.** To a presenter, this gives the impression that we aren't paying attention, we are disengaged, and, more than likely, we're multi-tasking (taking the dog for a walk? making lunch? answering emails?) We may not be doing any of these things, but it appears as though we might be, and that can make other attendees — and the presenter — feel disrespected or dismissed. And, well, that sucks!

2. **We forget that a virtual meeting/presentation is a professional event.** I love that the pandemic and "work-anywhere" cultures taught us to relax a bit and not take work too seriously, but it's possible for us to take virtual work and virtual conferences for granted as a casual experience that requires little to no forethought. I think that's a mistake and a slippery slope. When we're attending an online event, not taking into consideration the camera angle, our personal appearance, or background that others are seeing (our home or coffee house or car, our virtual or actual green screen, etc.) can decrease the quality of interaction for everyone and can leave the wrong impression on your colleagues. Many participants these days show up — often late — while driving their car with their phone in their lap (disrespectful? Yes! *And* ... dangerous).

3. **We neglect to take on the duties of "AV director" for our own audio connection and forget to mute the audio line when not talking.** Every noise in the background — dogs barking, kids screaming, car horns honking, Starbucks espresso machines screeching — will be heard by everyone else in the virtual meeting. And forgetting to mute can negatively impact everyone's experience. You might not be the presenter, but if the meeting isn't in "webinar" mode and your microphone is left open when it shouldn't be, you might suddenly find yourself "center stage" as the star performer who accidentally distracted and annoyed dozens or even hundreds of people. Yep, that definitely sucks!

These are the kinds of things that make virtual events suck. But here's the point — a virtual ANYTHING does not have to suck! And, while we've identified some ways for the audience to do their part to ensure a great experience, it's ultimately the presenter's responsibility to make sure a virtual meeting or presentation doesn't suck; as leaders and presenters, we do this by *engaging* the audience, deeply and at every opportunity.

> ## It's ultimately the presenter's responsibility to make sure a virtual meeting or presentation doesn't suck; as leaders and presenters, we do this by engaging the audience, deeply and at every opportunity.

So how can you be a better presenter or meeting leader?

For myself, the number-one challenge is remembering to look at the camera during the presentation. It is critical to make eye contact with your audience to help keep them engaged, and doing so in a virtual work is tricky in a new way. Think about it; in a live presentation, if the presenter never makes eye contact with you, would you feel that the presenter cared about you or their presentation? Probably not. So I try really hard to be focused and animated, and to use my hands and face because they're the only "body language" I can convey on camera unless I'm set up to show myself standing and full-body.

If you are the presenter or running the virtual meeting, here are eight tips to not suck and to ensure you engage your audience. As a special bonus, I'm throwing in two tips on how to improve your internet speed and stability. So, yeah — 10 tips! Ready?

How to Engage Your Audience and Not Suck as a Presenter

1. **Eye contact:** Raise your laptop or desktop monitor, so you are eye-to-eye with the webcam. You can achieve this by a stack of books under your laptop to raise it to your eye level. Also, remember to look into the webcam (rather than looking at your

screen or at notes on your desk) about 70% of the time. This will increase the engagement with the audience.

2. **Stand up:** Standing up in front of an audience and delivering your content is how presentations were done before the COVID-19 pandemic, so why should they be any different when giving a live "virtual" presentation? When we are standing (if we are physically able), we tend to increase our energy and passion. Go out and buy yourself a standing desk, a desk riser, or use your MacGyver skills to DIY a solution for making your technology work for a standing presentation. A colleague of mine took a basket and a lobster pot and put their monitor on top of it so they could stand and deliver their virtual presentation. Get creative!

3. **Music to their ears:** Purchase a good microphone without breaking the bank. Suppose your internet is running as it should, but the audience can't hear you well, or there are crackling noises in your microphone. In that case, your audience will stop listening to you or be too frustrated to really appreciate your message. Don't let a bad audio setup sabotage your results. You can get a decent microphone for less than $100 and it's worth the investment.

4. **Breakout rooms:** If you are using Zoom, Microsoft Teams, GoToMeeting, or Cisco WebEx, utilize the breakout rooms for discussions, role-play, brainstorming, debates, strategy discussions, improv exercises, or anything that requires a minimum of two people. Remember that at physical events, there's always a chance for networking and breakout communications; new technologies allow you to keep the benefit of those small-group or pair communications.

5. **Polling questions:** Poll the audience frequently and often to ensure they understand the concepts and content you deliver. Also, get to know your audience with some demographic information. The actual polling feature in online meeting software can be helpful, as can old-school "by a show of hands, how many of you have ...?" Talk *with* your attendees, not simply to them.

6. **Conferences i/o:** Audience engagement platforms are becoming more and more valued and even expected by event audiences. One of the most popular such platforms, Conferences i/o, improves attendee engagement, participation, and learning by inviting audiences to interact (with one another and with the event speakers) in real-time. Conference apps typically allow you to network with other attendees and submit questions to speakers; and other attendees can vote your question up or down so the speaker is able to address the questions that the entire audience thinks are most important. I used to rely on the chat box to have attendees submit questions to me and to share their answers to my questions; now, I'm using more of Conferences i/o. One of the things I like about the platform is that after my speaking, workshop, or coaching session is over, I can download a report to review and I can share it with my client. Now they have something tangible to review from my presentation.

7. **Use a multi-camera shoot:** For some of my presentations, I use two cameras — my webcam and my video recorder — and I have a video switcher. There are two reasons why I do this. I want the audience to be engaged and if I can switch to a different camera angle and speak to that camera, it helps with that engagement. Also, there are times when I use the second camera, and focus it on a flip chart or whiteboard in my office. That will raise some eyebrows and make it far more interesting and fun.

8. **Simplify your slides and tell more stories:** When I say "simplify," I mean to think like Abe Lincoln. Abe wrote the Gettysburg Address using only 272 words, and he is said to have delivered the speech in approximately two minutes. Then Secretary of State Edward Everett spoke before President Lincoln, and he spoke for two hours. And which speech is considered the more powerful and memorable of the two? We all know the answer. So I encourage you to believe in the power of brevity — to use fewer words on your PowerPoint (PPT) slides and to tell more stories in your presentations. That is how you keep the audience engaged. A data dump of facts and figures crammed onto a PPT slide with the font size of 12 is just another way of telling the audience to go ahead and read

their email and play their favorite app game because clearly you're not that interested in engaging them.

9. **Know your minimum internet speed, upload bandwidth, and network latency:** The minimum internet speed for delivering virtual presentations should be 200 megabits per second (Mbps), upload bandwidth of 5 Mbps, and network latency should be less than 100 milliseconds (ms). Latency refers to the time it takes for data to travel from a user's device to the server and back. The reason you should care about internet speed, upload bandwidth, and network latency (even if it's all Greek to you!) is because inadequate network performance can cause your online meetings to buffer or freeze or drop altogether.

10. **Improve your computer's overall performance by closing out of anything that's not necessary during your presentation.** Close extra browser tabs and windows, and shut down any programs running in the background (especially streaming music and social media).

*Improvise the scene you are in,
not the one you want to be in.*

CHAPTER 18

OFF KILTER: THE PANDEMIC AS THE ULTIMATE IMPROV EXERCISE

As I write this chapter, it has been 19 months since the onset of the pandemic. During this unique and terrible moment in world history, I have been interviewed on several podcasts and — at some point during every interview — I get asked to talk about how I'm dealing with the pandemic. I honestly answer that "most days, I am dealing with the pandemic with a positive mindset ... *and* I do have my days when I am not dealing well."

The pandemic temporarily up-ended my business, but my challenges have been far smaller than what many others have faced. It's early October 2021 as this book heads off to its readers and the United States just surpassed the grim milestone of 700,000 dead from COVID-19. For those families, these past two years have been a horror. All around me are people who have lost a family member, friend, business associate, or acquaintance due to the virus. Some of my readers have likely mourned tremendous losses too. I am very sorry for your pain.

Then there are the "frontline workers" — doctors, nurses, respiratory therapists, hospital support staff, grocery workers, postal employees, delivery drivers, hospitality professionals, funeral directors, and everyone who cared for the sick or tended to the billions of people who, while quarantined at home, had urgent and unique demands. If you are one of the many millions of people for whom the pandemic was emotionally and physically exhausting, I thank you for your service and sacrifice.

For lucky people like me — who found a way to keep working on my own (altered) terms, who stayed virus-free until a vaccine was available, and who has not mourned the loss of a loved one during the pandemic — 2020 and 2021 have been a time for what some people are calling "the great reassessment." And, with all my experience and even "expertise" as an improviser, the pandemic has pushed me to be my most artful and patient in the application of the tools I believe in and love. It has been hard, and I have learned a great deal.

Being an improviser prepared me, as best it could, for this moment in my life. The improv mindset affords me some extra tools for dealing with the consistent unknowns all around us, every day. I have thought, many times these past months, that I wish the entire world knew how to improvise because perhaps it wouldn't have been so scary or painful or disorienting for us all if we collectively had more practice in facing the "gifts" of unwelcome or unusual circumstances.

Being an improviser prepared me, as best it could, for this moment in my life. The improv mindset affords me some extra tools for dealing with the consistent unknowns all around us, every day.

Yes, indeed the pandemic has been the ultimate improv exercise. And it rages on. *And* this will likely not be the last major crisis we face together. So what can we learn, and how can we cope?

Here are three simple but powerful tips from an improviser's mindset to help you deal with the associated stress and anxiety:

1. **Focus on things you can control:** Too many times we get caught up in all the things we have no control over. For example, early in the pandemic, I lost 95% of my revenue in the months of March, April, and May of 2020. This had me worried but not scared. I tried to focus on what I could control, like taking the time to reinvent my business model. When we focus on the things we have control of, we often find a sort of peace in the stillness and a freedom in letting go of what's out of our hands. And we sometimes find that during a crisis, we find our footing — if we can — by helping others in their time of need. Throughout the initial chaos of the pandemic, we saw this spirit of community every day in the news, with stories of people making and distributing face masks (for free), people organizing street concerts and dance parties in "social distance" fashion, and people helping their neighbors and families by delivering groceries and running errands. I created a virtual improv workshop that I have offered to companies to help them to relieve stress for that one welcomed hour and to also teach them the improviser's mindset to improve their resilience. How have you — during the pandemic or during other traumatic moments in your life — controlled what you could and let go of what you couldn't? What did you learn and what were the silver linings? In learning to let go, patience is key. The systemic impact of mass unemployment, failed businesses, escalating mental health crises, and mass casualties has taught us all that when systems are stressed, it takes a long time for them to recover. As we wait, we must be patient and hopeful.

2. **Use this time to be creative:** The pandemic was not, as many have said, a "great equalizer." Some people found themselves working the longest sustained hours of their lives (in hospital ICUs and in Amazon warehouses and in factories working overtime to manufacture in-demand products like personal protective equipment).

And yet other people didn't know how to fill the hours left by job loss or furlough, illness, early retirement, or a reprieve from a work commute or business travel. Not everyone has had time to learn to bake sourdough, but most of us did find at least a few pockets of new time. If you had extra time, how did you spend it? And if you have unexpected time in the future (perhaps while recovering from surgery or experiencing another transition in your life), how might you improvise your way through it? If the "script" gets thrown away by circumstances or tragedy, then what? I encourage you to be creative. Literally. (Even if you're an accountant or a scientist or an IT expert.) Have you ever wanted to learn how to play the guitar, learn a foreign language, or learn how to dance? Have you been meaning to try out that "adult coloring book" you got for your birthday last year or buy some watercolor paints and channel your inner Van Gogh? If you are in business and your business has come to a complete stop, how can you reinvent yourself (and/or your organization) to withstand another situation like this in the future and keep revenue still flowing in? This is where I have spent a lot of my time during this pandemic. I am (as you know), finishing my third book, adding a new product line (Color Accounting Learning System) that I can do both live and virtually, and redesigning my presentations (which were previously built for a literal stage) so I can offer them virtually with the kind of engagement my audiences deserve.

> **The adaptive mindset of an improviser is the strongest attribute in their arsenal because they are typically more nimble than other people in times like these. They don't get tied to things in the past — the way things "used to be."**

3. **Be adaptive:** The adaptive mindset of an improviser is the strongest attribute in their arsenal because they are typically more nimble than other people in times like these. They don't get tied to things in the past — the way things "used to be." They see the

opportunity in front of them and adjust to the "now normal." Ever since this pandemic took over and my business began to spiral south, I have been working diligently on reinventing it so it will look different on the other side. I'm adapting, veering, turning to new opportunities and new attitudes. It's not easy, but I can do it. And so can you.

There's nothing I can say that will serve as an adequate salve to our collective wounds from the pandemic. For some people, it was hard. For many others, it was devastating. For all of us, there have been lessons. It is my hope that the lessons you've learned — first hand, from others, and through this book — will allow you to start thinking like an improviser in ways that help you manage your stress and anxiety.

BONUS BITES!

Every speedbump or brick wall is a chance to see the road to success from a different lens. Challenge yourself to look differently at the problem you are facing. A good friend of mine, John Kelley, Chief People Officer at White Castle Systems and a level 3 whiskey sommelier, puts on whiskey education and tastings for non-profits in the Greater Columbus area as a fundraising activity. When the pandemic hit, these whiskey tastings dried up (pardon the pun). Did that stop John? No, it didn't. He found a way to keep fundraising through his whiskey tastings by taking them virtual (thank you, Zoom!) and has help raise thousands of dollars for several non-profits who were struggling during the pandemic.

> *"I would unite with anybody to do right; and with nobody to do wrong."*
>
> – FREDERICK DOUGLASS

CHAPTER 19

OFF COLOR: AN IMPROVISER'S JOURNEY IN THE AMERICAN SOUTH

Throughout this book, we have sought to uncover our collective humanity — what we're afraid of, where we can be better as leaders, all that we have in common, and the fact that no matter how much life and work experience we have, there is still so much yet to learn. We know that the scripts and habits are appealing, and that "getting comfortable with the uncomfortable" requires commitment and hard work. Together, we've talked about letting go of our agendas and our egos so we can connect and achieve and thrive. Now, it's time for us to talk about letting go of something else — our biases.

I've told you many stories in this book, but I'm about to tell you *my* story — my story of growing up in a region, a culture, and a family awash in conscious and unconscious bias about race, religion, politics, and identity. I think it's important for me to tell you the truth about where I've been and how I am still seeking to evolve. Going "off script," for me, was a life-long venture and one I will never truly finish or master. I'm a work in progress, as they say, and if you're feeling like you've got a lot of work yet to do as a leader, I want you to know that you're not alone.

> **Going "off script," for me, was a life-long venture and one I will never truly finish or master. I'm a work in progress, as they say, and if you're feeling like you've got a lot of work yet to do as a leader, I want you to know that you're not alone.**

I grew up in the American south, where everything is bigger — the cowboy hats and farms, the long summers and deep love for college sports, and yes even the depths of our bigotry.

And what does bigotry have to do with a book on business improvision? A whole lot. It's a topic I would be remiss not to address because biases (including ugly ones like racism, xenophobia, sexism, or homophobia) prevent us from connecting and collaborating, leading and learning. The truth is that people with long-held or deeply rooted biases are inherently less open-minded than other people. Without an open mind, it's difficult to lead, to improvise, or to go "off script." So how do we open our minds? We get honest, we get vulnerable, we get introspective.

Improv as a Refreshing Revolution in Mindset

Call it what you will — racist, bigoted, racially insensitive, hateful — there's a legacy of white elitism where I come from. And I didn't recognize it at first. I was just your average Greek American, who blended into the crowd with my white skin and brown hair. As a teen, I headed off to study at the

University of Kentucky, an institution that is equal parts wonderful and mired in a racist history.

My father vehemently swore that there "would never be a black head coach at the University of Kentucky." When I pointed out that Tubby Smith was an assistant basketball coach at UK for what had been about eight years at the time my father made that comment to me, my dad said that "being an assistant was okay." In his mind, black athletes and employees were free to serve and entertain us, but apparently not to lead us.

It turns out that my dad was wrong when he declared that UK would "never" have a head coach who was black. When Rick Pitino left UK to coach the Boston Celtics in 1997, Tubby Smith was promoted from assistant coach to head coach, where he coached the UK Wildcats to the 1998 NCAA Championship. Smith was not just a good leader; he was an outstanding leader and ultimately a legend as collegiate head coaches go.

When I look back on that conversation with my dad, it strikes me not just as sad but as a little ironic. Because, you see, our family history involved being targeted by the KKK, the same organization that terrorized and murdered black people. In my family, we weren't the kind of white people who had all the power or privilege (though we eventually had enough of it to develop our own brand of racism, which saddens me). Back in the day, we weren't fully included or given equal access to the world of whites; we were kept "in our place" at the margins. My father once told me a story about his Greek stepfather trying to open a second business in Harlan, Kentucky, in the 1950s, only for it to be burned to the ground by the Ku Klux Klan (KKK) because, in the eyes of local white supremacists, a Greek could only have one business (anything more was perhaps "uppity" or gave too much power to immigrants). It's a devastating story and hard for me to think about — some self-appointed hateful and superior group telling someone else they are not allowed to do something and robbing them of their achievements through violence and intimidation.

So I remember 1997 distinctly. The rise of Tubby Smith to head coach at UK, shattering a racial glass ceiling. That was also the year I was introduced to improv comedy. As I began to recognize that improv was more than just being funny and it was actually a way of life, my attitudes and beliefs began to change immediately. The concept of "Yes, and ..." was teaching me to suspend my judgment, park my ego, listen to understand, and to be empathetic. I loved it, but it didn't all come naturally. I had grown up with certain biases and traditions and narrow mindsets — with scripts that needed to be thrown away and with beliefs that needed to be challenged.

I was a young man with a lot to learn and with some tired old beliefs I needed to shed.

Improv and "Yes, and ..." isn't about pushing a tired old belief forward just because that's the way it has always been. It's about breaking with the status quo.

Improv isn't about looking at others as second- or third-class citizens and making decisions based upon stereotypes. It's about equality and equity when examining the value of our ideas and our words and our individual humanity.

Improv isn't about listening and only responding to push your tired and outdated agenda. It's about listening to learn and understand, to become a team of collaborators where hierarchy, patriarchy, and seniority are obliterated.

"Yes, and ..." is just the opposite of blindly advancing and advocating for tired old ideologies. Improv requires a lot of empathy, which is a beautiful antidote to narrowmindedness. Empathy, as I have argued throughout this book, is not about putting yourself in someone else's shoes. Empathy is trying to understand how that person feels in *their* shoes. I wanted to understand and to feel differently. I was committed to trying.

> **"Yes, and ..." is just the opposite of blindly advancing and advocating for tired old ideologies. Improv requires a lot of empathy, which is a beautiful antidote to narrowmindedness.**

"Yes! And ..." and improv are all about humanity. So I've spent a lot of time trying to examine my own and to appreciate the humanity of others.

And, truth be told, I started this process with a lot to overcome. In recent years, the United States has elevated the conversation about social justice reform, racial justice, diversity, equity, inclusion, and the dream of eliminating racism. But our C-suites and universities and communities are still full of people (like me) who are products of their upbringings. I have come to believe that racism isn't an acquired trait, but that racism is something you learn — over time — through your family, culture, and environment. Growing up in Lexington, Kentucky, in the 1960s through the early 1980s, I witnessed racism in a variety of ways. However, back then, I never thought of those actions as racist because they were commonplace and part of the family, culture, and environment that raised me. The reality, however, (and I am sad to say it) is that at one point in my life, I was a racist.

Ask Yourself

➜ When it comes to tired old beliefs that you must shed if you are to become a truly gifted and impactful "improv leader," what do you need to overcome? What about your upbringing or vantage point might be holding you back?

Off Script and Off Kilter South of the Mason-Dixon Line

It was early 1984 (I was 24) when I recognized that my thoughts and attitudes had begun to change — that I wasn't as unapologetically racist as I was raised to be. I was the new general manager of Ken's Pizza in Griffin, Georgia, where I had the opportunity to interact with a lot of people (mostly white) of all ages and backgrounds. I ask people today if they know where Griffin, Georgia, is located and most don't. So I respond with "It's somewhere between Atlanta and the Civil War." The reason for that reference is rooted in an experience I had at the restaurant that was a shock to me.

It was on my first day on the job as general manager, after our lunch rush, when two little old ladies called me over to their booth. I came over and introduced myself to them and asked if they liked their pizza. They both said that they enjoyed the pizza. Then one of the ladies looked me in the eye and said, "It is nice to have a white general manager for a change." I was stunned. I didn't know what to say. I suspect I shook my head and furrowed my brows. I excused myself, saying, "I need to get back to work."

It wasn't until 13 years later, in 1997, that I had the conversation with my father about the potential hiring of Tubby Smith, African American, to be the new basketball head coach at the University of Kentucky. I was growing up and growing away from my racist history; I realized then that I had totally changed my opinions and mindset — not just about race, but about life and about humanity. I was going "off script." Not everyone around me liked it or understood.

So Far Yet to Go

When I talk about race and my past, I am often saddened to realize that not a whole lot has changed — that when it comes to racial justice in the United States, the past is not entirely in the past. Last year, a friend and I were talking just before my family's annual vacation to Sanibel Island, Florida, in August. We were talking about beaches and sunscreen. My friend is black and just before we hung up, he said, "Be careful that you don't get too dark; the police might pull you over." It was a joke but if I laughed, it was sardonically and sadly. I can't imagine getting pulled over by the police just because of the color of my skin, but we see and hear about it all the time. What would I feel like having a police officer pull me over just because he/she could? Especially when I know that I had done nothing wrong. That comment lingered in my memory for a long time. Clearly, it still does.

Reminders of our racial division are all around me. My favorite conference to speak at is the National Association of Black Accountants, and I spoke there for five years in a row. I distinctly remember the first time I was there; I was walking the halls with an African American woman who asked me, "Don't you feel nervous?" I replied, "About what?" She said, "You know, you kind of stand out from almost everyone attending." And she smiled. She was pointing out my whiteness. I smiled too. It was different for me to be a "minority" in this space. It was going to challenge me to put my money where my mouth was in terms of accepting my gifts, going off script, improvising, and getting comfortable with the uncomfortable. I had a phenomenal time at the conference ... and I was easy to spot in the crowd.

When it comes to achieving a more harmonious community, free from the poison of racism and bigotry, we still have a long way to go. We're still operating from our grandfathers' scripts. More change is needed and more voices are required.

> **When it comes to achieving a more harmonious community, free from the poison of racism and bigotry, we still have a long way to go. We're still operating from our grandfathers' scripts.**

I began this book with a story about the Reverend Dr. Martin Luther King, Jr., the March on Washington, and the "I Have a Dream" speech. And I'd like to begin bringing the book to a close with a reminder that what Dr. King was fighting for in 1963 is a fight that continues. As we throw away our "scripts" and habits — at work and in life — we get closer to the kind of respectful dialogue and equitable cultures that we seek. To enact positive change in the elimination of social injustice and racism, we all — regardless of our race — need to start asking more questions, listening, parking our egos and racial biases, and engaging in a dialogue to gain a better understanding of one another. We need to hear the conversation for what it is, not what we want it to be or assume it to be or fear it might be. We need to take an improvisor's mindset to search for a *solution* versus creating a bigger divide for our own self-interests (like when someone purposefully stokes division to play to a political base). I have heard many an improviser say, "If everyone would just take one improv course, this world would be a better place." It's an overstatement and a simplified solution, but I love the spirit of it.

As a fledgling or enthusiastic improviser, you are someone I see. And I see that — like me — you aren't perfect. If you're anything like me, there was a time (and you might still be in that time) when listening, empathy, and open-mindedness didn't come naturally. The truth is that it doesn't come naturally for *most* people! We all wear blinders. Some of us are (or were) racist or sexist; some of us are judgmental about the political leanings or religious beliefs of others; some of us are privileged financially or socially. Some of us are easily triggered by certain topics or ideologies or people who are different from us in some way. And that's okay. If you're feeling, as you're about to turn the page to read the conclusion of this book, that some of this work — learning to listen to others, to park our egos, to build upon the ideas of others, to empathize, to have fun at work — is going to be hard, you're right. Of course it's going to be hard! We're human, we're biased, we're flawed, we're arrogant. But we can — and must — peel back the layers of our unconscious biases and our out-of-date leadership practices so we can be better. It's time to go off script! Mastering the art of improv is challenging in a variety of ways but is so rewarding in the end.

> "*Improv is like The Hokey Pokey. Think about it. At the end of the song, what do we learn? What is it all about? ... You put your whole self in!*"
>
> **—MARTIN DEMAAT**

CONCLUSION

I
f you made it this far, thank you for investing the time to read this book. It is my hope that, early on in your reading of *Off Script*, you discovered with delight that you improvise every single day — that this work is fun and practical and easy to apply, and that you can master it. I hope you have already tested some of the exercises with your team and that you're beginning to change the way you think and talk. ("Yes! And …") The purpose of writing this book for you was to raise that awareness and to urge you to strategically use the foundations of improvisation to help your organization grow in productivity, profitability, and employee retention. No matter where you work or what you do, we are all in the people business — first and foremost — and improv is a method of inspiration and appreciation that we share with others.

To review, the 7 Foundations of Improvision can be visualized in this way:

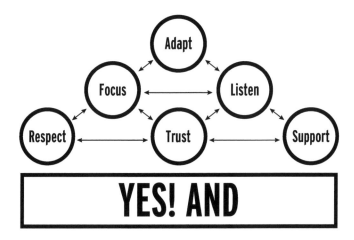

Improv is grounded in acceptance and in the intent to move the conversation forward in a positive direction with the philosophy of *"Yes! And ..."* The groundwork for becoming a master of the art of improv is learning to layer *respect, trust,* and *support* on top of the use of "Yes, and ..." This is really no different from any other type of relationship. If any of these elements are missing, the triangle falls apart. The next layer includes your superpowers — *listening* and *focus* (i.e., being present). When you do all those things right, you can *adapt* to any given situation.

Keep these principles in the forefront of your mind and practice them daily. Get an index card and write *YES! AND* on the card and put it somewhere where you will see it to remind you. In my early days of studying improv, I had index cards in my office, car, and home so that the reinforcement of the philosophy of improv was in my sights all the time. (These days, I have a pair of cufflinks that does the job — all I have to do is glance down to see "Yes!" on my left wrist and "And" on my right.) I also strongly encourage you to revisit the improv exercises with your team weekly. I have many clients who have carved out dedicated time on their calendars for solo or group work in this regard, including one client — Amanda Roselli, who you met in Chapter 16 — who spends time on Friday mornings using a random word generator online to give her words as prompts for stories she makes herself tell (i.e., improvise) in the moment. This work has made her more creative, nimble, and open-minded.

You Are Well on Your Way

Remember this question and answer: "How do you eat an elephant? One bite at a time." Take your time in implementing the foundations of improvisation into your organization. Start off slow, as we did in this book by busting the myth that improv is only about entertaining and comedy, and introducing "Yes, and ..." into the dialogues you have with your employees, peers, leaders, customers, clients, and other stakeholders. Then watch the magic of improv leadership grow from there almost overnight.

But Wait! There's More!

There is one more piece of the "off script" puzzle — one more skill to adopt that can help you round out this leadership style. And this recommendation might come as a surprise (or an "Of course! Look at Peter's professional background!")

When searching the internet looking for key words as it relates to the topic of leadership development, you will find the following:

➜ Confidence	➜ Influence
➜ Charismatic	➜ People
➜ Motivation	➜ Accountable
➜ Success	➜ Courage
➜ Inspiring	➜ Humor
➜ Trust	➜ Respectable
➜ Vision	➜ Making good decisions

(Just to name a few!)

I agree with all of these — these concepts, attributes, and values are all relevant to the development of strong leaders. Yet in every list of "leadership traits" I could find, there was one element missing: financial mastery

— the ultimate improv acceptance of leaning in, being comfortable with the uncomfortable, shedding bias, and accepting that this is a skill that is widely needed in all leadership development situations.

The best and most effective leaders have a good working knowledge of the company's financial health, and their decision-making process is established in the financial truths of the organization. Armed with this financial acumen, the effective leader can influence decision-making by conveying the tactical connection between the mission statement and the financial statements.

> ## The best and most effective leaders have a good working knowledge of the company's financial health, and their decision-making process is established in the financial truths of the organization.

Let me pause for a moment and stress that this financial acumen is not the sole responsibility of the CFO. It is the responsibility of everyone who is in a leadership role within the company, from the director level and up. Financial acumen should be the basis of understanding in every business conversation and in every decision made within an organization. This is a concept we explored in some detail in Chapter 7 and, because "the buck stops" in business where the buck literally stops, it's important for us to take a final moment to talk dollars and sense as they relate to leadership and the art of improv.

Hold on! Stay with me here. You might be thinking, "But I'm a marketer." Or "But I'm an engineer." Or "But I'm a social worker." Maybe numbers and money aren't your thing. But organizations exist for the purpose of existing perpetually, so understanding how the money is made (and kept and saved) is vital, no matter what you do and what your title is.

When it comes to the chief financial officer (CFO), it's his or her responsibility to become a better translator of the "foreign language" of business — accounting and finance. Yes, accounting/finance is often a foreign language to those in sales, human resources, information technology, distribution, public relations, etc. In addition, accounting/finance has an "image problem" for non-accountants. It's an image (or better yet, memory) of pages of mind-numbing numbers that make no sense. And that memory or stereotype can lead even the most well-meaning among us to "listener shut-down" — creating a phenomenon that, in turn, leads to lack of financial acumen within your organization.

Think about it this way: Who are the people in your organization who are making decisions? How many decisions are made every single day in an organization like yours? What percentage of those decisions have a financial impact on the organization? (75%? 80% 100%?) There are leaders within organizations who don't understand the fundamentals of accounting and finance, and I consider that to be a catastrophe in the making. For example, the lending department within a bank. Lenders are the salespeople of the bank. They're responsible for generating deals for customers so that they can lend money to them and grow the bank's business. We all know that, right?

However, these lenders can earn a bonus on the cumulative dollar amount that they lend. Do you see what is missing here? You are incentivizing the lenders on revenue generation (i.e., on interest earned from loans made) and not bottom-line profitability for the bank. This is and has been a recipe for loss in profitability. What is missing is taking into consideration what the bank's cost in booking and managing the loan (and the risks associate with borrower default).

I hear stories all the time from CFOs about how the sales team needs to grow their business by 25% and yet, in the process, somehow manage to lose 15% in profits. What's going wrong in organizations like this? And can it be fixed or prevented through the power of improv? (Yes! And yes.) In my podcast interview with Ken "Mr. Biz" Wentworth (Season 3, Episode 30, "How to Cut the Right Expenses & Make Your Balance Sheet a Fortress"), Ken calls this phenomenon "the silent killer" of all businesses. He shares a story of one of his construction clients wanting him to review a bid on a new piece of business. After he looked at the proposal, he advised the client not to bid on the work at that price and to raise the price by 25%. The pushback from the owner was that they needed to bid low so they could get the job. Ken, knowing the cost structure of his client's business, responded, "You can bid the job at the lower price and you will lose $40,000 on this job." The owner replied, "I am bidding it low to get my foot in the door for future work."

Let's stop right here. We all know that is a falsehood because when the owner — at some point in the future — asks for a bid on another project and we give our full pricing structure, what do you think the owner is going to do? That's right. He or she is going to feel a sense of "sticker shock," will think your prices have gone up with no notice or explanation, and they'll go find someone cheaper. I have used that strategy in the past and it hurt my business. As far as I'm concerned, it's never a good idea.

The silent killer of a business is ultimately a lack of financial acumen — the death knell of a company comes from having leaders (who are empowered to make important decisions) who don't understand the fundamentals of accounting and finance. We need this understanding and knowledge to make more informed, smarter, and more profitable decisions. If you understand accounting, you can understand finance. If you understand finance, you can understand your business.

If you understand accounting, you can understand finance. If you understand finance, you can understand your business.

But what does this have to do with improv — with respect, trust, support, focus, listening, adaptation, and the welcoming and additive "yes, and …" mindset? Well, without these key elements in place, we don't have the courage or safety to talk about the money. When your leaders are in meetings and the conversation shifts from operations to finance, are all your leaders participating in the conversation or are some of them just witnessing the conversation?

The solution is leadership. Financial leadership. The next time you have your leadership team participate in a leadership development program, add a day of high-level accounting and finance fundamentals. (I beg of you! And I promise that the subsequent results will speak for themselves.)

Oh, I know … I can see all your bitter Grinch faces. You are thinking: "An accounting and finance course. Oh, hell no! I'd rather have a root canal without any Novocain than sit through a full day of an accounting and finance." This goes back to the image problem accounting has — and it's a big image problem! And it exists because the traditional way of teaching accounting to non-accountants is the same way we teach accounting to accountants. That's like teaching any subject in a foreign language that the students don't understand — it's impossible to learn!

We need to teach accounting and finance to non-financial leaders in a different way. We aren't trying to turn them into accountants, but rather into leaders with financial acumen. We want to help them gain access to critical knowledge in a manner that removes the complexity of accounting/financial jargon and teaches them the fundamentals in plain English.

When you switch the accounting and financial light bulb on and include it as part of your improv leadership development, your leaders will make better business decisions because their business acumen has been fully achieved. Business acumen is built on a foundation of accounting acumen plus financial acumen and every leader should strive for this excellence. To build business acumen, you start with a foundation of accounting acumen (numbers, financial statements, etc.) and add on top of it the financial acumen (ratios, understanding what the numbers mean, leverage, economics, etc., and how they affect your business). Together, those two areas of understanding help you in developing your business acumen (running your business, forecasting, etc.).

Business acumen is built on a foundation of accounting acumen plus financial acumen and every leader should strive for this excellence.

Remember how several of the improv exercises in this book involved problem-solving scenarios that were about money (i.e., revenue, sales, costs, profit, budgets)? We talked about how to hold brainstorming sessions around cost-cutting ideas or revenue-generating ideas. We talked about creative (and even outrageous) ways to hire seasoned talent (so we could increase sales). We looked at how to solve problems that were expensive or that were keeping revenue at bay. We talked about problems and solutions, and — let's cut to the quick here — in business, problems and solutions are always about money.

The improv exercises in this book provide you with tools that can always make you stronger — regardless of your title or amount of work experience or your comfort in talking about the financials. But your ability to generate *big results* from these improv activities sometimes hinges on the participants' (yours and your team's) basic financial acumen to have these conversations in the first place. For that reason, I'm leaving you with a word about money — why it matters and why you need to understand it. The combination of the two — improv "off script" leadership skills and strong financial acumen — can take you (and your organization) to new heights.

It has been my great honor to introduce (or re-introduce) you to a world in which more "yes" is possible; a world in which respect, trust, and support underlie our every interaction; a world in which we can focus on what matters and listen to the people who matter; a world in which we can adapt to any contingency, opportunity, or crisis like a seasoned, talented improviser, ready to accept the gifts of change and forge forward into a story that's waiting to be written. Go write those stories — prepare and practice and then, if the occasion calls for it, go OFF SCRIPT!

ACKNOWLEDGMENTS

Writing a book appears to be singular in nature — something that one author does all alone and for which he takes all the glory in the end. However, it takes many people to help the author in creating their book — it took many people to help *me* in the creation and publishing of *Off Script*. So it's time for me to thank the many people who have helped me in various ways to get this book written and now in your hands.

I first want to start with thanking all the clients who have trusted me over the years and whose stories I have shared in this book. You make me a better improviser and servant leader.

Next, a huge THANK YOU to **Kate Colbert**, my publisher extraordinaire and this book's editor, and my super-talented graphic designer, **George Stevens**, who designed every aspect of the book, inside and out. Kate is a superhero who juggles a thriving business and a complex medical condition with both grace and grit. She rarely complains, has the *"Yes! And ..."* attitude, always has a smile in her voice and on her face, is a wonderful publisher, and is someone I am proud to call my friend. George was formerly on staff at a company that published my first book, *Improv Is No Joke*, and I won the graphic-design lottery when George was assigned as my book designer. Even after I chose Silver Tree Publishing to publish my next two books (*Taking the Numb Out of Numbers* and *Off Script*), I knew I wanted George to stay involved. A couple years ago, George started his own book-design company (G Sharp Design) and availed himself to develop the cover concept for this book and to design the new logo for my company. "The band was back together," as they say. The next thing you know, the vital position of art director opened up at Silver Tree Publishing and Kate called me to say, "Your designer, George, he's pretty great. *And*, do you think he'd be open to being our exclusive designer here at Silver Tree?" The rest is now history. George is extremely talented in the graphic arts and is deeply expert in creating books that serve their readers; he's a great guy, a new dad, and a friend for six years. Thank you both — Kate and George — for your desire to create *Off Script* with the "wow factor" I had in mind. I couldn't have done this without you.

I'd also like to thank **Jeffrey Hayzlett**, who wrote the foreword for this book and who has taught me a lot about the power of collaboration, service to others, and being bold while also being humble. Jeffrey was the one who got me thinking differently about the original title for my book. The original working title of the book was *Improv Leadership for the C-Suite*. As I was working on the subtitle, I had sent an email to 30 friends and colleagues, asking them to choose from among three subtitles. One email struck me, and it was from Jeffrey. He liked the title and one of the subtitles — *Mastering the Art of Business Improv*. However, being ever the masterful marketer, he pitched an idea on keeping the title short and punchy with something like *Wing It!* or *Spontaneity!* I loved the idea of the more concise title, and I felt that *Wing It* and *Spontaneity* were close yet not exactly the words I felt were the book's true essence. Thanks to his generosity of thought and time, Jeffrey put me on the path to the perfect title for this book.

I also owe a huge thanks to my improv coach and friend, **Jay Sukow** — from San Francisco — who wrote the preface for this book. Sorry about that; he lives in the Greater Los Angeles area. Ahem. (This is a callback to Jay's Preface. If you didn't read it, go back and read it. I'd hate for you to miss out on the joke.) Jay has taught me a lot about the world of improv — both from a business and a theatrical perspective. I remember the first time I met Jay in person. We were in Chicago. I had seen his picture before, but you know how people don't update their headshot regularly so I wasn't sure if

I'd recognize him in person. We were meeting Greg Conderacci (and his daughter Annie) at a restaurant called Eataly — an Italian grocery with various Italian restaurants under the same roof. So here I am walking around trying to find the specific restaurant, and I pass this guy and notice on his forearm he had a tattoo that read: *Yes And.* I looked at the guy, smiled, stuck out my hand, and said, "Jay Sukow, it is a pleasure to meet you." I had found my guy. Jay: It may finally be time for me to get the tattoo, too!

I'd like to express my gratitude to the editorial board who got the first glimpse at this book's manuscript. They read it, scribbled all over it, and provided me with great insight and direction about the book's content and flow. The team consisted of **Joselin Martin, Michael Sherlock, Roxanne Kaufman,** and **Merle Heckman.** Thank you all so very much for your time in helping us put out the best product we can for readers who deserve practical tools and inspiring stories. You four rock!

Then there are those who graciously endorsed the book and provided their thoughts for our readers to consider. Those who participated in offering early praise for the book were **Cathy Fyock, Lisa Braithwaite, Ken "Mr. Biz" Wentworth, Steve Morris, Don Craig, Brannon Poe, J. Clarke Price, Merle Heckman, Theresa Rose, Michael Sherlock, Alan Patterson, Michelle Wyatt, Jamie Richardson, Eddie Turner, Jeanie Price, Stacey Horan, Jay Young, Karen Young, Roxanne Kaufman, Jeffrey Hayzlett, Steve Makredes, Bob Dusin,** and **Adam Kratzert.** Oh wait, I forgot to mention my brother, **Steve Margaritis.** Thank you all (even my brother!) for your time and kind words.

A special thanks go to Ohio Retired Judge **Patricia Blackmon**. Judge Blackmon has publicly performed the "I Have a Dream" speech, and she graciously spent 30 minutes with me discussing the speech that Dr. King delivered at the March on Washington and sharing her thoughts on the "off script" vs. "on script" intentions of preachers/ministers who deliver sermons in primarily or historically black churches. She talked to me about how Dr. King — who had previously never veered from his written and memorized scripts — went "off script" more than once during the civil rights movement. Thanks to Judge Blackmon and Jeffery Hayzlett, the idea was taking hold in my mind, just swimming around. So, as I began to work on the introduction for this book, I got to the point of sharing Patricia's comment about King going "off script" and ... lights, bells, sirens went off, and I said, *"That's the title for this book!"*

I want to thank my mother, **Pauline**, my brother **Steve** (again), my sister **Stacie**, my brother-in-law **Rick**, and my nephew **Kayden James** for all their love, support, compassion, and humor.

I want to thank my wife, **Mary**, and my son **Stephen** (aka Chipper), and my two Labrador retrievers, **Midnight** and **MJ**, for putting up with me during this long process. Mary and Stephen: I could not have accomplished the task of writing a book (during a pandemic!) without your love, support, and carefully placed humor and sarcasm when I needed it the most. Midnight and MJ, your wagging tails always make me smile.

KEEP IN TOUCH!

💡 **Learn more about *Off Script*, access bonus resources, and quickly connect with Peter Margaritis on his website:**

PeterMargaritis.com

🔊 **Listen to the "Change Your Mindset" podcast:**

Listen on Apple podcasts, Spotify, C-Suite Radio, iHeart Radio, Audible, and everywhere podcasts are available and via https://PeterMargaritis. com/category/CYM-podcasts/.

✉ **Send an email:**

Peter@PeterMargaritis.com

💬 **To book Peter for a presentation at your organization:**

Visit PeterMargaritis.com/contact/ to fill out the booking form.

To order books in bulk and learn about quantity discounts:

Send an email! Interested in ordering 10 or more copies of Off Script for your organization or association? Inquire at Peter@ PeterMargaritis.com.

Find, follow, and share on social media:

LinkedIn.com/in/PeterMargaritis

Facebook.com/TheAccidentalAccountant

Twitter.com/pmargaritis

Instagram.com/pmargaritis

Become part of the "Off Script" revolution!

Reach out to Peter via email or social media to share how you and your organization are using the exercises and tips from this book. You just might find your team's story makes it into Peter's next book, which will be brimming with real-world stories about the art of business improv — stories about people like you!

ALSO BY
PETER A. MARGARITIS ...

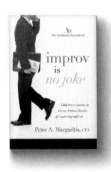

IMPROV IS NO JOKE: USING IMPROVISATION TO CREATE POSITIVE RESULTS IN LEADERSHIP AND LIFE

A must-read for accountants, bankers, and other financial professionals interested in sharpening the invaluable leadership and communication skills they need to successfully relate to clients and to communicate complex information in a user-friendly way.

Available in paperback, ebook, and audiobook editions.

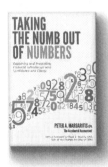

TAKING THE NUMB OUT OF NUMBERS: EXPLAINING AND PRESENTING FINANCIAL INFORMATION WITH CONFIDENCE AND CLARITY

An accessible, practical, inspiring book for mid-level and senior leaders who are tasked with presenting financial, technical, or complex information to key audiences. Learn how to...

- *Control Your Anxieties* — Peter shares tips to help calm your nerves and increase your confidence
- *Craft Your Story* — Learn the art of powerful storytelling to share complex information
- *Connect With Your Audience* — Discover how you can engage people and create interactive conversations

Available in paperback and ebook editions.

ABOUT THE AUTHOR

Peter A. Margaritis, CSP, CPA

During one of Peter's performance reviews, his boss said, "How in the heck did you ever become a CPA? CPAs can dig deep into the details, and you skim the surface. Peter, you are an 'accidental accountant.'" She was right.

Many of us are "accidental somethings" (you fill in the blank — accidental accountant, accidental engineer, accidental lawyer, accidental marketer, etc.). The world is full of people whose driving passion is not related to their title, credentials, or primary job responsibilities. They have found themselves in careers and lives accidentally or erroneously.

For Peter Margaritis, his passion is simple; he loves to make people laugh and he's felt that way for as far back as he can remember. That love to make people laugh took him down the path of performing stand-up comedy. It was an incredible learning journey for him, and he learned that the stand-up lifestyle wasn't something he wanted to pursue long-term.

Then came the life-changing discovery of improv comedy. It changed Peter Margaritis into the improv *leader* he is today.

Improv was mind-blowing for Peter not because of the humor aspects. It was because the teachings of improv aligned so strongly with the development of leadership skills.

This discovery — that leadership and improv go hand in hand — came later in Peter's career, after he had worked for organizations like Barnett Bank and Citizens and Southern National Bank as a consumer and commercial lender and after he had graduated from Case Western Reserve University with a master's in accountancy. This discovery of improv occurred during the years when Peter worked at Price Waterhouse, Victoria's Secret Catalogue (not as a model!), and Gap Inc. Direct.

When Peter left the corporate world for academia — teaching accounting at Franklin University and Ohio Dominican University — the three worlds collided: business, stand-up, and improv. In front of a classroom, Peter's passion reached nirvana. He was able to draw upon his accounting knowledge and deliver it engagingly and humorously. You heard that right — Peter used humor to teach accounting, and the students loved it.

Here is the epiphany: the students could retain the accounting knowledge and apply it to their accounting foundation because improv works differently from lecture or even regular discussion. Improv is about the ability to draw upon your experiences, knowledge, and education then apply your experiences, knowledge, and education in a way that meets the needs of the *other people* you are working with. Improv is teachable!

Peter Margaritis has a passion for making people laugh, helping them to see content in a different light, and inviting them to gain a better understanding of the application of the concepts taught. Along the way, he loves to see people laugh and have fun! In the workplace, this formula increases employee productivity because, simply put, people work better when they enjoy working in a fun environment.

In his career, Peter has held several leadership roles — the most prominent role as Chairman of the Ohio Society of CPAs Executive Board.

"Leadership has always been important to me," Peter explains. "And improv has accelerated that importance. I am a younger Baby Boomer whose corporate life involved being told what to do by senior leaders who looked at others in the organization as a number — not a person — who could easily be replaced. This mentality is what I refer to as 'ego leadership,' and it is *wrong* in so many ways."

Peter Margaritis is a strong proponent for the argument that "we are all in the people business" and that the sooner we accept that mindset, our organizations will prosper greater than we ever imagined. People are our greatest assets, and we need to start treating them that way. *Off Script* helps leaders do precisely that — master the art of business improv to achieve measurable, sustainable organizational results.

TWO OPPOSING FORCES
WORKING TOGETHER IN HARMONY
TO DRIVE RESULTS

Through his keynote presentations and customized workshops, Peter demonstrates the tools used in improv — listening to understand, being present, adaptability, and "Yes! And." These tools can change how a team interacts with each other and with their clients/customers. Peter helps team learn new methods to improve their communication and build stronger relationships with clients, customers, stakeholders, and associates. His programs and methods also help organizations reduce turnover while increasing productivity and profitability.

Off Script is Peter's third book.

Made in the USA
Columbia, SC
13 October 2021